Business Continuity Management

New technology creates new business risks. The rise of e-commerce has brought with it a rise in new forms of risk, such as the potential for attack by hackers. However, it is not only Internet-based companies that have experienced situations of this kind, conventional companies have similarly had to deal with interruptions or crises threatening normal operations. Our dependence upon 'hidden technology' only becomes clear when things go wrong, as was graphically illustrated by the Californian power failure of winter 2000/1.

Business continuity management (BCM) has evolved as an organizational response to such situations. Whilst computer mainframes were originally the focus of the crisis management strategies that have grown into BCM, now every aspect of business activity, including relationships with customers and suppliers, can be protected.

This book helps to define BCM from a strategic perspective, and demonstrates, with the help of case studies, how to undertake an analysis of the environment, prepare analytical frameworks, implement BCM and ensure it remains a continuous process.

Dominic Elliott is currently Senior Lecturer at the University of Sheffield's Centre for Risk and Crisis Management, UK. He has published widely in the fields of crisis and strategic management, and has worked with a number of organizations in crisis and strategy, including IBM, Philips, BNP-Paribas and the Government of Lesotho. He is co-editor of *Risk Management: An International Journal*.

Ethné Swartz is currently Assistant Professor at Fairleigh Dickinson University, US. She has published and taught in the fields of entrepreneurship, strategic management and crisis and continuity management, and has consulted with both small and large organizations in the UK, South Africa and North America.

Brahim Herbane is Senior Lecturer in Strategy at De Montfort University's School of Business, Leicester, UK. His main research interests are in strategic management, and crisis and business continuity management, and he has taught, published and consulted widely in both fields.

Business Continuity Management

A crisis management approach

**Dominic Elliott, Ethné Swartz
and Brahim Herbane**

London and New York

First published 2002
by Routledge
11 New Fetter Lane, London EC4P 4EE

Simultaneously published in the USA and Canada
by Routledge
29 West 35th Street, New York, NY 10001

Routledge is an imprint of the Taylor & Francis Group

Typeset in Times by RefineCatch Limited, Bungay, Suffolk
Printed and bound in Great Britain by
St Edmundsbury Press, Bury St Edmunds, Suffolk

British Library Cataloguing in Publication Data
A catalogue record for this book is available from the British Library

Library of Congress Cataloging in Publication Data
Elliot, Dominic, 1963–
    Business continuity management: a crisis management approach/
Dominic Elliott, Ethné Swartz & Brahim Herbane.
        p. cm.
    Includes bibliographical references and index.
    1. Crisis management. 2. Emergency management. 3. Business
planning. I. Swartz, Ethné, 1961– II. Herbane, Brahim, 1969–
III. Title.

HD49 .E44 2001
658.4′056—dc21

                                                    2001031999

ISBN 0–415–20491–7 (hbk)
ISBN 0–415–20492–5 (pbk)

To our parents
Barbara Elliott (RIP) and John Elliott
Frederick David Swartz (RIP) and Beatrice Swartz
Mahjoub Herbane and Maria Rodríguez Rodríguez Herbane

and dedicated to the memory of the victims of the attacks upon the World Trade Center and the Pentagon

26 February 1993
11 September 2001

Contents

Figures

Tables

Acknowledgements

This book is the result of collaboration with a number of institutions over a number of years. It has involved many people in both academia and in the emerging business continuity industry. We are therefore indebted to many individuals for their assistance in nurturing our research.

This book has drawn on a wide range of sources of ideas and inspiration. Numerous colleagues and friends have played a part, especially Professor John Coyne who provided much needed encouragement, some of it financial! Other notable supporters, in alphabetical order: Peter Barnes, Janette Beer, Fred Bell, Dr John Berman, Lyndon Bird, Eve Coles, Peter Davis, Brian Doswell, Nick Emery, Ian Gray, Steven Hall, Ricardo Herbane, Phil Hine, Steve Mellish, Dave Onyons, David Orton, Richard Pursey, Andy Rees, Mandy Robertson, Angela Robinson, Dr Michael Rouse, John Sharp, Nick and Gillian Simms, Professor Denis Smith, Professor Steve Tombs, Pam White, staff at Guardian DR (including Safetynet), Strohl Systems and Survive! have also assisted us over the years. Our students at a number of universities in the UK and US have helped shape our ideas, particularly those at De Montfort, Durham and Sheffield.

There were others who helped us in our endeavours but we promised you anonymity, you know who you are.

The project, which lay behind this book, arose from a chance exploration about ways in which we could combine our interests and expertise. It has been a long journey. We hope that this contribution to the field of business continuity will aid it in its own maturation. It seems clear to us that the need to ensure continuity has never been greater. The final eighteen months of this project saw us divided between two continents and we learnt at first hand just how valuable the Internet has become, as a tool for communication and as a resource. However, our dependence upon it made us vulnerable. This is perhaps the paradox of all new technologies and new ways of working, they offer great opportunities but dependence may also be a threat.

Many from the business continuity industry should be mentioned, but we promised anonymity – our special thanks to all who assisted us when we were collecting data.

We are also grateful to the reviewers of the book for the comments on individual chapters and wish to acknowledge how their input helped to shape our thinking and the overall content of the book. Of course, the final responsibility for the book in its final form rests with the authors.

Finally, for their forbearance and support, our love and gratitude to our families and children.

Megan, Hannah, Thomas, Lucy and Tracey Elliott
Philip and David Swartz-Saxon, and Tim Saxon

The authors and publishers would also like to thank the following for use of material in this book: Jossey-Bass Inc., a subsidiary of John Wiley & Sons Inc., for Pauchant, T. and Mitroff, I., *Transforming the Crisis Prone Organization*, San Francisco, 1992.

1 Business continuity in historical context

Introduction

When Nelson Mandela was released from prison in 1990 after twenty-six years, the world had changed dramatically. In the dozen years since Mandela's release the rate of change has, if anything, increased further. Consumers purchase goods with credit cards swiped through automated card readers. Purchase information is recorded and transmitted so that retail stocks can be replenished. Banks close their branches as customers withdraw cash through automated telling machines. Computers send out automatic letters to customers exceeding their overdrafts. Loyalty cards enable retailers to collect customer information from which detailed profiles can be drawn, electronically of course. Personal banking was superseded by telephone banking, itself now being chased by PC and internet banking. Indeed, personal banking is now being reintroduced as a 'value added service'. With a plethora of goods from which to choose, customers have become more demanding, less tolerant of sloppy service or of delays. As the change occurs incrementally we hardly notice it, but for Nelson Mandela the changes must have been immense. In his autobiography he describes how on his release a television crew 'thrust a long, dark and furry object at me. I recoiled slightly, wondering if it were a new fangled weapon developed while I was in prison. Winnie informed me that it was a microphone' (Mandela, 1994: 673). Change, fuelled by new information and communication technology (ICT) may be seen as a constant. Greater reliance on technology and on fellow members of the organizational supply chain has increased the potential for interruptions. The need to ensure business continuity has never been greater.

Business continuity management (BCM) is a new and evolving discipline. Its roots lie in Information Systems (IS) protection although it is argued that it has grown a long way from this. Although none of us remains untouched by technological change we are less concerned with the technology itself than with the changes to organizational processes, systems and operations which new developments have made possible. This book is written from the perspective that organizations are socio-technical systems and that continuity management must consider all elements to be effective. Our theoretical roots lie in a variety of sub-disciplines including strategy, industrial crisis and information systems. Inevitably these have shaped this book and our approach to BCM. Accordingly we define business continuity planning (BCP) as: 'Planning which identifies an organization's exposure to internal and external threats and synthesizes hard and soft assets to provide effective prevention and recovery for the organization, whilst maintaining competitive advantage and value system integrity' (Herbane *et al.*, 1997).

This definition of business continuity is firmly rooted in a crisis management approach (see Shrivastava, 1987; Smith, 1990; Pauchant and Mitroff, 1992) and is broader in scope than more traditional approaches, which emphasize hard systems (see for example, Doswell, 2000). The next section outlines what is meant by a crisis management approach. Following this, Chapter 1 considers the strategic importance of being able to deal with crises and interruptions effectively; how service continuity might be a more appropriate term than business continuity; finally we examine the historical development of business continuity management.

A crisis management approach to business continuity

A key part of this book's contribution to the development of business continuity management lies in its crisis management approach, which underpins all aspects of this text. For our purposes a crisis management approach may be defined as one that:

- recognizes the social and technical characteristics of business interruptions
- emphasizes the contribution that managers may make to the resolution of interruptions
- assumes that managers may build resilience to business interruptions through processes and changes to operating norms and practices
- assumes that organizations themselves may play a major role in 'incubating the potential for failure'
- recognizes that, if managed properly, interruptions do not inevitably result in crises
- acknowledges the impact, potential or realized, of interruptions upon a wide range of stakeholders

Figure 1.1 illustrates how a crisis management view of business continuity acknowledges that the organization is part of an environment characterized by uncertainty and change, leading to new challenges. Within the environment regulation, legislation and stakeholders help to shape the business continuity process within individual organizations. That process will be shaped by the historical legacy of the continuity process and the accumulated knowledge within an organization. In addition, a key driver will be the strategic importance that business continuity management assumes both within the organization as well as externally.

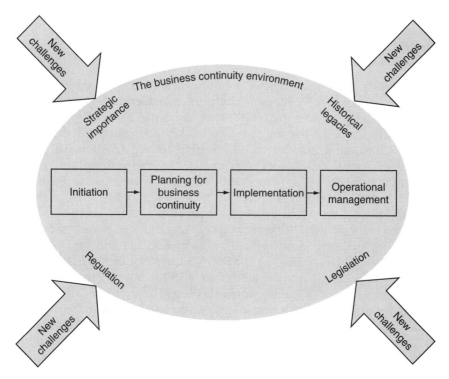

Figure 1.1 The continuity management process in context

Earlier business continuity publications (see for example Ginn, 1989; Anderson, 1992; Strohl Systems, 1995) have restricted their attentions to IS management and protection. More recent practical guides and case studies have a broader range of interests extending to all facilities (see for example, Hiles and Barnes, 1999; Vancoppenolle, 1999) and in some cases to reputation management (Elliott *et al.*, 1999).

This broadening of business continuity reflects the underlying assumption that crisis incidents or business interruptions are systemic in nature, comprising of both social and technical elements. Such a view has been well developed within the field of crisis management (Turner, 1976; Turner and Pidgeon, 1997; Shrivastava, 1987; Smith, 1990; Pauchant and Douville, 1993; Perrow, 1997). For example, the Challenger disaster (1986) arose from the convergence of technical failure (faulty seals) and a NASA culture which made assumptions about the ability of staff always to succeed. The organization became 'deaf' to concerns about safety and, when specific safety issues were raised, the culture conspired to push ahead with the launch, resulting in tragedy (see Schwartz, 1987; Starbuck and Milliken, 1988; Pauchant and Mitroff, 1992). Within such a framework, the focus of disaster recovery upon hardware is inherently flawed in that little or no consideration is given to human, organizational or social aspects of the system, nor to the interaction between components.

Strategic importance

The environment in which organizations operate is very complex, with change and innovation driven by increased competition and technology change. The judicious management of technology and the exploitation of Information Systems (IS), in particular, are recognized as key skills which will determine organizational advantage in the 'information society' (Bangemann, 1994, quoted in Crowe, 1996). Pilger (1998) disputes the label 'information society' arguing that 'media age' is more apt. Pilger's central argument is that much information is managed and filtered for good or ill. Such a view recognizes that the technology which makes information-processing so easy is pro-grammed and controlled by people and organizations; that is, there are social as well as technical dimensions. This is depicted in the case of Fear Uncertainty and Doubt (FUDs) and Sun Microsystems, shown in Box 1.1.

The prominence given to the protection of IS has been highlighted earlier and forms a key consideration within this text. However, we challenge the view that this is the extent of scope for business continuity management. An underlying assumption is that BCM permeates all areas of organizational activity. Box 1.1 highlights two high-profile 'interruptions' with far-reaching consequences for the organizations involved.

Mercedes (Chrysler-Daimler) and Ford achieved ongoing success for much of the twentieth century and look well-positioned for the twenty-first. Both cases highlight how interruptions can be self-induced, in even the most suc-cessful of companies. Few commentators would deny that the crisis responses of Mercedes, Ford and Firestone were perceived to be inappropriately slow. Although continuity management is closely associated with ensuring that organizations can recover quickly from the loss of key facilities, we argue that the same principles can be applied to interruptions of a strategic nature. Breaks in continuity represent an interruption in the provision of products or services to customers. Facilities are restored in order that an organization can continue to meet the needs of its customers and other stakeholders; recovery is a means to an end rather than an end in itself. Key lessons emerging from these two cases include:

- the potential threat to continuity from moves into new markets
- that technical failures arise from the complex interaction of factors including scientific knowledge, management interpretation and the demands of achieving business objectives, quickly
- the potential transfer of damage from one product market to threaten an organization's reputation in all areas
- that a slow and ineffective response may exacerbate the impact of an interruption

- the dangers of ignoring early warning signals
- the relevance of continuity management to new product development

Although finance, marketing and operations have been subsumed within general management they have retained their professional distinctions. It is our view that continuity management will follow and be one of those areas for which all managers have some responsibility. Of course there will always be the need for discipline experts but success requires that a continuity mind-set be absorbed by managers of all types and at all levels.

Box 1.1 FUD – Fear, uncertainty and doubt

Emerging from the early days of the personal computer industry, 'fear, uncertainty and doubt' (FUD) is a term used to describe the actions of rivals that seek to propagate misinformation about a product or technology. In so doing, the FUD factors will lead consumers to disregard the product or technology, thereby protecting the position of incumbent suppliers of the technology.

The FUD technique is said to have originated at IBM during the 1970s, when one of its most senior managers, Gene Amdahl, left the company to set up a rival concern. He in turn became a victim of FUD as the salespeople of his former employer sought to undermine Amdahl products, giving rise to the term 'fear uncertainty and doubt'.

By the 1980s, FUD had become a widespread marketing and sales technique within the computer industry. When Amstrad launched a range of home computers, it found that rivals (whose rival products were often twice the price) quickly pointed out that the computer did not have a cooling fan and this could lead to the overheating of internal components and a subsequent loss of data. However, the Amstrad computer had been designed to operate without cooling fans because the power supply unit was not housed within the main case. Nonetheless, rivals' FUD tactics seemed to have generated reluctance and doubt in consumers' minds. Consequently, Amstrad was forced (unnecessarily) to install a cooling fan into its computers, at great expense and market damage to itself (given the unnecessary recognition of the unwarranted criticism).

FUD shows no signs of going away. Indeed, the tensions between Microsoft and Sun Microsystems have given rise to the official and ongoing monitoring of statements relating to their products. Sun Microsystems, for instance, has a website dedicated to FUD statements, alongside official comment and rebuttal. Clearly, in either consumer or corporate markets, wherever there is the threat of FUD activities emanating from a rival, so too does the propensity for a crisis to arise.

Sources: Irwin (2001), Sun Microsystems (2001)

Mercedes A-Class

More than a billion Deutschmarks had been invested in the development and manufacture of the 'Baby Benz', formally known as the Mercedes-Benz A-Class. Scheduled for launch in late 1997, this radical new vehicle marked a major shift for the company into smaller-sized vehicle segments, thereby capturing mass-market sales revenues. However, such visions soon became a nightmare for the company when, on 21 October, five Swedish motoring journalists managed to topple the vehicle at a mere 60 kph during an object avoidance manoeuvre, known as the 'elk' test.

Alone, this widely reported handling shortcoming represented a major crisis for the company famous for its quality and safety. But, the lack of an immediate response to an incident perceived by the company to be inconsequential (given that the car had been tested for over 8 million kilometres) merely served to increase the media interest in the story. When, a few days later, the company made its first public comments about the Baby-Benz, the company sought to deflect attention from Mercedes' contribution to the failed elk test, suggesting instead that the blame resided with Goodyear's tyres, which, it suggested, were insufficiently stiff for the vehicle's requirements.

Eight days after the initial failure of the vehicle in Sweden, Mercedes began to accept some responsibility for events and the behaviour of the vehicle by offering an expensive electronic modification to the car and tyre changes. In the aftermath of the crisis, the company spent an estimated £100 million on retrofitted components and delayed re-launch for twelve months. Furthermore, the crisis had wider effects. Daimler-Benz, the parent company and one of Germany's largest industrial conglomerates, found its stock price diminished, at its worst point by nearly 32 per cent.

Opinion is divided over whether Mercedes-Benz (now part of the Daimler-Chrysler group) will have suffered in the long term over the A-Class crisis. Production and order books have now reached target levels (180,000 vehicles per year), and the company's hi-tech Rastatt factory, along with the innovative vehicle, is widely admired within the motor industry. Mercedes' response to the crisis is, however, less so.

Sources: Olins and Lynn (1997), Prowse (1998)

Firestone – precedented crisis, unprecedented changes

Product recalls in the motor industry are far from unusual. In the early 1970s, Ford faced public outrage following its unwillingness to respond to fatal design flaws in its Ford Pinto vehicle. Later in the decade, Firestone, the tyre manufacturer, was forced to recall 14.5 million tyres, said to be at risk of exploding under normal driving conditions. The magnitude of these crises suggested that neither of these companies would be found wanting again.

Never in the history of the car industry had production plants been closed in order to generate surplus stocks of new components for customers until the onset of one of the largest tyre recalls in history. Ford's plant closures released

70,000 new tyres, but this was not enough as against the 6.5 million tyres recalled by Firestone (part of Japan's Bridgestone) in August 2000. The fault that led to tyre tread separation has been linked to 150 deaths and hundreds of accidents in the USA, Venezuela and the Middle East with repercussions for tyres fitted to Ford's Explorer and Ranger 4 × 4 models across the world.

Sharing in both the effects of the crisis and its causes, Bridgestone and Ford now face several hundred lawsuits arising from individual and collective litigants. In spite of their shared exposure to significant out-of-court settlements or court-imposed damages, the companies continue to wrangle over the blame and response to the crisis. Ford has been criticized for not acting quickly and being more open with the public media and authorities, having ignored early warning signs and having failed to recognize the role of the vehicle as a contributory factor. Equally, Firestone has been criticized for its perceived supporting role in the crisis, and by Ford for its lack of openness and communications during the crisis.

The closure of the three plants to release the 70,000 tyres is estimated to have cost Ford $100 million and the redeployment of Ford employees to assist in the replacement of tyres at motor dealerships has proved to be one of the largest logistical operations of its type for the Ford motor company. Furthermore, in 2001, Ford announced that the company would offer, for the first time, its own warranties for tyres to supersede those offered by the tyre manufacturer, offering a first step on a long road to corporate image recovery.

Meanwhile, the cause of the fault remains a mystery.

Sources: Taylor (2000), Bowe (2001), Tait (2001)

From hardware continuity to service continuity

Box 1.2 describes how Royal Sun Alliance recovered quickly in restoring 'business as usual' when its offices in Manchester (UK) were destroyed in an explosion. This is a typical scenario and highlights the dependence of organizations upon their facilities, obvious as it may seem. Organizations increasingly depend upon each other and upon key services and technologies; this has been a major development of the late twentieth century. A negative aspect of this is that the growing dependence upon IS requires that they will always be available for use. Inevitably, this is not always the case and, when problems arise, 'drastic' solutions may be sought. For example, the failure of privatized electricity companies in California led that state to embark on transferring the utilities back to public ownership.

We make assumptions about the dependability of technology-based systems. Technological breakthroughs quickly become absorbed into daily routines because of the ubiquitous nature of technology and IT systems. Such systems eventually become used by all and questioned by none. The case of EPOS (electronic point of sale) is instructive here – most people only notice their dependence upon such systems when they are unable to pay for their

---

Box 1.2   Manchester: Royal Sun Alliance, 1996

Manchester's business and retail quarter was devastated by a bomb, although early warnings enabled police to evacuate shoppers and workers. The Royal Sun Alliance's offices were severely damaged, with the loss of hardware, data and paperwork, communication systems were destroyed. Also, thirty-four people had been working in the building that day, all of whom were mentally or physically injured in the blast. There seemed little chance of business as usual the Monday after the blast. Royal's recovery plan swung into action within 24 hours and by Monday alternative office space had been found although access to the blasted building was not possible for some days. By chance the Royal's headquarters in Liverpool had some space. Other Royal departments were split across offices in Manchester and a Comdisco recovery site at Warrington. A warehouse was set up to deal with recovering data from damaged hardware and documents taken from the ruins.

Source: Royal Sun Alliance (1996)

---

goods in a store due to a breakdown in computer systems. The extent of an organization's 'hidden technology' such as its IS may only be highlighted when things go wrong. Pauchant and Mitroff (1992) describe how a fire in a Chicago telephone switching centre caused disruption to 1.5 million business and domestic customers. The immediate effects lasted for some three weeks at an estimated cost of $200–300 million. The pre-incident attitudes of many were summed up by the comment of one manager: '*I always thought the dial tone came from God!*'

If it is accepted that ICT will help determine organizational advantage (Earl, 1989), the protection of such systems has become vitally important. It is important that managers approach the protection of such systems from a strategic perspective so that opportunities presented by new technologies can be better exploited. There is a danger, however, that protection of the system becomes the objective, rather than seeking to ensure that the desired outcomes are achieved, as Thames Water's case in Box 1.3 indicates.

Box 1.3 indicates that organizational continuity should be extended beyond merely IS. It clearly indicates that business continuity is incomplete when it is internally and hardware-focused. Facilities and IS offer a means to an end, they are not ends in themselves. Service continuity, as a concept, emphasizes that organizational assets, soft and hard, are a means to the end of satisfying customers.

This chapter now turns to examine the development of business continuity as a discipline. It is not our intention to introduce the reader of this text to a prescriptive approach, as we do not subscribe to the view that there is 'one right way' of doing continuity planning. All organizations differ and it would be foolhardy to presume such an approach as at all feasible. Rather, we present a perspective that we hope will stimulate debate and new ways of under-

---

Box 1.3   Continuity as a means to an end

Thames Water in London, UK relabelled business continuity as 'service continuity'. When a water main burst, interrupting supplies, the company originally defined this as a technical problem to be solved by repairing the burst pipe. Reconsidering this, Thames Water realized that customers were less concerned with repairing the water pipe than with ensuring that clean water was delivered to their properties, by tanker if necessary. Service continuity was best reflected in the story told of how a burst water main had flooded a garden due to host a wedding two days later. Service continuity included not simply fixing the pipe but restoring the garden for that weekend in order that the wedding could go ahead.

When Sunderland City Council, in the north-east of the UK prepared for possible disruptions triggered by the millennium bug it identified alternative power generation as a key vulnerability. Initially, key sites were held to be security lighting on Council premises and building developments. Slowly, there was the recognition that, if power supplies were interrupted, Council residential homes for the elderly and disabled would be without electricity and that protection of human life was a higher priority than the protection of property. The Council had simply not considered the possibility of a major power failure in its residential care homes.

(Elliott *et al.*, 1999a)

---

standing the issue. Our approach regards people as being at the heart of the issue of ensuring organizational preparedness. Without a body of committed employees who enact whatever continuity plans the organization has constructed, organizational preparedness will remain a chimera. Second, we regard an organization as forming part of a wider system and highlighting this interdependence is crucial. Business continuity management should therefore, we think, be based upon the recognition of these issues and the planning process should reflect these realities. However, too often, texts in the area do not appear to take into account these issues and the resultant business process is therefore the poorer for it.

Historical legacies, evolution and stages of development

It is well recognized that products and services often follow common life-cycle patterns (see, for example, Levitt, 1965; Gibson and Nolan, 1974; Shipley, 1998). Even the diffusion of management ideas appears to follow such common patterns of development and demise (see, for example, Egan, 1995). With regard to information systems, such an evolution, in this case from a technical to a broader organizational focus, has been observed (see, for example, Nolan, 1979; Earl, 1989; Galliers and Sutherland, 1991). An organization's underlying assumptions concerning the nature of IS and strategy will be revealed by the approach taken. For example, technocratic approaches emphasize ICT hardware and the importance of control by IT professionals.

Despite their limitations, life-cycle models have been extremely influential because they highlight a well-recognized pattern – in the IT field they document the switch from focus upon technology to resource management and value extraction as development moves beyond the initiation stage. Put simply, concern switches to seeking ways of exploiting IT for competitive advantage. The speed of change may be determined by the nature of the technology (Earl, 1989) or by the degree to which the management team understands the importance of systems to the success of their business (Hirschheim *et al.*, 1988).

Within the IS management literature the use by Galliers and Sutherland (1991) of Waterman *et al.*'s (1980) Seven S framework may be seen as both reaction to and development from earlier evolutionary models (see also Pascale and Athos, 1982). Developed by McKinsey and Company during the 1970s the Seven S framework emphasized the systemic properties of organizations. Sutherland and Gallier's (1989) resulting stages-of-growth model mapped out the organizational characteristics associated with the six stages of development identified.

In an attempt to apply the 'stages-of-growth model' to business continuity management, Swartz *et al.* (forthcoming) identified at least three stages from a study based on data collected from six organizations, shown in Figure 1.2.

Two mindsets dominate the BCM literature, and organizational practice, which Swartz *et al.* label the 'technology' and 'auditing' mindsets. A third, arising from their study analysis, is described as a 'value-based' mindset. Figure 1.2 depicts the evolutionary path of BCM over the last two decades, extending from a technology-focused activity to a value-based activity found within some organizations today. These mindsets are historically contingent and, to be properly understood, should be considered against the context of the dominant technologies and organizational forms of the different periods. In presenting Figure 1.2, it is not suggested that these perspectives are

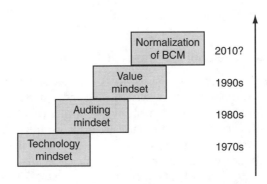

Figure 1.2 Evolution of BCM concept and practice

restricted to specific decades; it is argued that each mindset represents the dominant paradigm for a particular period. Accordingly, mindsets coexist within the population of organizations and even within any one organization. Key characteristics of each mindset are summarized in Table 1.1.

In Table 1.1 *scope* refers to whether BCM is regarded as functional or organization-wide in its focus. *Triggers* indicate the nature of the event that led to initiation of the BCM process within an organization. *Process* refers to whether BCM is regarded as a technocratic or business activity, to the degree of involvement of key staff and the underlying assumptions made about how BCM should be embedded within the organization. We discuss the different stages and mindsets below.

Technology mindset

The technology mindset focuses exclusively upon the protection of computer systems and facilities. During the 1970s, a common assumption was that business disruptions were triggered by a technology failure; thus priority was placed upon protecting hard systems such as corporate mainframe systems (Pritchard, 1976; Broadbent, 1979; Kuong and Isaacson, 1986). Ginn (1989) reports that disaster recovery originated from the desire of US banks to

Table 1.1 Exploring assumptions about business continuity management provision

Emerged during this decade	Mindset	Scope	Triggers	Process
1970s	Technology	Limited to technology Focus upon large corporate systems e.g. mainframes	External physical triggers, flood, fire, bomb	Contingency measures focused on hard systems
1980s	Auditing	All facilities All systems – both corporate and departmental offices	As above and legal or regulatory pressures	Contingency measures outsourced Compliance driven
1990s	Value-based	Maintain competitive advantage Includes customers and suppliers Entire organization, including human, social issues	Organizational stake-holders in value system	BCM developed as business process focused on business managers

protect corporate data centres during the early 1970s. Kuong and Isaacson (1986) explain how BCP started in electronic data-processing (EDP) depart-ments as computer systems became integral to the operation of businesses such as airlines, financial services, retailing, etc. They point out that the con-sideration behind providing security for such systems is often the need to protect the technical systems rather than any sound management consider-ations that aim to protect the whole enterprise. In the UK, the main triggers for the 'technology' perspective have been external failures and, during the 1990s, the perceived threat of terrorist attacks. Ginn (1989) is at pains to show that the focus upon recovery and disaster events differs from what he calls 'continuity planning', which focuses upon disaster prevention for the entire organization. Ginn (1989) asserts that IT disaster recovery (recovery of sys-tems after disruption has taken place) can be traced back to the US banking industry in the early 1970s. This was when the Vice-President for IS of a major US bank sought a solution to being disturbed at night by telephone calls from the data-processing centre about potential disasters threatening IT security. Out of this arose the idea to systematically plan back-up or recovery sites and many of the concepts and practices which are still used today in disaster recovery. The 1970s were years where IS was dominated by main-frame systems whilst the 1980s saw a change to technology which allowed end-user computing to become established (Panko, 1988). This provides the basis for the auditing mindset, with computing becoming distributed and control shifting to end-users. It then became necessary to police compliance.

Auditing mindset

The auditing perspective regards business continuity as a 'cost' required by regulations or corporate governance initiatives. For example, specific federal legislation has acted as a driver in the USA. This mindset assumes a broader scope for BCM than its predecessor. It is regarded as vital insurance. This functional perspective, however, can see no other opportunity or purpose for business continuity within the process of value creation. Consequently, the business continuity process is still concentrated upon contingency measures for hard systems protection, perhaps outsourcing certain tasks to disaster recovery consultants. The major focus of the auditing perspective is still on the technology, the plan itself, and how continuity can be established through protecting essential business activities. This became increasingly important as end-user computing spread through organizations during the 1980s. For Ginn (1989) this type of continuity planning has two distinct phases:

* Phase 1, planning to lessen the risk of disaster
* Phase 2, concentrating on the development of a survival plan to ensure survival and recovery from a disaster

Whilst phase 1 might concentrate on IT systems and the corporate data centre, phase 2 is concerned with how to prevent and survive disruption through the loss of buildings, people or other resources required to conduct business.

The main BCM triggers acknowledged by the auditing perspective appear to be regulation; for example, the US Foreign Corrupt Practices Act which requires that publicly owned organizations have internal control provisions to safeguard assets (Kuong and Isaacson, 1986). More recently, in the UK, Turnbull's (1999) guidance on internal controls and the IS Security Standard (BS7799) promoted by the UK Department of Trade and Industry have triggered consideration by organizations of information systems and security.

While the auditing perspective does consider people as part of the BCM process, the focus is principally upon how to 'engineer' compliance. There is no elaboration of the impact of the human contribution to disruption (either as cause or prevention) or of its influence on implementation of the business continuity process. In the value-based approach it is proposed that these factors are regarded as central to the process (Herbane *et al.*, 1997).

Value-based mindset

The value-based perspective is concerned less with compliance, regulations or technology failure than with the needs of the business itself. Crucially, in this mindset BCM is regarded as having the potential to add value to the organization, not just consume revenues.

The 'value-based' perspective departs from the technology and auditing perspectives in the assumptions that are made about the scope and purpose of BCM. The scope is perceived as constituting the entire organization including employees, who are regarded as presenting the biggest challenge in terms of implementation and management of the business continuity process. Organizational stakeholders are regarded as being the most important driver for change and hence for BCM. In essence, business continuity is regarded as the integration of social and technical systems that together enable effective organizational protection (Swartz *et al.*, 1995). In organizations which adopt this approach, BCM expertise is often brought into the new product development process, and actively exploited in marketing strategy. Therefore, BCM not only protects but also is seen to contribute to the value adding process through more efficient systems or providing value-adding benefits to customers through superior responsiveness, reliability and security.

In an earlier study (Herbane *et al.*, 1997) a continuum was developed which subsequently evolved into the three mindsets identified above (see Figure 1.3). It is argued that what we now term a value-based mindset constituted 'better practice' compared to the 'standard practice' of the technology mindset.

The continuum depicted in Figure 1.3 identified a number of dimensions against which 'practice' might be assessed. The first two dimensions refer to the types of staff employed on continuity projects and to the scope of their work. Standard practice is concerned with IT systems and employs only IT

'Standard practice'	'Better practice'
Old	New
Disaster recovery	**BCM**
IT focus	Value chain focus
IT staff	Multi-disciplinary team
Existing structure	New structures
Protect core operations	Protect entire organization
Sustain current position	Create sustainable advantage
Parochial view	Open system view
Recovery emphasis	Prevention emphasis

Figure 1.3 Old and new BCM approaches compared

Source: Adapted from Herbane *et al.* (1997).

staff whilst better-practice organizations employed staff from a diversity of backgrounds on a project business-wide in scope. A range of forces, including a board level champion, managerial appraisal and a persuasive communications strategy, drove effective continuity. Better-practice organizations combined these and other measures to drive the business continuity process successfully; standard-practice firms had little use for such initiatives because continuity management was seen as a task for IT alone. In such organizations there was little need for new structures. In better-practice cases, new structures of coordinators were identified, with responsibility for the continuity process, and were delegated to each business unit, with the dedicated continuity team providing a supporting role. The final differences between the two extremes concern strategy. Better practice saw continuity as a strategic issue both in terms of protecting its place in the supply chain but also in marketing activities. The continuum provides a snapshot of continuity practice.

The plan of the book

This book is structured around the key concept of business continuity management and the underlying assumptions that accompany theoretical and practical approaches to this process. It is logical that the book should be structured in line with the strategic management process, starting with the main environmental issues first and then focusing on the internal, organizational influences and process. Figure 1.1 illustrates the business continuity management process and factors that influence the activities necessary to put continuity management in place within an organization.

In Chapter 1, we have considered why organizations should adopt BCM through a consideration of the strategic importance of being able to deal with crises and interruptions effectively. Furthermore, we examined the historical legacies and antecedents of business continuity management.

Chapter 2 considers the regulatory and legislative environment within which continuity planning and management must operate. The ethical and legal responsibilities of organizations must work in parallel with continuity management, particularly as organizations' liability in the event of a crisis may have consequences for its survival. Although there is little specific legislation for business continuity a wider range of rules and regulations can influence the responsibilities of an organization before and after an interruption.

Having considered the strategic and regulatory/legislative need for continuity management, Chapters 3–6 introduce and detail the four stages of the business continuity process, from initiation to implementation as depicted in Figure 1.1. Chapter 3 examines how organizations initiate continuity management and put into place structural, managerial and resource requirements in order to proceed with planning for business continuity (Chapter 4). Following this, Chapter 5 examines how organizations can and should implement business continuity management by exploring change management. From this, organizations are in a position to proceed to the operational management of business continuity (Chapter 6) in which they continuously maintain and test their plans. In addition, Chapter 6 examines how organizations manage recovery operations in the event of a crisis.

Chapter 7 concludes with an examination of the new challenges and developments that are shaping the current and future business environment. In so doing, we identify the prospect of such developments having an influence on continuity management in the future.

Summary

This chapter has introduced the concept of business continuity and has identified a range of different approaches to it. We have argued that effective continuity management needs to be focused upon business processes and assets as means to an end. The growing reliance of organizations upon one another, and upon technology and infrastructure, has also been cited as supporting the view that continuity management matters more today than at any other point in history. The approach in this book is founded upon what has been termed as a crisis management approach; this assumes that soft and hard system elements must be considered together and that organizations themselves may incubate the potential for interruptions. Managerial intervention plays a vital role in causing crises or in mitigating their effects. Whilst no methodology can guarantee that interruptions will be avoided, it is argued that adopting the broad methodology developed in this book will assist organizations to be better prepared.

References

Anderson, R.E. (1992) *Bank Security*, Woburn MA: Butterworth (Publishers) Inc.

Bangemann, M. (1994) *Europe and the Global Information Society*, Recommendations to the European Council, Brussels: European Commission.

Bowe, C. (2001) 'Ford and Firestone settle high-profile lawsuit', *Financial Times* 8 January.

Broadbent, D. (1979) *Contingency Planning*, Manchester, National Computing Centre.

Crowe, M.K. (1996) 'Information and business process', *Systems Practice* 9(3): 263–72.

Doswell, B. (2000) *Guide to Business Continuity Management*, Leicester: Perpetuity Press.

Earl, M.J. (1989) *Management Strategies for Information Technology*, Hemel Hempstead: Prentice Hall.

Egan, C. (1995) *Competitive Advantage*, London: Butterworth-Heinemann.

Elliott, D., Swartz, E. and Herbane, B. (1999) *Business Continuity Management*, Report for Income Data Services (IDS), London.

Galliers, R.D. and Sutherland, A.R. (1994) 'Information systems management and strategy formulation: applying and extending the stages of growth concept', in R.D. Galliers and B.S.H. Baker (1994) *Strategic Information Management: Challenges and Strategies in Managing Information Systems*, Oxford: Butterworth-Heinemann.

Gibson, C. and Nolan, R.L. (1974) 'Managing the four stages of EDP growth', *Harvard Business Review* 52(1).

Ginn, R.D. (1989) *Continuity Planning: Preventing, Surviving and Recovering from Disaster*, Oxford: Elsevier Advanced Technology.

Herbane B., Elliott, D. and Swartz, E. (1997) Contingency and continua: achieving excellence through business continuity planning, *Business Horizons*, 40(6): 19–25.

Hiles, A. and Barnes, P. (eds) (1999) *Business Continuity Management*, London: Wiley.

Hirschheim, R., Earl, M., Feeny, D. and Lockett, M. (1988) 'An exploration into the management of the information systems function: key issues and an evolutionary model', *Proceedings Information Technology Management for Productivity and Strategic Advantage, IFIP TC-8 Open Conference Singapore*, March, cited in R.D. Galliers and A.R. Sutherland (1991) *Information Systems Management and Strategy Formulation: Applying and Extending the Stages of Growth Concept*, Oxford: Butterworth-Heinemann.

Irwin, R. (2001) *What is Fud?* [on-line] www.geocities.com/siliconvalley/hills/9267/, accessed 29/01/01.

Kuong, J. and Isaacson, J. (1986) *How to Prepare an EDP Plan for Business Contingency*, Wellesley Hills, MA: Management Advisory Publications.

Levitt, T. (1965) 'Exploit the product life cycle', *Harvard Business Review* 43: 81–94.

Mandela, N. (1994) *The Long Walk to Freedom*, London: Abacus Books.

Nolan, R. (1979) 'Managing the crises in data processing', *Harvard Business Review*, 57(2): 115–26.

Olins, R. and Lynn, M. (1997) 'A class disaster', *The Sunday Times* 17 November: 14.

Panko, R.R. (1988) *End User Computing*, New York: Wiley.

Pascale, R.T. and Athos, A.G. (1982) *The Art of Japanese Management*, London: Penguin Books.

Pauchant, T. and Douville, R. (1993) 'Recent research in crisis management: a study of 24 authors' publications from 1986 to 1991', *Industrial and Environmental Crisis Quarterly* 7(1): 43–66.

Pauchant, T. and Mitroff, I. (1992) *The Crisis-prone Organisation*, San Francisco, CA: Jossey-Bass.

Perrow, C. (1997) *Normal Accidents*, New York: Basic Books.

Pilger, J. (1998) *Hidden Agendas*, London: Vintage.

Pritchard, J.A.T. (1976) *Contingency Planning*, Manchester: NCC.

Prowse, R. (1998) 'A legal moose on the loose?', *Motor Industry Management* October: 17.

Royal Sun Alliance (1996) *The Manchester Bombing Incident*, Video. London.

Schwartz, H. (1987) 'On the psychodynamics of organisational disaster', *Columbia Journal of World Disaster* 22(1): 59–68.

Shipley, D. (1998) 'Marketing strategies for growth, maturity and decline', in C. Egan and M.T. Thomas (eds) *The CIM Handbook of Strategic Marketing*, London: Butterworth-Heinemann.

Shrivastava, P. (1987) *Bhopal*, London: Ballinger.

Smith, D. (1990) 'Beyond contingency planning: towards a model of crisis management', *Industrial Crisis Quarterly* 4(4): 263–75.

Starbuck, W.H. and Milliken, F.J. (1988) 'Challenger: fine tuning the odds until something breaks', *Journal of Management Studies* 25: 319–30.

Strohl Systems (1995) *The Business Continuity Planning Guide*, King of Prussia, PA: Strohl Systems.

Sun Microsystems (2001) *Official Fudwatch Index* [on-line] java.sun.com/features/ fudwatch/, accessed 29/01/01.

Swartz, E., Elliott, D. and Herbane, B. (1995) 'Out of sight, out of mind: the limitations of traditional information systems planning', *Facilities* 13(9/10): 15–22.

Swartz, E., Elliott, D. and Herbane, B. (forthcoming) 'Greater than the sum of its parts: business continuity management in the UK finance sector', *Journal of Strategic Information Systems*.

Tait, N. (2001) 'Firestone in wider tyre recall', *Financial Times* 2 January.

Taylor, A. (2000) 'Jac Nasser's biggest test', *Fortune* 142(6): 71–4.

Turnbull, N. (1999) *Internal Control: Guidance for Directors on the Combined Code*, London: Institute of Chartered Accountants in England and Wales.

Turner, B. (1976) 'The organizational and interorganizational development of disasters', *Administrative Science Quarterly* 21: 378–89.

Turner, B. and Pidgeon, N. (1997) *Man-made Disasters*, 2nd edn, London: Butterworth-Heinemann.

Vancoppenolle, G. (1999) 'What are we planning for?', in A. Hiles and P. Barnes (eds) *Business Continuity Management*, London: Wiley.

Waterman, R.H., Peters, T. and Phillips, J.R. (1980) 'Structure is not organization', *Business Horizons* June: 14–26.

Further reading

Billings, R., Milburn, T. and Schaalman, M. (1980) 'A model of crisis perception', *Administrative Science Quarterly* 25: 300–16.

Herman, C.F. (1963) 'Some consequences of crisis which limit the viability of organizations', *Administrative Science Quarterly* 12: 61–82.

Turner, B. and Pidgeon N. (1997) *Man-made Disasters*, 2nd edn, London: Butterworth-Heinemann.

Study questions

1   What are the advantages of applying a business continuity approach to strategic decisions?
2   Examine the newspapers for a fourteen-day period and identify examples of service continuity.
3   How does service continuity differ from business continuity?
4   What are the characteristics of good business continuity practice?
5   How would you expect to see this implemented in:

- a large retailer
- an Internet service provider
- a football club

2 Regulatory and legislative issues

Introduction

Despite the uncertainty which managers may face in determining the types of crises which an organization may face (which we address in Chapters 3 and 4), regulations and legislation affecting the organization in the context of a crisis or business interruption are well known. In this chapter, we navigate through some of the important areas of legislation of which managers should be aware. We also consider the role of regulations and self-regulation as an influence upon business continuity management. It is important, prior to any attempt to plan for crises, that managers are aware of those legal and regulatory issues that will influence or affect the plans they seek to develop. After all, a business continuity plan which leads to a subsequent breach of law or regulation merely serves to cause a further crisis.

We begin with the importance of control systems within the context of business continuity within an integrated framework, which identifies their source, type, purpose and appropriateness, and proceed to evaluate the influence that stakeholders have upon external controls such as legislation and regulation. The evaluation of external controls proceeds with a consideration of three major areas of legislation: employment law, health and safety law and product liability law. These are major influences on crises and their outcome, but should be central considerations within a business continuity plan in an attempt to pre-empt and prevent crises from occurring. From this we introduce regulations and self-regulation as alternatives to legislative provisions. Whilst having many benefits compared to legal provisions, our analysis highlights the problematic nature of regulatory approaches and examines how the role of regulators has evolved. Finally, we consider two embryonic approaches to the development of business continuity management (BCM) standards which seek to address the absence of BCM-specific standards, although their scope and specificity has yet to evolve.

The context of control

Contingent upon their origin, controls influence or determine an organization's actions. Control systems are processes that enable an evaluation of whether objectives and goals are being met in four major ways: coping with complexity; coping with and adapting to environmental complexity; enhancing efficiency by minimizing costs; and maintaining standards (Herbane and Rouse, 2000). Controls are important in guiding and determining the behaviour of organizations and their employees. The types of control examined and evaluated in this chapter (such as regulation and legislation) determine the degree to which behaviour is *guided* or *determined*. The need for control systems in the implementation and integration of BCM within an organization is subject to the same exigencies as the actions needed to incorporate improved quality programmes or new administrative processes.

The provenance of controls can be both external and internal. With differing degrees of influence and appropriateness, an organization is faced with many reasons why its processes and actions must adhere and conform to prescribed standards. Figure 2.1 presents a hierarchy of controls, which organizations are subject to, and provides a framework for this chapter.

Legislation, regulation and internal controls are the three control *types* which have been identified. We can observe from Figure 2.1 that the *source* of control types ranges from externally derived sources, such as regulation and legislation, to those developed internally, such as administrative systems, procedures, mentoring, appraisal systems, budgets and rewards. Such internal controls are highly tangible yet will vary between organizations. Control types also vary in terms of their *appropriateness* and their *purpose*. *Appropriateness* is considered in terms of the congruence of control types within an organization, given the unique nature of its resources, operations and history. This varies from generic legislation, to which all organizations

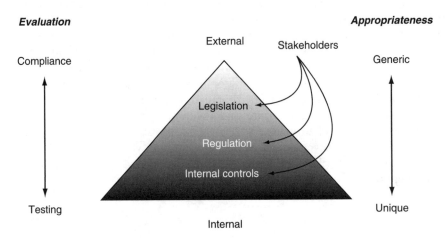

Figure 2.1 Hierarchy of controls

within the boundaries of a jurisdiction must conform, to regulations which may deal with specific industries, activities and processes, and finally to the unique control systems which individual organizations have in place and which are determined by factors such as age, history, environment and leadership. *Purpose* refers to the rationale behind the control type, such as whether organizations are meeting the expectations determined externally about their behaviour, such as compliance, or whether activities are achieving internally established goals, reflecting performance aspirations.

Stakeholders and control

In the previous chapter we introduced and examined the relationship between stakeholders and organizations, with the attendant requirement for organizations to be aware of their ability to ensure not only the continuity of commercial trading and production but also the continuity of stakeholder relationships. Stakeholder groups are not only unique between organizations, but their relationship with an individual organization can be characterized by dynamism, particularly during crises. Crisis events serve not only to challenge day-to-day operations, but may also change the relationship between stakeholders as the effects on differing stakeholder groups may vary. In the process of an organization invoking continuity plans, the necessity arises for the organization to implement a series of planned activities designed to achieve the resumption of operations (often referred to as a 'time-line of recovery'). This may shift stakeholder relations from the existing dynamic complex of relations with a large group of stakeholders to a more limited set of groups which has been designated as those on whom the organization must rely, or who are in turn reliant upon the organization during the recovery phase. The shifting dynamics of stakeholders during a crisis not only play an important role in the subsequent turnaround period but also influence the controls which prevail within the organization. For instance, a car component manufacturer facing a product recall will prioritize the media and franchised dealership network more highly that the university with which it has an ongoing, but unrelated, research and development programme since this latter group, albeit an important stakeholder in a different context, does not constitute a priority in the activities designed to resolve the aftermath of a major product recall. The role of stakeholders is significant for each type of organizational control. New legislation may arise due to the influence of stakeholders, such as in the introduction of a Treasury funded re-insurance scheme following intense lobbying by the UK insurance industry soon after the Baltic Exchange bombing in 1992.

Regulations (from governments and industry groups) may reflect changing public tastes and social change, like the ban placed upon the testing of cosmetics products on animals imposed by the British government in November 1998. The stakeholder influence on internal controls is equally discernible. Stakeholder expectations in competitive industries with publicly quoted companies create a form of market control whereby the expectations and actions of equity holders drives the need for organizations to have in place controls that ensure that expectations (such as investment returns, but increasingly in terms of socially responsible conduct) are met.

Legislation and business continuity management

Legislation and control

Statutory provisions in law are generic in appropriateness to organizations (Figure 2.1) and have compliance as their purpose. At present, legislation specifically directed at continuity management practices do not exist in the UK. However, this is not surprising since business continuity management is concerned with how individual organizations plan to prevent, deal with, recover from and manage crisis incidents. Furthermore, this absence most likely exists because the overriding concern of many aspects of legislation is the outcome rather than the process, that is, culpability rather than motive (although the latter forms *prima facie* evidence of the former). It is in cases where an organization or its agents are considered to be negligent that litigation ensues.

However, a wider examination of legal provisions yields a variety of statutes and precedents, which provide a legal framework in which organizations should operate, and therefore have an influence upon business continuity management. We consider three areas of particular importance: employment, health and safety, and product liability law. In each of these areas, those with involvement in continuity management should consider (in consultation with legal expertise) whether current practices and processes comply with statutory minimum requirements, and whether all aspects of the business continuity plan reflect and mirror legal provisions.

Employment law

Employment law governs the fundamental relationship between employer and employee and imposes controls on the relationship, performance, conduct and behaviour of parties, with implications for business continuity management. Under English law, both employees and employers have implied duties and obligations. These are not absolute duties which render all organizations liable for harm and injury to their employees. Rather, the duty is of reasonable care. Within this fundamental and implicit common law provision continuity issues can be considered. For instance, the duty to ensure employees' safety in common law provides a foundation upon which statutory legislation (such as the Heath and Safety at Work Act 1974) is built. The current view of the standard of care has been set down since 1951, when Lord Oaksey interpreted this as 'the care which an ordinary prudent employer would take in all [reasonably foreseeable] circumstances' (Selwyn, 1988: 172).

Here, prudence can be seen within a context of risk assessment and monitoring in the working environment of risks that can be reasonably foreseen. Whilst the risks of a working environment, materials or substances may not be known at a given point in time, employers must ensure that they protect their employees against injury or damage as knowledge of such risks becomes known. Hence, the common law duty of employers is extended; they must be cognizant of new risks that their employees may be subject to. The plea of ignorance is an insufficient defence.

Employers are also required to provide safe plant and equipment, a safe system of work and engage reasonably competent fellow employees. If an employer does not take reasonable precautions to ensure that plant and appliances are safe, the lack of care can constitute common law negligence. Should an employer procure equipment, resources or services from a supplier which then cause injury or harm to an employee, the employer is considered negligent in relation to the employee. This could arise where an organization uses the services of a disaster recovery provider offering alternative premises. In turn, however, the employer can then initiate litigation against the supplier. A safe system of work includes systems, training, instructions, supervision and protective equipment in place whilst employees carry out their tasks in an employment relationship. Employees must be told explicitly about safety precautions, and safety equipment must be available to use. Where injury and harm to an employee has arisen because of an incompetent person, an employer will be held liable for failing to take reasonable care of employees.

Issues such as those noted above are of vital importance where a business continuity plan requires employees to undertake activities which are required for business recovery such as equipment and data salvage, or where a company is forced to use new premises. It is, therefore, important that, when organizations develop and test their business continuity plans (Chapter 4), legal compliance with employers' statutory duties is maintained in circumstances where alternative locations are used to restore operations, away from an inaccessible building or facility.

Equally important in the contract of employment (and with implications for business continuity management) are the implied duties and obligations of the employee to his or her employer. The duty of faithful service requires employees to undertake 'duties carefully and competently, with due regard for the interests of the employer' (Selwyn, 1988: 183). Unless an order or instruction is unlawful or falls beyond established contractual obligations, employees have a duty to obey lawful and reasonable orders from employers, otherwise a breach of contract will occur. Employees must also use skill and care in carrying out their work and in using the company's property. Employees are also duty-bound to refuse bribes and commissions and to protect confidential information and intellectual property. The disclosure of confidential information (unless disclosure is a requirement, such as for health and safety compliance) by an employee could give a rival an advantage and is an act which could precipitate a crisis for an organization. Clearly such actions by an employee could be construed to be fair grounds for disciplinary action.

Employment law is an important issue to consider within the context of continuity management, since not only might the duties of the employer be related to a crisis arising, but they may also govern the content of the business continuity plan, in which employees are required to undertake tasks which are not part of normal procedures. There is a fine line between what can reasonably be expected to be foreseen under normal circumstances as opposed to non-routine but reasonably foreseeable circumstances (since they are specified in the continuity plan) and what would constitute exposure of employees to undue risk in non-routine circumstances.

Health and safety

The Health and Safety at Work Act (1974) formed the basis for the integration of several acts (such as the Factories Act 1962 and the Offices, Shops and Railway Premises Act 1963) that were gradually repealed. A major change occurred in the emphasis of the legislation, away from a focus on premises towards employees and non-employees within places of work. An additional, yet original, intention of the legislation was to promote better health and safety practices within a regulated environment, with the Act serving as an introductory set of statutory duties for employers. The Act is supplemented by a series of regulations (a breach of which is punishable generally as a criminal offence) which apply either to all employment premises and environments, or to specific risks and hazards, or, finally, specific hazards in designated industries. Selwyn (1988: 365) suggested that:

> The use of regulations as a device for laying down legal standards [is] a superior method to legislation, for regulations are simpler and more flexible; they can be altered more readily in accordance with experience and technological progress, and will be more manageable to those who have to implement them.

Under the Act, Health and Safety Inspectors are given wider powers of access, investigation and enforcement. Where a contravention of statutory provisions is found, an inspector can enforce an improvement notice, in which a specified period is given to remedy the contravention (a minimum period of 21 days is allowed in order to allow appeal). If the inspector considers the contravention to be one where there is a risk of serious injury if an activity is not ceased, a prohibition notice can be served.

Within the Act itself, duties are either absolute, in which case the person with the duty is obliged, without discretion, to carry out the duty, or 'so far as is reasonably practicable' whereby an organization must consider the cost and time involved in adhering to the duty. In legal proceedings, the burden of proof is placed on the employer to show that it was not reasonably practicable to meet the duty, or that it could not have known the implications of a given contravention. In addition, some duties include obligations to use the 'best practicable means' which sits between the two degrees of obligation noted above. The duties of the employer include:

- to provide safe systems of work (including handling and transportation, training and information, maintenance and employee welfare) for employees
- to not charge employees for the costs incurred in meeting statutory health and safety requirements (VDU filters, specialized clothing, etc.)
- to produce a written safety policy (except for organizations with fewer than five employees)
- to consult with a safety representative and to establish a safety committee as requested, and
- to ensure the health and safety of non-employees when using the employer's premises

Controllers of premises that are non-domestic are also responsible for ensuring that there is no risk to the safety and health of users of the premises. Controllers must also ensure that atmospheric emissions from the premises are harmless. Manufacturers and suppliers of materials and substances have additional duties to those indicated above. These duties extend to the design, manufacture, testing and examination of equipment which, as far as is reasonably practicable, should be safe and not create risks to health and safety. The provisions of the Act extend to the disassembly and disposal of equipment. The additional duties of material and substance producers/suppliers include safe handling, storage and transportation of substances, and testing, research and training in relation to substances used by the employer.

Under section 7 of the Act, employees also have statutory duties which include cooperating with employers/controllers and taking reasonable care of the safety and health not only of him or herself but of others also. They have a duty not to interfere with measures taken or with facilities or equipment provided by an employer to maintain or improve the health and safety conditions required under the Act.

The Health and Safety at Work Act (1974) includes provision for Codes of Practice, where the Health and Safety Commission (HSC) can produce practical guidelines for organizations to comply with the types of statutory duties listed earlier. Codes of Practice must have government approval following consultation with the relevant state departments. The authorship and revision of Codes of Practice is not the sole preserve of the HSC. Individual organizations, trade unions and industry associations are also entitled to submit draft codes for Home Office approval. The failure of an employer to meet the standards of a Code of Practice does not by itself constitute a breach in the duties of care, but could be considered to be evidence of negligence nonetheless.

Product liability

One of the major crises which an organization can face is the recall of a defective product. Product recall crises should be a central consideration in the continuity plans of all organizations, particularly since the liability of organizations for their products is well-established in legal systems world-wide. Table 2.1 provides a small sample of product recalls.

The legal liability of organizations selling products which cause injury is known under the umbrella term 'product liability'. The US legal provisions of product liability stem from the precedent laid down in *Greenman* vs. *Yuba Power Products Inc.* (1962). Since then, both the European Union (through the 1985 Directive on Liability for Legally Defective Products) and Japan (Product Liability Law 1994) have come to broadly reflect the US legal framework for product liability (McCubbins and Mosier, 1998). Each system is underpinned by the concept of *res ipsa loquitur*, whereby a plaintiff must show that they were injured by a product in such a way that would not have occurred had the manufacturer not been negligent.

From the Ford Pinto to Perrier mineral water, all products sold carry an implied warranty that they are safe and fit for use. In the food industry, ranging from production to catering, the requirement for inspection, hygiene and training cannot provide a reasonable defence against a litigant. Sirignano (1997) argues that commercial product liability litigation in the USA is problematic giving rise to frivolous and opportunistic lawsuits, whereupon the defendant has the burden of proof to show that their duty of care to the buyer has been maintained. For example, R.J.R. Nabisco successfully defended a case in which a child had eaten a snack which contained a pin by

Table 2.1 Product recalls

Year	Product	Defect	Company
1998	A-Class	Unstable vehicle	Mercedes-Benz
1998	Aluminium cans	Tin lining unstable	Various food companies
1990	Mineral water	Benzine contamination	Perrier
1986	Lawn mower	Battery close to fuel tank	John Deere
1984	Pharmaceuticals	Limited warnings on label	Ortho Pharmaceuticals
1974	Dalkon shield	Birth control device caused pelvic disease	A.H. Robins
1967	Cola	Exploding bottles	Coca-Cola Company
1963	Fireworks	Powerful firework found in a domestic firework set	T.W. Hand Fireworks Company
1944	Cola	Mouse found in bottle	Coca-Cola Company
1941	Bread	Contained fragments of glass	Canada Bread Company
1985	Breast implants	Causes auto-immune disease	Dow Corning

Source: McCubbins and Mosier (1998), Nocera (1995), Authors.

showing that the incorporation of the pin into the product could not have taken place at any stage in the production process:

> The raw ingredients were filtered and carefully inspected for foreign materials, the finished products were passed through metal detectors, the wrapped bars were placed in sealed cartons, the type of pin was not used in the manufacturing facility, and all employees were prohibited from wearing jewellery.

> (Sirignano, 1997: 7)

The application of product liability law in the USA has undergone several changes in recent years, with a re-examination of the interpretation of why a plaintiff may have wilfully destroyed a defective product, thereby destroying the central evidence in a product liability suit. Where this is found to be the case, the jury can be directed to favour the defence's case and/or the exclusion of the plaintiff's expert witnesses (Goetsch, 1996). A second change has occurred in the liability facing companies which fail to provide adequate warnings about the use of a product or its hazards. No longer is it a requirement for juries to consider whether warnings could have been better (strict liability), but rather if such warnings were unreasonable (negligence). Siegfried (1998) argues that closer involvement of legal experts in the development of labelling and instructions for buyers will not only prove to be precautionary but also enable a strong defence, helping a company to better defend against litigation. This should reduce expensive settlement payments and discourage others from litigation. This requires extensive data to be collected, under the supervision of legal experts, of information associated with the product (substances, materials and packaging) and potential hazards, but once these are known, comprehensive, clear and accessible information on usage should accompany the product. In practical terms, we can see this in many household items. Take, for instance, a food item which is labelled that it 'may contain nuts', safety caps and dosage instructions of pharmaceutical products, and Braille text on cleaning products.

The implications of a product recall crisis and product liability litigation are clear. Not only may an organization face the costs of legal action, the revenue losses from direct sales, the cost of public relations activities and the costs of redesign (where design is at fault) increase the expense of such crises. Moreover, the reputation of an organization and its brand may have further repercussions beyond the ambit of a single recalled product. In being intangible, the effect of a crisis upon a reputation is immense. It should be remembered that a corporate and product reputation takes many years of investment and effort to build, yet little time to destroy. Reputation may be central to an organization's competitive advantage (Hall, 1992). Even where an organization has managed to recall products without injury to customers, the organization will find itself in an inferior competitive position than prior to the recall. A closer link between lawyers specializing in product liability and research and development (R&D) teams has been suggested by Goodden (1996) as a way in which organizations can not only pre-empt the likelihood of a product failure leading to injury to users but also provide documented evidence which can provide a 'state-of-the-art defence'. This refers to where an organization can claim that it was reasonable in ensuring the safety of the product given the best prevailing knowledge it had at the time it designed and produced the product. Furthermore, as Siegfried (1998) indicated earlier, accrued benefits could also include a deterrent and cost-saving effect. The approach suggested mirrors the Failure Mode and Effects Analysis (FMEA) process used in R&D and seeks to factor out any actions which could be seen as negligent should a product subsequently injure a consumer. Furthermore, documentation supporting this process can be used as evidence that a company has taken reasonable steps to prevent foreseeable product liability and should be known to business continuity managers whose role may involve managing the media during a crisis. The types of questions to be considered include:

- What are the reasonable and foreseeable uses of the product?
- What might end-users do with the product that the manufacturer has not anticipated?
- What are the various ways that the products could injure users or cause property damage?
- Are such dangers obvious?
- To what unusual and climatic or environmental conditions might the product be exposed?
- What kinds of warning labels or instructions should be included in the product?
- What legal implications can reasonably be predicted following the launch of the new product?
- What types of testing should be done to ensure that products or their materials will be reliable?

(Goodden 1995, 1996)

Industry associations and liability

The link between professional and industry associations, their members and product liability has recently been highlighted with the pedicle bone screw litigation in the US (Jacobs and Portman, 1998). Around 2,000 patients had found that the screw (used in spinal fusion surgery) had broken, leading to further painful and protracted surgery for the removal of the device. This case is of particular importance because, not only does the manufacturer of the pedicle bone screw face litigation, medical societies (the equivalent of an industry association) have also found themselves facing prosecution since it has been alleged that the screw was not approved by the Food and Drug

Administration for spinal fusion surgery and that they were responsible for the promotion of the screw on behalf of the manufacturer. Specifically, it was alleged that the manufacturer and medical societies had worked together to organize seminars, attended by doctors and spinal surgeons, to promote and sell the product. In addition, the societies received financial incentives for recommending the product to fellow medical practitioners. Despite several unsuccessful attempts to have proceedings dismissed, the medical societies now face prosecution for recklessly selling a product that was not approved for the use suggested by the societies' promotional activities, and liability for injury, pain and lengthy convalescence of spinal fusion surgery patients. The implications of this case reach far beyond the medical industry and its representatives. It marks the extension of liability from companies whose products are defective to industry associations which have provided assistance in the promotion of members' products:

> The best precaution that associations can take to reduce the risk of such liability is to ensure that full disclosure is made to seminar participants about financial relationships with corporate sponsors and the regulatory status of products, discussed, displayed or exhibited at such events. Although these precautions cannot prevent a law suit from being filed, having a documented record of disclosures of financial interests and regulatory status of featured products can discourage product liability plaintiffs from including associations in such litigation.
>
> (Jacobs and Portman, 1998: 82)

Another development concerns mass torts in which plaintiffs group together and enact legal proceedings against an organization, as highlighted in Box 2.1.

The mass tort approach, with many hundreds, if not thousands, of plaintiffs represented simultaneously, offers several advantages to prosecution lawyers by creating legal economies of scale that would counteract the corporate legal resources of large organizations who are better equipped to defend against a single litigant and lawyer.

The effect of a product recall quite clearly threatens the continuity of an organization's operations. The causes of such recalls may arise from supplier defects, errors in research and development, and poor manufacturing. During such a crisis, several functions of an organization undertake higher levels of involvement: legal affairs, in dealing with the threat or actuality of litigation; marketing, in its attempt to restore the image and reputation of the organization and its products; and the manufacturing function, in resolving physical causes of defects. Equally, services can face their own equivalents of product recalls. The UK's pension mis-selling scandal in the late 1980s has led to many pension houses compensating customers for losses incurred in switching from occupational to private pensions. The business continuity team/plan has a major role to play in coordinating the activities of these different

---

Box 2.1   Mass torts as crises

Litigation against the manufacturers of silicon breast implants illustrates the major impact of large-scale product liability (mass torts) and how the reaction of an organization prior to, during and following a crisis can influence the outcome of judicial proceedings. A salient issue in the breast implant case from a product liability perspective is that conclusive and comprehensive medical research to support the link between silicon breast implants and anti-immune disease has yet to be produced. Yet, mass torts and their subsequent settlements have been responsible for the bankruptcy of Dow Corning and the major settlements paid by Bristol-Myers Squibb, 3M and Baxter healthcare. The product has been available in the US since 1964, a time in which it was deemed to be a medical device rather than a pharmaceutical product, and thus not subject to the same stringent testing, licensing and approval procedures by the Food and Drug Administration.

Within Dow Corning, the largest manufacturer of implants, several memoranda (subsequently used in evidence) had questioned the long-term safety of the product, but these had not been informed by formal medical study. These speculative documents (known later as the 'Dow Documents'), whilst inadmissible as proof of medical risk, were used as evidence to convince a jury that Dow Corning had been negligent. In July 1985 plaintiff Maria Stern was awarded $1.7 million damages. As Nocera (1995: 64) notes, 'for any complicated law suit to sprout into a mass tort, something more is needed than a victory or two against a company. There has to be a climate of fear . . . and a group of angry users.' The outcome of this case was significant, as the medical risk of the product had still not been established. In fact, in November 1991, the Food and Drug Administration publicly (but largely ignored) announced that silicon breast implants should not be withdrawn from sale.

In January 1992 the FDA became privy to the 'Dow Documents' and imposed a temporary restriction on silicon breast implants for cosmetic uses, thereby augmenting the number of litigants.

---

functions in the course of a crisis turnaround. Prior to this, the continuity plan (Chapter 4) should include a consideration of, and a contribution from, these important functions. As we have seen, a parochial approach is counter-productive to prevention and recovery of business operations in the wake of a product recall and could indicate, *inter alia*, negligence, unreasonableness and a failure to act with due care.

Intellectual property

The threat to intellectual property represents the propensity for a crisis to occur in a wide variety of ways. Patents, copyright, trademarks and trade secrets represent major investments; such patents can be undermined, or emulated by rivals and malicious parties. Accordingly, organizations with intellectual property that is central to the company's success should be aware how this type of resource could be threatened.

A salient example of the effects of intellectual property violations by an employee is the feud between General Motors (GM) and Volkswagen (VW) over José Ignacio Lopez de Arriortua between 1993 and 1997, which exemplifies how the problems of commercial secrecy can lead to claims of industrial espionage and racketeering. Lopez had resigned from GM and allegedly taken with him purchasing information for 60,000 parts, technical data for new GM models, materials for cost-reduction programmes and a detailed study of a super-efficient car manufacturing plant. Following several years of claims and counterclaims, the companies settled their dispute out of German and US courts, with a $100 million payment to GM, a mutual statement of apology, an agreement by VW to buy $1 billion worth of GM parts over seven years and an undertaking from VW to not re-employ Lopez until the year 2000 (Elkind, 1997).

More recently, the theft of Microsoft's source code in 2000 may have compromised the secret elements of the Windows operating system. The wider ramifications of the crisis have been to threaten future product developments, require the company to invest in further security measures, and expend resources to mitigate effects of the crisis.

In the case of physical inventions (protected by patent), the litigation between Dyson and Hoover, in which Hoover was found to have infringed the patent for the bag-less vacuum cleaner invented by Dyson, has forced Hoover to withdraw certain models from sale and return to bag-based technology. Furthermore, the reputation of the company could be considered to have been tarnished, as it is no longer considered an innovator but an imitator instead.

Increasingly, as organizations move or commence their operations in an e-commerce environment, the threat to them in terms of intellectual copyright breaches is likely to increase as trademarked and copyrighted material is made available on-line. In such cases, it is imperative that the business continuity manager work closely with legal advisers to ensure that there is, at the very least, an understanding of how the international dimension of such threats can be addressed.

Regulation and business continuity management

Regulation and control

Regulation is a further set of controls upon organizations and their behaviour. They are developed and supervised by extra-organizational authorities, and are designed to control the decisions and actions of individual organizations operating within specified economic sectors of activity. They are still external, generic and compliance-based controls, but to a lesser degree than legislation, although, as we have seen previously, regulations may supplement a more generic set of legislative instruments within specific contexts (industries and activities). Equally, regulations may have elements of wider law associated with them in order to ensure compliance. In having their origins beyond the boundaries of an organization, such controls coexist in the context of the controls which have developed from within organizations during its growth and development. The source of such controls determines the way in which they are assimilated into an organization's everyday process.

By their very nature, controls originating from outside an organization are *imposed* since the regulatory authority in question will normally have statutory powers to enforce compliance with their regulations (Table 2.2). In contrast, internal controls may develop in a *voluntary* manner, reflecting a more organic process of bargaining, consensus and human resource practices which differ between organizations. In making a clear distinction between imposed controls and voluntary controls we can acknowledge fundamental differences between them and identify how their integration into processes and activities vary.

Both voluntary and imposed controls coexist in the organizational environment in which business continuity management prevails. The composition of controls (whether external or internal) will clearly vary according to the organization's operating context. However, the imperative facing business continuity managers is the need to understand the balance between controls. This will not only determine the content of business continuity provisions in place, but may also affect the necessity to have specific provisions in place.

We initiate our discussion of regulation with an overview of both statutory and self-regulated approaches to the control of corporate and individual behaviour and highlight its relevance for business continuity. In so doing, it will become clear that little, if any, regulation is specifically directed at business continuity management or related provisions (such as plans, emergency equipment, etc.), although regulations have consequences for BCM and are therefore an important consideration in planning and implementation. We then turn to an evaluation of regulators and regulation.

Table 2.2 Voluntary versus imposed controls

	Imposed	*Voluntary*
Source	*External*	*Internal*
Organizational fit	Homogeneous controls applied to heterogeneous organizations	Reflects existing organizational systems and controls
Purpose	Achieve standardized compliance and behaviour between organizations	Achieve standardized compliance and behaviour within an organization

The development of regulation

Regulatory approaches

Regulation can exist in two forms: *statutory regulation*, underpinned by statute, or *self-regulation*, underpinned by voluntary agreements between organizations. A two-tiered regulatory regime can be observed where both types of regulation are used to govern the activities of organizations. A further distinction is provided by Hemphill (1996) between 'industry regulation' which focuses upon an individual industry, and 'social regulation' which is 'issue-related and non-economic in nature, crosses industries in its impact, and affects the manufacturing processes and physical characteristics of products' (1996: 27). Smith and Tombs (1995: 620) define self-regulation as where organizations 'ensure that they comply with current legislative requirements, without the direct policing of, and subsequent interference by, the various regulatory bodies'. The existence of regulators, in their view, is testament to the inability of employers to regulate themselves without compromising safety or responsible behaviour.

Reflecting the view that safety through compulsion is unlikely to be achieved without an organizational desire to change, a number of studies have advocated varying degrees of self-regulation (Mintzberg, 1983; Braithwaite and Fisse, 1987; Kharbanda and Stallworthy, 1991):

> In industry, management inevitably know more than anyone else about the type of risk involved in the operations within their plants, and the implications for the community at large. . . . It is in their own interest for management to self regulate . . . their own affairs and to do their best to ensure that such disasters never occur.
>
> (Kharbanda and Stallworthy, 1991: 88)

For Mintzberg (1983) trust alone is insufficient. He argued that managers should be relentlessly pressured and constrained by a framework of regulation. In addition, efforts should be made to integrate a range of stakeholders into decision-making processes. Braithwaite and Fisse (1987) argue that self-regulation must be made to work and that the basis for an effective system requires that compliance personnel be given informal authority and top management support; that line managers be given clearly defined responsibility for compliance and careful monitoring of performance; and that effective communication of problems is made to those capable of acting. What is evident from these studies is the range of opinion regarding the most effective means of controlling organizational behaviour.

The relevance of regulation in a continuity management context is salient. The improper, imprudent, impudent, careless or negligent behaviour of organizations and their agents can promulgate or cause crises for which continuity plans must be invoked. In order to prevent, or reduce the propensity towards the occurrence of crises regulatory systems of both an internal and external nature must be thoughtfully considered.

Doyle (1994) suggests that the need for regulation of either type should be determined by whether detailed and formal legal contracts are required to undertake an economic transaction. In many cases of economic exchanges, formal contracts are incomplete or missing altogether. The structure of competition of an industry will provide a partial solution to inappropriate behaviour should a vendor not fulfil their obligations to the purchaser. If an organization behaves in such a way that it fails to protect its consumers, a highly competitive market would provide an incentive (yet not a guarantee) to improve and sustain better working practices, since to do otherwise would lead to inferior financial performance. In effect, the invisible hand serves, partly, as a tacit regulator. In a less competitive market, there is a lower competitive incentive for organizations to ensure that their business practices meet public expectations. The appropriateness of regulatory approaches can be determined by competition, structure, activities, innovation and information (Figure 2.2) where we highlight the context and position of self-regulation.

Certain activities within organizations and economic sectors may be required by statute or regulation to have certain data available at all times. In Hearnden's study, around a quarter of respondents had contingency arrangements in place due to the legislative or regulatory environment in which they operated (Hearnden, 1993).

The problems of regulation are exacerbated where industries and organizations operate both within and beyond national boundaries, and have to manage the (often major) differences between accounting, legal and supervisory systems. Moreover, in a sector such as financial services, different product types may fall within the remit of different regulatory bodies whose level of supervision and authority may differ. Two subsidiaries of the same organization operating in the same product, but different geographic markets will have similar operations yet face a different statutory environment, which is, in turn, determined by different legislatures, which are in part influenced by differing stakeholder groups. The challenge for business continuity planners is to develop internally consistent continuity systems operating within

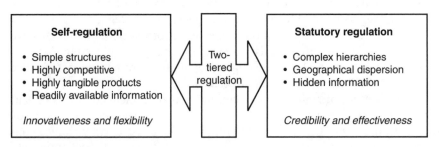

Figure 2.2 Regulatory approaches

differing industrial, geographical, operations and legal domains. As we discuss in Chapter 4, clear structural linkages must exist between the BCM team and functional representatives to ensure contextual relevance in continuity provisions.

A *regulatory cost advantage* arises when an organization has lower costs of regulatory compliance than rivals located in another country. Such costs include health and safety expenditure, environmental protection measures and legal liability (O'Connell, 1998: 547). This could, in part, elucidate the actions of many governments, which seek to portray themselves as anti-bureaucracy in an effort to attract Foreign Direct Investment. O'Connell suggests that the US legal system, with its high litigation and insurance costs, compounded by uncertainty, has led to the relocation of several companies outside US territory. Equally, within the same industry and country a *competitive regulatory advantage* will arise when an organization has in place better practices than its rivals; where it has amortized the cost of compliance and has a history of investing in resources for compliance.

Self-regulation

In the quagmire that remains, the introduction of standards for product testing, ethics, certification and accreditation are increasingly being used by industry associations as criteria for membership. Such actions by industry and trade associations represent a process of self-regulation that is becoming increasingly popular. However, as Jacobs and Portman (1997) found, self-regulation may serve the public interest but equally expose associations to legal liability in areas such as anti-trust laws, negligence, discrimination and defamation. Associations will be liable if their self-regulation guidelines lead to anti-competitive activity, particularly where membership of the association (contingent on meeting standards) leads to distinct groupings of competitors (members and non-members). Associations will also be liable should procedures for ethics, standards and membership be shown to be unfair. Due process in common law should be seen not only in the criteria upon which organizations are evaluated but also the clarity of the decision-making process undertaken by the association in determining conformity with standards or membership entitlement. Where self-regulation is undertaken by an industry association, it may also be liable to third parties affected by the actions of a member that has been certified as compliant with the association's standards. The element of associations' liability forms an extension to the legal liability that may transpire in the case of a product recall, as seen earlier in the pedicle bone screw case in the USA.

It is in the context of liability and the embryonic nature of business continuity that there is an absence of regulation directly associated with business continuity. In its place, a piecemeal consideration of legislative provisions and their impact upon continuity issues has occurred. For instance, the *IT Law Today* publication produced a guide to legal liability and the Y2K problem, highlighting issues such as contracts and express warranties, liability, mounting claims, implied contract terms and guidance on who is liable in disputes between two or more parties (*IT 2000*, 1997).

Self-regulation in UK financial services

The UK financial services sector provides a salient example of the problems facing regulatory organizations and commercial organizations. The system of self-regulation was introduced in 1986 alongside the Financial Services Act (1986) and the Conservative government's credo of increasing self-regulation throughout the British economy. The SIB (Securities and Investments Board) became the main regulatory organization in the finance sector, with responsibility for another five self-regulatory organizations (SROs), nine professional bodies and a small number of specialized regulators. In 1994, four of the SROs merged. In the first, the Life and Unit Trust Regulatory Association (LAUTRO) and the Financial Intermediaries, Managers and Brokers Regulatory Association (FIMBRA) became the Personal Investment Authority (PIA). In the second, the Association of Futures Brokers and Dealers (AFBD) and the Securities Association (SA) became the Securities and Futures Authority (SFA).

Under this two-tiered system, each SRO would register an institution in a contractual arrangement that could only be rescinded in court. As an interim measure, organizations could be given formal reprimands, but no statutory provision was in place for levying fines on organizations found to have broken the SRO's rules. In contrast, the US financial services sector has in place a statutory regulation regime under the remit of the Securities and Exchange Commission (SEC). Founded in 1934 and still active today, US federal law made malfeasances such as insider dealing both a civil and a criminal offence, and substantial fines – up to three times the profits made by the insider trader – can be imposed. In the UK, insider dealing only became a criminal offence in 1980. Moreover, US federal law requires conviction on the balance of probability rather than beyond all reasonable doubt as in the UK (Doyle, 1994).

However, in the wake of several financial scandals, by the early to mid-1990s, several financial institution executives openly began to question the effectiveness of the self-regulation approach. A further exacerbation of the situation occurred with increasing public dissatisfaction due to the lack of punitive measures available to regulators. The lack of a coercive regulatory environment has led to one in which regulatory bodies became an administrative adjunct to the industry's structure without being the catalyst for changes towards good working practices, improved industry performance and the protection of the public interest, as had been originally intended.

The shortcomings of the two-tiered system operating to govern the UK financial services industry can be seen in the aftermath of the Barings scandal of 1995, where the SFA and the Bank of England were criticized for their lack of vigilance. Furthermore, the inability of the SFA to impose punishments on Barings' executives exacerbated the problem. In contrast, the employee at the centre of the crisis, Nick Leeson, received a rapid conviction in a Singaporean court. The nature of the industry and the system of self-regulation arguably contributed to an environment in which crises such as the BCCI and Barings collapses, and the Maxwell pension scandal, could occur:

> The complex hierarchical structure of a modern merchant bank operating on exchanges across the world also presented difficulties for internal governance, let alone external governance. . . . The reliance upon a cumbersome system of considerable self regulation in UK financial services would seem to have enabled more rather than less unacceptable practices. . . . The preponderance of SROs certainly exacerbated the problem of inconsistency, expense and duplication.
>
> (Doyle, 1994: 41)

When Gordon Brown, Chancellor of the Exchequer introduced plans for reform of the system of self-regulation on 20 May 1997, he indicated to Parliament that the two-tier system was 'inefficient, confusing for investors and lack[ed] accountability and a clear allocation of responsibilities' (Imerson, 1997). The new Financial Services Authority (FSA) has replaced the separate SROs for the UK financial services industry and re-emphasizes consumer protection. Unlike its predecessors, the new FSA has a statutory obligation to measure the cost effectiveness of its regulations, in order to prevent the augmentation of bureaucratic costs which had previously encumbered the self-regulation of the industry. The UK financial services sector highlights the complex and dynamic environment in which SROs attempt to create minimum standards of behaviour without having sufficient authority to impose heavy sanctions upon organizations which fail to conform. The crises that have precipitated reform of the regulatory environment are high-profile cases in the public and media eye and difficult to observe and control by outside parties. These conditions, in conjunction, provided a formula for a failure in the supervisory regime in this sector and the subsequent lack of credibility which ensued.

Stakeholders and self-regulation

The US approach to deregulation in the mid-1990s began with the 'reinventing government' programme aimed at simplifying and reducing state-directed regulation. Changes in the areas of environmental protection and health and safety were introduced in parallel with simpler documentation for businesses, a lower use of punitive fines and greater flexibility in interpretation of federal rules (Hemphill, 1996)

Stakeholders play an important role in developing self-regulation following crisis incidents. The Coalition for Environmentally Responsible Economies

(CERES), established in 1989, developed a voluntary code comprising ten principles designed to improve the environmental protection practices of organizations. Named after the oil spill in the same year, the 'Valdez Principles' have been adopted by over eighty companies, including Mobil, General Motors and Polaroid. CERES is a coalition of thirty-two environmental and pressure groups, including investment and pension funds. Similarly, the Aerospace Industries Association of America, the Chemical Manufacturers Association and the American Petroleum Institute have incorporated environmental, health and safety (EHS) codes of conduct into their by-laws for membership (Hemphill, 1996).

The existence of regulation within an economic sector of activity may indeed be one of the main influences upon the formal establishment of a BCM team. It is also evident, from a study of better practice organizations, that organizations (in this case a US bank) regarded regulation as constituting a starting point for internalizing control systems:

> About six years ago it was first of all, 'the regulations say we have to have it', then it became, 'well, there is some impact on us financially if we don't operate in a certain period of time' and then, 'well, I suppose our customers would be a bit upset' . . . Last year that had completely turned around, now it is customer expectation first, the financial impact second and federal requirements third. . . . the reason for that is that federal requirements should not be driving your business, your business should be driving your business.
>
> (Herbane *et al.*, 1997: 24)

In other sectors, the will to implement BCM as a formal business function may arise from factors such as learning from crisis incidents, the influence of best-practice rivals and the requirements of buyers and/or suppliers.

Problems with regulators and regulations

The conflict between regulation, self-regulation and stakeholders can be seen in the recent move by the British government to make UK-based chemical companies more responsible for the risk assessment of chemicals. At the European Union level, an absence of funds has led to only ten of some 10,000 'recognized' chemicals being assessed since 1993. Moreover, the total number of man-made chemicals is known to number around 100,000. The government favoured an approach in which policy would be developed in consultation with stakeholders comprising chemical companies and the Chemical Industries Association (CIA), researchers and the general public. In contrast, the move toward a two-tiered approach was seen by the environmental group, Friends of the Earth, as a concession to businesses that would compromise the nation's health and the environment (*Chemical and Industry*, 1998).

The actions of regulators themselves have contributed to crises. A drastic fall in saccharin use followed the US Food and Drug Administration's announcement in 1977 that the artificial sweetener was linked to cancer in laboratory rats. Typical of the regulatory logic that has be called 'Condemn now, nail down the science later' (Huber, 1997: 114), the announcement from a regulator precipitated a crisis for saccharin producers. This case was not accompanied by vast numbers of litigants in the intervening period, before saccharin was found to be non-carcinogenic, but more recently, as we have seen earlier, the legal liability of regulators is growing. Huber argues that the blame for the actions of regulators is attributable to lack of accountability that regulators have for their claims. The absence of any requirement for regulators to evaluate both *ex ante* and *ex post* the scientific evidence supporting an announcement is clearly different from a situation in which 'regulators who take things out of the food supply should be held to the same standards as private companies that put them in' (1997: 114).

Goodhart (1998) argues that the failure of regulation is not due to the regulators themselves, but rather of the inherent conflict between and separation of the external regulatory activity and the internal management controls within organizations. Regulations which compare financial measures between players in the same industry are susceptible to the differences in accounting practices, business operations and the reliability of information provided to regulators. In order to ensure comparability of data between organizations, the role of the regulator would have to become increasingly costly and officious. The impositions on, and disturbance for, organizations would also generate a greater resistance towards cooperation with regulators. Furthermore, the dynamism of change within many industries also renders the controls and regulations used by regulators redundant at worst, or minimal at best. Goodhart argues that many of the highly publicized crises have arisen from poor internal controls rather than regulation, but the latter tends to attract blame since its fundamental role is one of supervision in the public interest. This problem is exacerbated due to the asymmetry of information between regulators and the regulated, leading to a problem of causal ambiguity (Reed and DeFillippi, 1990). Under such conditions, the cause-and-effect relation cannot be fully understood unless all the factors in the relationship are known.

A distinction should be made between an organization's control systems and the behaviour it successfully or unsuccessfully elicits. The systems of control through procedures, meetings and measures can be in place, but in circumstances where improper or careless behaviour is not identified, the system and its agents are negligent. Conversely, where, in spite of controls, such behaviour is condoned, the control system can be deemed to be irrelevant in shaping employees' behaviour and, indeed, could be construed both as clouding the actions of employees and as a veil beneath which improper practices are obscured. As Goodhart points out, 'internal risk [or other] control mechanisms, however technically advanced, cannot be more reliable than those humans who manipulate them' (1998: 23). Even where regulators develop complex techniques for supervision and control, the lack of compliance (deliberate or otherwise) needs to be addressed predominantly as an internal matter. Were a regulator to pursue a change in the culture of behaviour and practices within an industry, the intangibility and subjectivity of culture and decisions derived on the basis of it would expose regulators to charges of lacking due process and bias and could in return leave regulators facing litigation (Goodhart, 1998). Moreover, the causal ambiguity over how an organization's culture contributed to improper behaviour would, *inter alia*, be great and could lead to speculative decisions regarding conduct and performance: 'everybody may have "known" that BCCI had a shady reputation, but the Bank of England needed objective proof before it could act' (Goodhart, 1998: 23). The process of both internal and external supervision could be improved by increasing the amount and extent of supervision. This, however, is hampered by the further problems of resistance. Both internal and external auditing may not be considered value-creating activities, and those responsible for them may be relegated to a lower status than those who are the subject of supervision and who are better remunerated and regarded. This lower relative status makes this profession unattractive, demoralized and in some cases, under-qualified. Regulators, however proficient, are in a perpetually unenvious position. In their role as a supervisor of the penultimate resort (the judiciary represents the final resort), their inability to identify improper behaviour will be met with criticism. Equally, the improper behaviour of an organization deemed to be proficient and compliant by a regulator will meet with a similar response toward the regulator concerned.

The British government tacitly abandoned the introduction of a new Food Safety Agency through its omission from the Queen's speech in November 1998, although it had been promised to the electorate in the party's 1997 election manifesto. Whilst the intention of creating such an agency had been to prevent a recurrence of food scares and threats such as salmonella and BSE, criticism of a 'nanny-state' approach may have proved a deciding influence upon its abandonment. Only a month later, the government-funded Action 2000 body underscored the precarious relationship of regulators and government agencies in continuity issues. Action 2000, which was responsible for making organizations become Year 2000 IT compliant, faced severe criticism in the press when a representative of the body commented that British citizens should stockpile food in case of problems with food supply chains.

Ask *et al.* (1995) also address the issue of the level at which standards (set by regulators) should be set. The difficulty here is two-fold: level and its evaluation. How readily do regulators know what the worst and best standard of practice are within an industry? In order to achieve this (ignoring the issue of causal ambiguity for the moment) it would require a 'long-standing rigorous programme of basic inspection or a highly interventionist form of regulatory knowledge and information gathering' (1995: 625). Such efforts, undertaken to make regulation supposedly more effective, would run counter to the development of internal controls and supervision, whose objectives may be to develop practices superior to those in competing organizations (corporate responsibility as competitive advantage, e.g., Body Shop). The view that regulators should have greater influence on organizations is predicated on their ability to impose penalties upon those which transgress. The problems of the reliance of regulators on the accuracy and veracity of information provided by organizations for the purpose of compliance is exemplified by the case of Union Carbide, which made available data indicating (to the Occupation Safety and Health Administration) that the company had a good safety record. In fact, the company's real position in occupational safety terms was far below the average within the chemical industry (Smith and Tombs, 1995).

With changes in economic, financial and trading circumstances, organizations may change their priorities *vis-à-vis* issues which could influence the propensity for a crisis to occur. A further problem of self-regulation at an organizational level is the assumption that existing customs and practices are acceptable and, in being so, create an endorsement which regulators may find difficult to challenge given the 'limitations' of their knowledge of specialized businesses. Smith and Tombs (1995) offer the example of the *Herald of Free Enterprise* ferry disaster in 1987, caused by the long-standing and accepted practice of departing from ports with bow doors still open.

The focus of regulatory requirements in specific areas of activity within an organization may also affect the efforts of organizations in a wider ambit of improving and sustaining appropriate levels of parsimonious and proper behaviour. Since organizations have limited resources over discrete periods (budgetary and accounting periods), this may be reflected in sustained spending in areas required to comply with regulations but a curtailment of expenditure on peripheral activities which do not fall within the boundaries of those required for compliance. From their study based on safety issues in the UK chemical industry, Smith and Tombs (1995) concluded that a greater degree of regulation is required, with an attendant shift towards more powerful regulators. This would encompass four central themes. In the first, regulators should become more 'punitive-oriented' than 'compliance-oriented', involving well-publicized and immediate enforcement designed to prevent further infractions which require additional investigation, administration and enforcement. Second, the costs of regulatory bodies should be addressed by having commercial organizations contribute to the costs of the regulator itself. Additionally, through a dialogue with government, penalties for con-compliance (fines) should be reviewed in order to ensure that the cost-benefit ratio of a regulator pursuing litigation is appropriate. As they point out, where fines are low, the legal costs in pursuing a case against a plaintiff do not warrant the action, and this limits the ability of the regulator to use other enforcement approaches in its place. Third, a dual strand empowerment of trade unions through legislative provision, so that employees have a legal right to refuse to undertake dangerous work (as is the case in Sweden and Norway), and the right of trade unions to report safety concerns to regulators would offer some protection for employees against employers that disregard safety concerns. Fourth, a wider variety of stakeholders should be involved in the development of regulation in a move away from an organization-centred approach to its development: 'a central element of current practice has been the role of technical expertise in both *validating* the claims of corporations and *undermining* the concerns of local residents and workers who are exposed to the risk' (Smith and Tombs 1995: 633, original emphasis).

The need for regulation should be extended to disaster recovery (DR) companies, since their services often form a vital part of an organization's business continuity plan (Herbert, 1995). In the UK, no such quality verification standards exist for evaluating companies within the disaster recovery industry. Without them, the only manner in which to evaluate a DR supplier is to test plans regularly to establish whether a supplier of recovery services could successfully resume its client's operations. It is suggested that minimum standards for DR suppliers should include reference to avoiding single points of failure (telecommunications, power, security and ventilation), high client densities, and exposed locations of facilities. To consider the capabilities of a DR supplier on the basis of size and reputation alone would be unwise and imprudent.

What is clear from the regulatory and legislative environment is the increasing liability of regulators, not in place of organizations, but in addition to them. The role of regulators is increasingly limited due to the trade-off between comprehensiveness and complexity whilst attempting to facilitate the dynamism of economic, operational and legislative forces.

BS7799 and the BCI: a new era for BCM standards?

Whilst the absence of regulation addressing business continuity practices is marked, we have already seen that a wide variety of such external controls have a major impact on the consideration, content and conduct of business continuity. Increasingly, however, the growth of business continuity within organizations as a formal and strategic (rather than facilities- and security-focused) undertaking has led to several developments which are designed to improve business continuity. Within this, the BCI certification standards and BS7799 have a central role to play.

In the UK, the Business Continuity Institute (BCI) has developed a certification standard for business continuity practitioners. This members' organization emphasizes ten key areas:

1 Project initiation and management
2 Risk evaluation and control
3 Business impact analysis
4 Developing business continuity strategies
5 Emergency response and operations
6 Developing and implementing business continuity plans

7 Awareness and training programmes
8 Maintaining and exercising business continuity plans
9 Public relations and crisis coordination
10 Coordination with public authorities

(BCI, 1997)

Although embryonic and generic in form, the BCI standards recognize the importance of regulation and legislation within a business continuity plan.

The Department of Trade and Industry (DTI) established the Commercial Computer Security Centre in 1987 to establish a set of internationally applicable and recognized standards for IT users in supply chains. Following several codes of practice and in consultation with leading UK companies such as Marks & Spencer, Nationwide Building Society, Prudential, Shell UK, Unilever and BOC Plc, a code of practice for 'information security management' was published and became the foundation for BS7799. BS7799 is a British Standard (adopted in Australia, New Zealand and the Netherlands) which focuses on how organizations should store, process and handle information in paper form and in electronic form using computers and networks. It consists of two parts. The first is a voluntary code of practice which addresses ten major areas of security controls, business continuity and legal obligations. Originally intended for IT and electronic records, recent revisions have included paper-based records since, although they are decreasing in volume, they have equal importance should they be lost, stolen or damaged. Additionally, the standards have sufficient flexibility to be revised periodically to reflect developments in information technology.

The second part details guidance and requirements for management standards. This second part was developed to ensure that organizations and managers have undertaken a systematic appraisal of information protection policy. The process involves five stages:

1 Defining the information security policy
2 Defining the scope of management concerns
3 Risk assessment
4 Managing risk
5 Selection of controls

(Gamma, 1998)

Central to the certification scheme is risk assessment, which includes a consideration, not only of the financial and economic damage of information loss, but also the penalties that could be imposed by regulators. Clearly, however, as a voluntary scheme, regulatory considerations in a BS7799 risk analysis will have a small impact upon the compliance of the majority of organizations to regulations since the area of focus is small and the scheme is relatively new. However, as with many BSI (British Standards Institute) and ISO (International Standards Organization) standards, certification gradually becomes a minimum competitive criterion as more organizations achieve certification and a greater number of organizations upstream and downstream in the supply chain require certification standards as a necessity for supply chain partners. The UK certification scheme is overseen by the BSI on behalf of the DTI with a series of registered assessors (who cannot work as consultants) carrying out assessments within organizations with subsequent periodic review.

BS7799 and the BCI standards represent the leading voluntary standards in an otherwise under-developed framework for business continuity, although it is clear that commercial vendors of business continuity 'solutions' have for some time offered methodologies, hardware and software for business continuity mainly targeted toward IT/IS protection. An evaluation of these two new standards would be premature, but it should be noted that they are very recent developments, operating within the same legal, regulatory and economic domains seen above that have made improvement, enforcement and control difficult to harmonize and impose.

Control and BCM

The absence of continuity management-specific legislation and regulation should not be interpreted as meaning that organizations are free to introduce (or otherwise) controls of their choice. With wider reference to legal and regulatory prerequisites, continuity planners do not operate under conditions of absolute uncertainty. What is clear, however, is that a wider set of external controls relevant to business continuity has developed, and that the planning process should involve an analysis of changing legal and regulatory requirements. To do otherwise would expose an organization to greater prosecution (legislation), higher penalties (regulations) and a loss of competitive advantage (certification standards). If continuity management is to be seen as a value-adding (rather than value-diminishing) activity a wider set of organizational controls needs to be considered in order to pre-empt and prevent crises and their consequences, both legal and financial. This requires planners to achieve higher levels of integration between business functions (marketing, R&D, production and procurement) and external bodies (regulators and SROs).

Summary

In this chapter we have examined some of the external pressures which require or encourage organizations to adopt business continuity management. Chapter 1 examined the competitive and strategic implications of having BCM processes in place within an organization or otherwise. The pressures examined in this chapter arise from the regulatory and legislative environments in which all organizations must operate. In whatever geographical location an organization undertakes its activities, it will find itself having to adhere to legislation pertaining to health and safety, employment rights, product safety and corporate negligence. In the course of this chapter, we have shown that whilst such areas of legislation do not have an explicit relationship with business continuity management, careful examination of these legal provisions will reveal the need for organizations to consider carefully how a crisis or interruption may give rise to legal issues and litigation, or influence their ability to respond once they have formal business recovery processes in place.

Legislation, however, forms only one type of control (which in this case is imposed) over the activities of organizations, with attendant consequences for business continuity management. The existence of regulation at an industry level which may be statutory (imposed) or self-regulatory (voluntary) is another. Equally, where an industry has experienced business interruptions and crises, organizations within a single industry may adopt a self-regulatory approach. By using the example of financial services in the UK, it is clear that, in the absence of legislation which is specific to business continuity, relationships between governments, regulatory bodies and individual companies can lead to the widespread introduction of crisis prevention and recovery measures. Self-regulation in itself, as this chapter discussed, does not provide a complete solution to the raising of standards (or indeed the adoption) of business continuity management. Often it is pressure from stakeholders which has led to organizations embracing a more proactive approach to dealing with crises.

In this and the previous chapter we have seen that, in a business continuity context, organizations are exposed to competitive, strategic, regulatory, legislative and stakeholder pressures, which increase the need for the adoption of business continuity. In the next chapter, we examine, in the light of such pressures, how the business continuity process is initiated prior to planning.

References

BCI (1997) *The Ten Certification Standards for Business Continuity Practitioners*, London: Business Continuity Institute.

Braithwaite, J. and Fisse, B. (1987) 'Self-regulation and the control of corporate crime', in C.D. Shearing and P.C. Stenning (eds) *Private Policing*, London: Sage.

Chemical and Industry (1998) 'UK warned over risk assessment', *Chemical and Industry* 3: 587.

Doyle, P. (1994) *Marketing Management and Strategy*, London: Prentice Hall.

Elkind, P. (1997) 'Blood feud', *Fortune* 135(7): 24–33.

Gamma (1998) *BS7799 – An International Management Standard*, London: Gamma Secure Systems Ltd.

Goetsch, S.D. (1996) 'Products liability', *Defence Counsel Journal* 63(3): 399–401.

Goodden, R.L. (1995) *Preventing and Handling Product Liability*, New York: Marcel Dekker.

Goodden, R.L. (1996) 'Lawyers can provide unique product-liability perspective', *Hydraulics and Pneumatics* 49(2): 10–12.

Goodhart, C. (1998) 'Regulation from the inside – the politics of managerial control', *Chartered Banker* January: 20–23.

Hall, R. (1992) 'The strategic analysis of intangible resources', *Strategic Management Journal* 13: 135–44.

Hearnden, K. (1993) *Corporate Computing 1993: Key Business Issues*, London: Computing Services Association.

Hemphill, T.A. (1996) 'The new era of business regulation', *Business Horizons* 39(4): 26–31.

Herbane, B. and Rouse, M.J. (2000) *Strategic Management: An Active Learning Approach*, London: Blackwell.

Herbane, B., Swartz, E. and Elliott, D. (1997) 'Contingency and continua: achieving excellence through business continuity planning', *Business Horizons* November–December: 19–25.

Herbert, P. (1995) 'Is it time for regulation?', *The Business Continuity Magazine* May: 43–4.

Huber, P. (1997) 'The health scare industry', *Forbes* 160(7): 114.

Imerson, M. (1997) 'Helen Liddell: taking a tough approach to regulation', *Chartered Banker* December: 10–15.

IT 2000 (1997) *A Legal Guide for Users and Suppliers*, London: Monitor Press.

Jacobs, J.A. and Portman, R.M. (1997) 'Risks of self-regulation', *Association Management* March: 89–90.

Jacobs, J.A. and Portman, R.M. (1998) 'Beware the threat of product liability litigation', *Association Management* June: 81–2.

Kharbanda, O. and Stallworthy, E. (1991) 'Industrial disasters – will self-regulation work?', *Long-Range Planning* 24(3): 84–9.

McCubbins, T.F. and Mosier, G.C. (1998) 'Effects of product liability laws on small business: an introduction to international exposure through a comparison of US and Canadian law', *Journal of Small Business Management* 36(3): 72–9.

Mintzberg, H. (1983) *Power in and around Organisations*, Englewood Cliffs, NJ: Prentice-Hall.

Nocera, J. (1995) 'Fatal litigation', *Fortune* 132(8): 60–74.

O'Connell, J. (1998) 'Regulatory cost advantage', in C.L. Cooper and C. Argyris (eds) *The Concise Blackwell Encyclopedia of Management*, Oxford: Blackwell Business.

Reed, R. and DeFillippi, R.J. (1990) 'Causal ambiguity, barriers to imitation and sustainable competitive advantage', *Academy of Management Review* 15(1): 88–102.

Selwyn, N.M. (1988) *Law of Employment*, London: Butterworths.

Siegfried, W.A. (1998) 'Guard against suits', *Design News* 53(11): 230.

Sirignano, M.A. (1997) 'Unsafe hamburgers and unreasonably hot coffee', *LI Business News* 14: 7.

Smith, D. and Tombs, S. (1995) 'Beyond self-regulation: towards a critique of self-regulation as a control strategy for hazardous activities', *Journal of Management Studies* 32(5): 619–37.

Further reading

Freeman, R.E. (1994) 'The politics of stakeholder theory: some future directions', *Business Ethics Quarterly* 4: 409–21.

Larsson, G. and Enander, A. (1997) 'Preparing for disaster: public attitudes and actions', *Disaster Prevention and Management* 6(1): 11–21.

Nerht, C. (1998) 'Maintainability of first mover advantages when environmental regulations differ between countries', *Academy of Management Review*, 23(1): 77–89.

Schneider, R. (2000) 'Knowledge and ethical responsibility in industrial disasters', *Disaster Prevention and Management* 9(2): 98–104.

Study questions

1   Here are some figures:
    We have sold 12.5 million units of product XYZ but there is a fire hazard fault in the product.
    The cost to remedy the defect will be $11 per unit.
    The total cost of the *recall* and defect repairs will be *$137.5 million.*
    However, we have forecast the following deaths, injuries and damaged products:

	Deaths	Injuries	Damaged
	180	180	2,100
Costs	$200,000	$67,000	$700
Total	$36,000,000	$12,060,000	$1,470,000

Total cost of compensation: *$49.5 million*

Would you recall the product and why?

2   Think about the implied duties of the employers and employees. Then write down some examples.

3   Think of an example of where a breach of intellectual property rights has led to a crisis.

4   Identify an industry or sectors where regulation has followed some time after privatization.

5   Think about what you have read about BS7799. Does it offer a complete crisis management solution?

3 Initiating and planning for BCM

Introduction

The purpose of this chapter is to investigate the preliminary steps in the business continuity management process. Our aim is to demonstrate that whilst the generic process is applicable to most organizations, the starting point in that process will differ between organizations. The point at which an organization commences the continuity process will depend on the specific experiences in the field of continuity management that an organization might have had, as well as the nature of the industry within which an organization operates.

Several strategies may be adopted by organizations in their efforts to establish continuity management within their organizations. Each of these – reactive, proactive and interactive – are introduced as a precursor to the sequence of activities that have been found to provide the most suitable foundation for the initiation of planning for business continuity (Chapter 4).

The chapter then considers the sequence of activities regarded as important to the initiation of continuity management within organizations. Following this, the chapter concludes with a consideration of why a shift in the mindset which influences the way in which crises are looked at is needed for planning to focus on both recovery and prevention whilst continuously learning from the organization's experiences and those of others.

The continuity management process

Figure 3.1 portrays the business continuity management process as comprising of four distinct phases – initiation, planning, implementation and operational management. This is a similar approach to the planning approaches used for business or strategic planning, where managers establish corporate goals and then undertake a strategic analysis of the organization and its environment in order to choose the most appropriate strategy. This is, in turn, followed by the implementation of the chosen strategy. Typically, this process of analysis, choice and implementation is known as the process of 'strategy formulation' (Mintzberg, 1994). This formulated approach to planning (i.e.

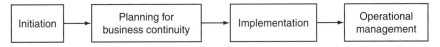

Figure 3.1 The continuity management process

analysis + choice = the successful implementation of strategy) is not without its pitfalls. Changes beyond the control of the organization may render the choice of strategy a failure. Equally, unexpected opportunities may lead to a change in the organization's intended strategy.

The BCM process portrayed in Figure 3.1 differs in two important respects from the wider activity of strategic or business planning. In many cases, organizations have long-established departments, activities and experiences of strategic planning. This tends to be less the case with BCM; many organizations are currently only just embarking upon the introduction of BCM. Accordingly, the initiation of the process, which is critical to the success of BCM planning is not necessary for strategic planning which is widely considered to be an activity of long-recognized value. In contrast, as a relatively new activity, BCM seeks to put into place resources, activities and processes that, it is hoped, will never be used. The challenge of initiation is to establish need, interest, support and a clear remit for subsequent continuity planning activities (Chapter 4).

A further difference is the inclusion of operational management in addition to implementation in Figure 3.1. Implementation (Chapter 5) considers the matter of how organizations can manage the process of change to incorporate and integrate continuity management where previously it did not exist. The operational management of continuity management (Chapter 5) refers to the instigation of recovery activities in the event of a crisis.

The continuity management process should be regularly reviewed and updated to ensure that the resulting plans remain appropriate. However, before we begin our examination of initiation, it is appropriate to examine some general principles of planning which apply equally to this chapter and the next, in which the planning processes specifically concerned with business continuity are considered in greater detail.

Planning to plan

Planning without discovery is a time-consuming and expensive self-fulfilling prophecy. After all, if, *ex ante*, we understand the issues that will give rise to the plan itself, why should the manager undertake any analytical activities? Planning, therefore, and planners themselves should be immersed in the discovery of what is *not* known, often found in places where they were *not* expected. For instance, a business continuity manager in a car manufacturing company might assume that there is no risk of virus attack to the long-established electronic purchasing system used with its suppliers of components, only to find that the company has decided to introduce Internet-based purchasing. Not only has the technology changed, the threat of attack and the linkages between one department (purchasing) and others (administration and central data storage) have now been created. The planner can only plan once she or he has *discovered* that such changes have occurred.

One of the first issues facing an organization setting out to develop a business continuity plan is that of who should be primarily responsible within the organization for the research, planning, analysis and drafting of preliminary plans.

Although the planning process requires a dedicated project manager it also normally needs senior management support. Progress in relation to BC activities should be reported regularly to the Top Management Team (TMT) or appropriate committee. Elliott *et al.* (1999a) suggested that this project management task should not be undertaken by an IT specialist within an IT department. It is argued that the appointment of an IT specialist communicates to employees that business continuity planning is merely an information technology issue, with little human impact or involvement, and is temporary in its nature. Given that the planning process requires information which can only be gathered and ascertained from individuals across many parts of the organization, participation in the process is considered essential.

Many successful organizations place business continuity within a central department that has responsibility for strategic planning and analysis amongst other tasks. A useful model includes a steering group to support the project manager. This steering group should include senior and influential staff from different business units or departments.

A further problem which arises from the outset of any planning process, whether this be strategic, functional or business continuity oriented, is the 'legacy hindrance'. Organizations are complex socio-technical systems which reflect antecedents such as decisions, systems, structures, values and beliefs. The influence on strategy of an organization's structure has long been recognized (Chandler, 1962) and, despite considerable debate in this respect, structure should remain a focus of attention since it offers one manner in which the organization can be viewed and, therefore, analysed. The way in which one perceives an organization can often determine the decisions and actions that are taken (Snyder and Ebeling, 1992; Herbane and Rouse, 2000).

In a business continuity context (and in practical terms) many organizations find themselves in a 'brownfield' planning context. This means that managers involved must recognize that they cannot make sweeping changes to the organization and its social and technical systems. They must plan in their context. This does not necessarily mean that they should eschew possibilities for greenfield planning. For example, in the early 1990s a US bank made the decision to locate its European headquarters in the UK. Rather than seeking a building in the City of London, where the majority of rivals, suppliers and customers were located, it decided to locate the headquarters some distance away. This provided more scope for the company to exploit building designs which accommodated business recovery requirements and reduced the (albeit perceived) threat of interruption to the business arising from transportation strikes and indiscriminate terrorist activity. Similarly, Facer (1999) observed that organizations may 'design in' redundant computer-processing capacity and facilities as a contingency for business interruptions. Hence, the challenges facing planners in brownfield and green-field situations are not dissimilar from those which emanate from business process redesign (Hammer, 1990; Mumford and Hendricks, 1996).

The perception of failure may also influence the discovery process that precedes the development of business continuity plans. In some organiza-tions, failure is considered to be a positive side-effect from which discovery and subsequent improvements can be effected. Kumar *et al.* (2000) recount that Sony's failure in the development of products such as the 2-inch diskette produced avenues to the development of games consoles. Equally, planners should be aware of the symbolism that failure can bring. The plan itself could be blamed, or specific individuals could be blamed. The failure itself is more nebulous, and unless it is thoroughly understood, there could be little, if any, improvement should similar circumstances arise in the future (see Box 3.1).

Furthermore, the implication that a systematic and formulated approach to planning is a rational one does not always hold true. Long established are studies which suggest that decision-making can be distorted through a phe-nomenon known as 'Groupthink' (Janis, 1983), where individuals coalesce around the ideas of influential persons in group decision-making.

The notions of rationality in managerial behaviour and decision-making have been challenged since the early work of Simon (1957) through the notion of bounded rationality, whereby the individual (or a collective) is cognitively impeded due to the inability to process infinite amounts of infor-mation in a limited period of time, compounded by the differing perspectives that individuals may have of a situation or environment. Although this should not be taken to suggest that managers act irrationally in decision-making, limited rationality presents what Eisenhart and Zbaracki (1992: 22) term a 'heuristic perspective', whereby aspects of the decision-making process can be rational whilst others cannot.

More recently, the view that perceptions influence behaviour (i.e., decisions and actions) has been refined to include a consideration of experiential influ-ences, values and beliefs, and the filtering of information in the development of managers' perceptions (Day and Lord, 1992; Finkelstein and Hambrick, 1988). Others have examined the links between managers' perceptions of the environment and organizational performance (Dutton and Dukerich, 1991; Thomas *et al.*, 1993), suggesting that there is a clear link between how man-agers perceive their organization and environment and how they sub-sequently act to achieve predetermined goals, and that external influences have a greater impact on managers' perceptions than functional experience and conditioning (Chattophadhyay *et al.*, 1999).

In short, those involved in the planning process should be aware of the

---

Box 3.1   Who's to blame? What's to blame?

On 5 May 2000, computer servers and e-mail systems were shut down. The 'love bug' virus spread from South-East Asia at the rate of the dawn and the log on. Primarily affected were computer systems using Microsoft Outlook programs and users quickly found that the 'worm' had buried itself in their hard drives. Struck by the virus, Germco (a fictional name) quickly invoked its plans for widespread virus disruption. The virus type had not been seen before and therefore could not be stopped. Users logged in as usual and, intrigued by the 'love letter', opened the message with disastrous effects for seven working days. A few days later the 'inquiry' began. Germco managers blamed the IT division for a lack of systems protection. The IT division refuted this, arguing that user 'naivety' generated, propagated and compounded the problem. The solution, it seemed, was a simple one – to update virus software and prevent similar viruses entering the systems in the future. In early July 2000, the e-mail systems closed again for three days. The virus had remained dormant in the in-box of an absent colleague and upon his return, began to spread. This time, preparedness was not to blame. Instead, a lack of communication and willingness to change led to the re-occurrence. Staff had not been told how to upgrade their desktop virus software and still continued with the inappropriate practices of using the preview window in their software and opening unusual messages. People's behaviour – specifically a reluctance to learn positively from failure – led to the loss of 4 per cent of the working year.

The experience of Germco indicates the need for continuity management to be an ongoing, iterative, process. The lessons from the first interruption were not heeded. Unsurprisingly, therefore, the preconditions for a subsequent interruption remained in place. Furthermore, the misdirection of blame can serve as a misdirection away from the real causes of a crisis.

---

limitations of any planning methodology which they employ. Rather than dismiss the formal planning process out of hand, creative solutions should be sought. Nonetheless, there are many activities which characterize business continuity planning (Chapter 4). Prior to that, however, we turn to how planning can be initiated.

The interim goal of the planning process is to develop a business continuity plan (or set of plans) which can be invoked (used) in the event of an interruption. Planning marks neither the start nor the end of the BCM process (Figure 3.1). The ultimate goal of the planning process is to improve the resilience of the organization to business to interruptions, thereby protecting the organization's operating or trading position.

Basic strategies underlying business continuity provision

Figure 3.2 outlines the nature of the basic strategies underlying the business continuity provision found in companies.

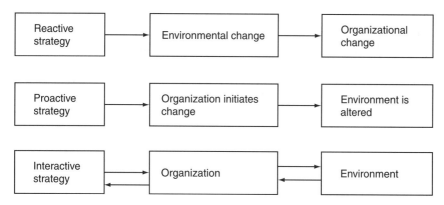

Figure 3.2 Basic strategies underlying business continuity provision

In an ideal world, business continuity management should be driven by an interactive strategy where companies consider business needs in relation to organizational and environmental pressures and make appropriate provision. Leading up to the advent of the year 2000 it became evident that certain industries such as the finance sector had employed a sophisticated interactive strategy to safeguard their computer resources. Clearly, within the sector, some organizations were better at doing so than others, but on the whole it emerged that most financial sector organizations had realized the importance of the issue months or years in advance. Appropriate technological changes were made to systems and staff were trained in these and also in terms of what to do should there be a problem once the date change occurred. Indeed, one UK retail bank had completed their Year 2000 changes and tested their systems well in advance of others. It publicized this during the spring of 1999 and was able to capitalize on this by stealing a public relations march on competitors. Similarly, other UK organizations that could identify an early start to their BCM programmes included the following:

- 1995: British Telecom, Lloyds TSB, Nationwide
- 1997: British Airports Authority, Great Universal Stores, Royal & Sun Alliance and Woolwich

However, it should be remembered that business continuity can be costly and time-consuming. Indeed, planning for the Year 2000 computer problem three years in advance of it potentially occurring indicates the time and investment required for continuity management in an instance where the threat and the date of the potential threat were known. The planning response of an organization is thus often related to the degree to which time and investment are perceived to be scarce organizational resources. This fact is illustrated by the case of the small business community response, not only in the UK but also elsewhere. Small companies are resource-poor and frequently cannot afford to devote the financial or human resources to the business continuity activities examined in this chapter and the next. It is clear that this sector could be divided into those that were found to be proactive and those that simply reacted to government demands to make changes to their information systems.

Should it not be feasible to have an interactive strategy, the organization should at least be proactive and put in place measures which take into account the range of internal and external factors the organization might be exposed to. In practice it is perhaps inevitable that all organizations will, in the first instance, initiate business continuity provision as part of a reactive strategy to cope with a crisis triggered by a specific event, either internal or external. Some organizations might then move towards being more proactive. It has been found that many finance sector organizations (investment banks and insurance companies) in the UK had experienced some form of interruption prior to setting up a business continuity unit and capability. These interruptions varied from the secondary effects of bombs and a major fire at a site in Europe, to parcel bombs and telecommunications lines being severed by construction equipment during building works. What is interesting, however, is that continuity managers may be rather less concerned about external and physical threats than about issues such as supplier failures, European Monetary Union, transport strikes, flu epidemics and the attendant effects on staff availability for work (Elliott *et al.*, 1996).

Clearly, an interactive business continuity strategy is best suited to the development of plans to be used in the event of a crisis or disruption. Resource limitations may impede the ability of organizations to take such an approach given the internal, market and macro-environmental pressures placed upon them. It is in this context that, for the organization to develop an interactive BC strategy, the initiation of the planning process must be treated as a high priority, for it is at this stage that the remit, commitment and resources for subsequent activities is determined. Consequently, the focus for the remainder of the chapter is the initiation of the continuity management process.

The initiation of business continuity planning

Initiation is the stage at which strategic decisions are made to undertake business continuity management, to set policy, define structures, allocate resources and agree specific projects and monitoring mechanisms. From this, the organization can establish the objectives and scope of continuity activities and begin the shift the mindset of employees away from recovery to one of recovery *and* prevention.

Business continuity management sets out to change the behaviour of managers and employees. The object is to sensitize everyone to the possibility of business interruption and the need to take active steps to guard against it. The initiation stage, with its strategic perspective and broad brush approach, is the appropriate arena in which to consider how business continuity will be managed. Careful consideration of these issues at the outset will facilitate operational management during the implementation stage (Chapters 5 and 6).

Figure 3.3 sets out the business continuity management process and identifies what must be done to initiate it. Decisions made at this first stage will determine fundamentally the approach, or mindset, adopted by the organization to continuity management.

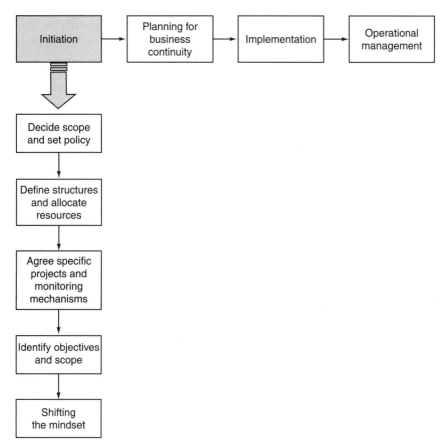

Figure 3.3 Initiation in the continuity management process
Source: Adapted from Elliot *et al.* (1999a).

Decide scope and set policy

The role of the management board is to decide how broad or constrained the focus of business continuity provision is to be. This will involve a consideration of the business processes that are to be covered by continuity provision, and the extent to which external continuity services will be used.

The Top Management Team (TMT) also has to determine the mindset that will drive business continuity management in a strategic sense. The mindset adopted by the TMT will determine what kind of business continuity practitioner it wants the organization to be. The UK government reiterates this view in its advice to companies: 'Board-level commitment is vital. Without top down direction, support and ownership, success in both the BCM process and activating the BCP will be difficult, if not impossible' (Power, 1999: 4).

Once the TMT has made these policy decisions it should issue a clear statement about the importance of business continuity management, and make sure that it appears in communications channels such as the annual report, the company newspaper and the company Intranet. In this respect, practice varies widely amongst different companies. Calor Gas uses human resources managers to drive awareness, while the Royal Bank of Scotland uses both informal and formal communication forums (including 'roadshows', videos, newspapers and the annual report) to communicate the importance of business continuity. Both these organizations acknowledge that the extent to which the TMT is seen as giving business continuity a high priority affects the ease with which implementation occurs (Elliott *et al.*, 1999a).

Clearly, additional policy recommendations will be made once plans for business continuity have been drawn up for the first time. This continual process, whereby the understanding reached at the end of the planning process is fed back into a discussion of the original objectives set for the process, is an extremely important part of business continuity management. The best means of ensuring this feedback loop is through the business continuity organizational structure and formal links with the TMT. This is discussed in the next section.

In addition to the formulation of a policy document, the TMT/board may appoint business continuity 'champions' (in addition to a dedicated business continuity team) to drive the process at local or departmental level. The role of such champions is to support, in a tangible and practical manner, both the business continuity planning process and the implementation of any planning recommendations (see Box 3.2). These champions should therefore have a certain amount of power and command the respect of their colleagues. This gives the process legitimacy, and it can help to persuade the unconvinced of the need to implement business continuity practices. In many organizations, the business continuity function is treated as the last stop for IT personnel before they retire or are made redundant. The assumption is that these employees have technical skills and are therefore well placed to be the guardians of efforts to protect technical systems. Consequently staff may suffer from low morale because they are aware of the organization's perspective on their unit and of their potential contribution. Often these individuals are extremely well trained in facing some of the technical challenges required by their roles, but they may lack critical people-management and leadership

---

Box 3.2 Senior management reluctance in flames

In one organization, based in the City of London, we interviewed executives who admitted to the frustrations they felt at the assumptions about business continuity that existed in their organization. They illustrated this with the example of a senior executive who had paid little attention to their efforts to obtain her support – she alleged that there were more important business issues to be attended to. During the conversation, however, it became clear that there was a major fire taking place at a bank very close by. In fact, they could see the smoke rising from the building through the window of the office in which the meeting was taking place. This incident was reported widely that evening and could therefore be used by the team to convince the reluctant senior executive of the importance of being prepared.

Source: Elliott *et al.* (1999a)

---

skills. This is due to the fact that in their previous roles they would not have been expected to interact in a persuasive and influential capacity and will therefore not have had the opportunity to develop these capabilities. Another assumption is that these plans will most likely never be invoked, and that it is therefore necessary to spend as little money as possible on the employees in the business continuity function.

The example of the frustrated BC manager is instructive as it is not only in the BCM field that senior managers adopt this type of attitude. An analogy may be drawn with the response of senior managers in large companies to the challenge posed by the Internet. Research by Moss-Kanter (2001) concerning the strategic responses of corporations to the Internet mirrors the type of attitude and cultural response that we observe in respect of BCM. This attitude speaks of mixed messages – on the one hand senior managers are aware that they have to be seen to be responding to the Internet, but, on the other, they are not entirely comfortable with this and lack a strategic understanding of exactly how this new technology might be exploited for organizational advantage. Moss-Kanter calls such organizations 'wanna-do's' and she illustrates how those in charge of on-line strategy and ventures are set up in a manner which can only lead to failure. We have used her lessons about how to sabotage on-line ventures as a blueprint to show how the same process is at work for continuity teams (Table 3.1).

Define structures

It is important that the structure through which business continuity management is to be implemented is considered at the initiation stage. From observations of company practice (Elliott *et al.*, 1999a), the structure featured in Figure 3.4 represents a useful model. The key feature of this organizational structure is that it ensures close contact between the business continuity

Table 3.1 Five ways to sabotage business continuity management!

---

1   Recruit IT staff with poorly developed leadership skills and who lack understanding of the potential of business continuity. This often means that a lack of understanding of business areas will translate into a highly technically focused initiative; sadly it also often means that the initiative becomes reduced to essentially a series of lists of telephone numbers and rules on what to do after an incident.

2   Recruit staff who do not have political influence and who do not have well-developed relationships across functions.

3   Sprinkle responsibility for business continuity in an uneven way across organizational functions. (Be inconsistent in which functional or divisional heads have to assume responsibility for business continuity. This way there is much scope for such individuals to shirk responsibility and handle the activity in a sceptical manner.)

4   Form a committee to develop the organization's policy on business continuity management. Recruit to this committee staff who are already highly committed to many other important projects and do not allow them time to devote to this new initiative. This will ensure that not enough time will be devoted to business continuity and at critical times all you have to do is to produce your lists to satisfy any regulatory requirements.

5   Treat each business unit as a separate entity and do not link rewards into achievements in business continuity. In fact, within business units, do not link reward systems to the team effort at all. This ensures that business continuity is regarded as something that has no value at all to individuals or teams.

---

management team and the board on an ongoing basis. It also makes provision for all business units to 'own' their plans and implement these themselves.

Allocate resources

The business continuity strategy will determine both the financial and the human resources required to facilitate the business continuity process. To a large extent the commitment made will depend on the mindset that the board adopts and its assessment of the perceived risks versus the potential business impact that such risks might have. This type of risk assessment will often involve judgements based on historical data.

Some immediate costs will be incurred by the execution of the planning stage of the business continuity management process. They will be determined by the extent of the planning process, and whether or not external assistance is required with it. In some organizations, external consultants are used to take the business continuity management team through one full cycle (covering the most critical parts of the business) of the planning process. The in-house team will work alongside the consultants and build up a knowledge base. Once a pre-determined period has passed, and the in-house team has

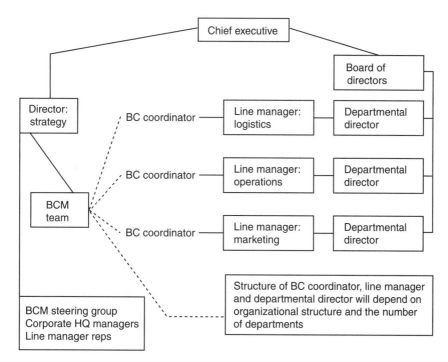

Figure 3.4 Model for effective business continuity management

been trained, the work is executed internally and external experts consulted only for very specialized areas of the process. Such areas may include data-vaulting and mirroring, and activities where equipment from a third party may be used (e.g. office space and telecommunications).

The issue of knowledge and skills is clearly very important in the planning process – both for the business continuity team and the coordinators at the business unit level. It is becoming apparent that, as continuity management becomes more focused on interruptions that are not solely IT-related, all those involved in this area should have the following skills and attributes:

- good communication skills
- a good understanding of how the business operates as a whole

In a study of the stages organizations move through as they approach greater IT maturity, Hirschheim and Verrijn-Stuart (1996) found that the skills cited above, rather than technical skills, were the requisite capabilities that enabled IT to be managed for organizational advantage.

The business continuity team requires (in addition to the above) the following capabilities:

- strategic analysis and risk assessment skills, to conduct the business continuity planning stage
- project management skills
- change management skills, to manage the implementation and operational management stages
- an understanding of how to manage quality issues

Agree projects and monitoring mechanisms

Specific projects must be agreed and a decision has to be taken on how business continuity management is to be 'rolled-out' across the organization. Figure 3.5 sets out a suggested structure for the control of projects.

The project team should be led by a project manager, drawn from the business continuity team, who will work as a facilitator and coordinator of working groups. The project team should consist of appropriate staff from the business continuity team/unit or external consultants, the business unit coordinators and business continuity champions, and other managers from the business units.

The project team should drive the process through the use of regular progress reports, which, in turn, should be submitted upwards to the business continuity management board and ultimately the board of directors. The Central Computer and Telecommunications Agency (CCTA, 1995) also suggests that project plans should contain the following:

- specific project outcomes and quality assessment criteria
- start and end dates for each stage
- the clear allocation of responsibilities for each stage

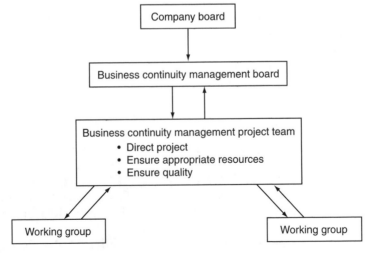

Figure 3.5 Suggested business continuity project management structure

- the identification of important dependencies
- dates for project meetings, presentations to the business continuity management board and quality review meetings

Initiation is clearly a crucial part of the business continuity management process, as it determines the cultural environment within which implementation and operational management will take place. Business continuity managers comment on the difficulties that they often experience at the implementation stage with embedding the process within business units. The seeds for success in implementation are sown during the initiation phase. Arguably, this is where the organization's attitude towards business continuity will be set and it is vital that the issues raised during this first stage of the process be given due consideration. This is the phase of the planning process where the leadership of the organization will create certain assumptions about the nature of business continuity management. These assumptions will permeate the entire organization and establish the mindset or cultural attitude of the organization towards business continuity management (Schein, 1992). Furthermore, without an 'executive sponsor' for business continuity, it is argued that insufficient financial and management support will be given to the activity (Fitzgerald, 1995). It is therefore imperative that the planning process, beginning with initiation, be approached in a strategic manner.

Identifying objectives and scope

Organizations establish their objectives, which vary in terms of scope and time. The broadest and longest-term objective – the mission or vision – is often the best-known of those generated by an organization. The desire to be number one in a market, to reflect social, ethical and environmental values, or to innovate continuously may seem far removed from business continuity planning. Such objectives do not conflict with continuity management. Without business continuity provisions, an organization's vision or mission could be threatened and, without a linkage between an organization's strategy and business continuity, efforts directed at the latter can be perceived as of lesser importance. However, due regard to the organization's mission gives rise to the term 'mission-critical', referring to processes, resources and people that are most directly associated with the accomplishment of the mission.

For e-commerce companies, information technology is a 'mission-critical' resource which ought to receive early attention in a business continuity sense. However, such attention is highly variable. For example, a UK-based on-line travel agency operated for nearly a year without any disaster recovery provisions, only to find that a server failure was the trigger to seek further assistance in protecting the company's systems. Feldman (1998) reports that many US companies failed to manage short-term interruptions, introduce alternative facilities, develop detailed recovery plans or continuously evaluate emergency procedures.

A further 'mission-critical' resource is postal and distribution systems. Many companies have partnership arrangements with courier and delivery companies. Accordingly, managers should give due regard to their exposure to an interruption arising with their delivery partners. For example, Petroni (1999) found that the Banca Commerciale Italiana's involvement in a system of inter-bank settlements led to the introduction of continuity planning for information systems in 1992. The objective of this planning was to ensure the objective of 'zero downtime' (1999: 104).

The use of Information and Communication Technologies (ICT) is now commonplace. Indeed, companies are now increasingly reliant on shared technology or information from their suppliers, not just in their country of origins, but overseas as well. Table 3.2 shows the use of ICT for purchasing operations, using a variety of technologies, including the web, e-mail, Extranets and electronic data interchanges (EDI). From the table, we can see that there are high rates of usage of such technologies across all sectors and across many industrialized nations, and thereby discern the potential vulnerability of such systems to interruptions. Furthermore, as companies move toward lean models of production and just-in-time stockless production, the need for continuity in the supply chain is increasingly critical as companies tend, no longer, to have large warehouses of stock available to continue operations in the event of a disruption at a supplier's facilities.

Beyond the broad remit and purpose of the mission or vision, organizations set detailed objectives because they provide a focus for action, generate benchmarks which serve as a control system, and enable managers to evaluate performance over a specified period. In addition, it has been argued that specific goals improve the motivation of the individual to attain a predetermined level of proficiency (Locke, 1968). This is particularly

Table 3.2 Technology and the supply chain – an international perspective (year 2000)

Country	% of businesses ordering supplies on-line	% of businesses' on-line orders	% of businesses making on-line payments	Technologies used to order goods from suppliers on-line (%)			
---------	----	----	----	E-mail	Web	Extranet	EDI
UK	45	14	28	77	85	9	18
France	21	13	7	55	61	18	27
Germany	45	24	20	82	85	13	13
Italy	28	14	10	88	61	7	7
Sweden	50	21	23	73	89	16	12
US	53	28	19	72	91	20	18
Canada	43	24	21	83	87	22	17
Japan	15	45	6	62	56	14	40

Source: Compiled from UK Online for Business (2000).

important for business continuity planning in organizations where the activity is new and/or where the planning is being undertaken by a project manager whose responsibilities vary more widely than simply business continuity. It is therefore advisable for organizations to set goals for business continuity planning (BCP). For instance Elliott *et al.* (1999b) researched the BCP objectives for several UK and international companies (Table 3.3).

Table 3.3 Examples of BCP objectives

Company type	BCP objective
Public authority	Protect mainframe systems
Energy supply company	Protect head office functions
Water company	Maintain supply to customers
Bank	Protect head office and branches

In each case a clear rationale existed, reflecting organizational priorities and resources. What is also noticeable is that the objectives shown in Table 3.3 vary in terms of each organization's experience and approach to BCP. The protection of mainframes reflects a disaster recovery philosophy (Chapter 1) whereas the protection of the head office marks the organization's attempt to slowly introduce BCP, starting with the most important building. The most experienced company (the bank) has extended its BCP to the entire organization, including the smallest of its branches. Objectives can also be phrased not only to refer to what is included and protected but also to encompass the philosophy of the company's approach to business continuity. King (1997: 17) found that the objective of one US credit card company's business continuity resources was to 'make sure that the customer doesn't see anything they shouldn't ... [and] making sure what could become a disaster doesn't become one'. For this company, it is about maintaining the credibility of 'business as usual' in the event of a disruption.

The objectives of BCP will, in turn, influence the scope of planning activities. 'Scope' refers to the staff, systems, facilities, business processes, suppliers and stakeholders to be included within the analysis and subsequent plan (see Box 3.3). The assurance of continuity has extended in scope, in recent years, from buildings, computers and information systems to include people and business processes. As the bombings and transport strikes of the early 1990s in the UK have indicated, there is little value in having buildings and working information systems if staff cannot access them.

Preliminary steps

Where an organization has no business continuity plans in place, it is advisable for a preliminary brief on the objectives, scope, investment requirements

Box 3.3   Using objectives and scope as foundations for planning

Standard Chartered Bank, an international financial services company, manages the continuity management process from its Singapore headquarters. The company has formally defined the scope of continuity management activities as follows: 'To develop a business continuity plan for the main business units so they will be able to resume effective operations within an acceptable timeframe in the event of a disaster.' It continues by defining the meaning of a disaster in the context of the bank's operations: 'A sudden, unplanned calamitous event which results in a great amount of damage or loss. Any event which prohibits the bank's business units/critical business functions from gaining access to their premises for a period of a week or more.'

From this, a series of objectives have been developed from the scope noted above:

- provide for the safety and well being of people in the branch at the time of the disaster
- establish management succession and emergency powers
- identify critical businesses and supporting functions
- minimize immediate damage and losses
- resume critical business functions in temporary premises
- return to normal operations when the primary facility is restored.

The objectives can be seen to complement and support the scope of BCP. Furthermore, having established this series of objectives, continuity managers at Standard Chartered developed a number of assumptions designed to ensure that planning activities and investments would be focused to meet the most likely continuity needs:

- no access to the affected building for seven days
- no more than one building will be affected concurrently by a disaster
- disaster occurs at the most vulnerable time for each function
- IT recovery plan or disaster recovery plan is in place and tested
- only critical business functions are recovered and the less essential business functions can be postponed
- alternative staff and replacement equipment are available within planned timeframes.

In establishing scope and objectives for business continuity, it is apparent that this organization recognizes that in the event of a disaster or interruption it may not be possible to recover all operations immediately and simultaneously.

Source: Heng (1996)

and timing to be prepared at this stage. This briefing document (or draft business continuity policy) should identify the following important themes which are necessary for the successful completion of the first business continuity plan:

- the objectives of the process

- its scope
- board level champion
- involvement of third parties (suppliers, stakeholders)
- the intended level of detail and sophistication of the analysis
- timing, including a realistic draft timetable
- likely costs
- budget

It is essential that the rationale for introducing and retaining BCP, in addition to the briefing document, be communicated as fully as possible to all concerned. The involvement of as many people as possible will make it more effective. At this stage the involvement of staff from around the organization is sought and negotiated. Problems of securing their input should be resolved, with board level support if necessary, as soon as is practicably possible. This requires that the BC project manager possesses not only access to a senior executive but relatively high status and good quality communication and negotiation skills. Such skills are particularly important since planning teams often work best if they comprise participants from different business areas (information systems, human resources, facilities, etc.) rather than only from one functional area (Herbane *et al.*, 1997). In Chapter 1 we noted that the predecessor of BCP, disaster recovery planning, was dominated by participants with IT backgrounds.

Shifting the mindset

Once the objectives and scope have been decided, a worthy step is to develop an understanding of the type of crisis which an organization could face, i.e. those which could reasonably be expected to occur. This is an important activity since there is a need to develop parameters of the organization's exposure to interruptions/crises and associated needs. In addition, an understanding of the types of potential disruptions can be used to develop scenarios which are important for plans and their testing.

It has been argued that organizations themselves incubate the potential for accidents or business interruptions (Greiner, 1972; Perrow, 1984; Pauchant and Mitroff, 1992). That is, while the final trigger might be an uncontrollable external element (e.g. earthquake, terrorist bomb) the weaknesses that permitted such a trigger to cause a crisis are within the control of the organization that experienced the failure.

For example, lax management, poor procedures and a lack of appropriate investment were cited as key causes at Bhopal in 1984 (Shrivastava, 1987) and at Chernobyl. The organizational crises triggered by the IRA's City of London bombs were largely determined by internal factors – the degree of centralization, hardware and software back-up routines and out-of-hours staff communications. A gas explosion or earthquake might have had similar effects. Following the Bishopsgate bombing, the National Westminster's data transfer routines were cited as a key factor in its ability to maintain operations. Conversely, the routines of the Hong Kong and Shanghai Bank Corporation did not facilitate a quick return to normality. The trigger, created by the bomb, only caused crises for some organizations (Herbane, 1997).

The critical issue here is that many crises (and in most cases the success of recovery efforts) are influenced by events, decisions and actions that precede the crisis. Whilst such causality may seem to be a statement of the obvious, planners should be aware that much can be learned from an examination of the events, decisions and actions that led to a crisis, and set into place measures which reduce these or similar malevolent events, decisions and actions occurring in the future. In addition to examining crises faced by the organization in the past, it is often useful to learn from the experiences of others (see Box 3.4). Such learning is illustrated shortly from the experiences of Perrier. You will recall that a critical difference between DR and BCP is that the latter balances its focus on both prevention and recovery.

Smith (1990) proposes that a crisis comprises three stages (see Figure 3.6). Based on this, the stages can be conceived of as the before, during and after phases.

The pre-crisis stage refers to the period in which the potential for failure is incubated. In the years and months before an incident occurs, decisions will be made that make the organization more or less vulnerable to crises. Such decisions might include (in)appropriate staffing levels, the timing and frequency of back-up routines, the discrediting or ignoring of internal and external safety reviews, or a focus upon profit to the detriment of safe working practices.

The second stage refers to the immediate organizational handling of an incident and includes the immediate period of the crisis, between the crisis taking place and the resumption of operations or activities. Clearly, this period will vary according to the nature of the crisis itself and the ability of the organization to respond. In the next chapter, business continuity plans are shown to include details of which operations should be resumed, in which order and when (e.g. 1 hour, 4 hours, 24 hours, 3 working days, etc.). The period following the advent of a crisis has been called a 'glide path' (Fitzgerald, 1995). This analogy has been used because aircraft will vary in

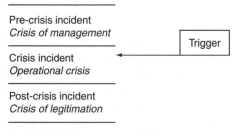

Figure 3.6 Three stages of crisis

Source: Adapted from Smith (1990).

Box 3.4   Crisis management strategies – the airline industry

Recent tragedies in the airline industry demonstrate the importance of preparedness in the event of a disaster. In September 1998, Swissair Flight 111 crashed near the coast of Nova Scotia. Within an hour of learning of the crisis, the Regional Vice-President, Walter Vollenweider, was answering press questions at New York's JFK airport. Furthermore, a 24-hour call centre was brought into use immediately and information, media and counselling services were offered during the aftermath of the crisis. Months after the incident, families and affected parties had access to their own 'care-givers' employed and trained by Swissair to ease the post-crisis phase.

Swissair, having faced a crisis, recognized that not only was the immediate crisis recovery important to the company, its image and its stakeholders, the longer-term actions of the company would add to those upon which it would be judged.

The ValuJet crash of 1996 highlighted the importance of the pre-crisis phase and how the use of third parties in the provision of a service can lead to a crisis. SabreTech. Inc had been used by the airline to undertake routine maintenance. It was alleged that maintenance employees were poorly trained and that (subsequent to the crash) the company had made misleading statement alleging that SabreTech had improperly handled and loaded oxygen canisters, which was seen as the primary cause of the crash. Since little was seemingly done to mitigate against the potential for a disaster to occur in this instance, the post-crisis phase of the crash led to the first criminal prosecution against the company and employees of a company associated with a maintenance failure. As Chapter 2 indicated, the widening of corporate liability along supply chains will increasingly require a more proactive, interactive strategy toward continuity provision.

Although the company has not faced a major incident involving fatalities, another airline which recognizes the importance of being seen to be prepared, responsive and responsible in a crisis is Virgin Atlantic. The company has in place a website area that can be brought 'on-line' in the event of disaster. The web page (www.virgin-atlantic.com/emergency) presents the following text:

A Virgin Atlantic aircraft has been involved in an accident: The plane was flying from X(PLACE)X to X(PLACE)X on X(DATE)X. It took off from X(PLACE)X at X(TIME)X local time. The flight number is VS X(NUMBER)X.

The page continues: 'We are already working closely with emergency authorities involved and are channeling all our efforts into collecting information about the accident.' The existence of such a provision may not be unexpected. However, it indicates that the company is not complacent in terms of its safety record since its foundation.

Each of these short illustrations shows (to varying degrees) the preparations that companies within the same industry have in place in the event of a crisis. They are a measure (albeit a partial one) of the degree of crisis preparedness in place within organizations. Although it is hoped that a crisis will not occur, a continuity management approach necessitates a focus on the preparation and prevention in addition to recovery.

Sources: Parris (1999), Carrington (2000), Schneider (2000)

their ability to glide based on environmental conditions, design, load and pilot skills. Similarly, following an interruption to their operations, organizations may be able to continue their operations albeit for a short period of time. In general terms, the so-called 'glide path' connotes the manner and speed at which operations are recovered.

The third and final stage refers to the period in which an organization seeks to consolidate and then re-position itself (see Box 3.5). Of course, stage three feeds back into stage one as organizations may or may not learn from their experiences.

Having considered the 'process' of crisis using Smith's (1990) model, the next step in the planning process is to identify the types of crisis which an organization is likely to face. It is, at this point, where planning for business continuity begins in earnest.

Box 3.5   Perrier and Tylenol – a contrast of approaches

In 1990 Perrier recalled 160 million bottles of its sparkling mineral water when traces of benzene were found during tests. However, nobody died or suffered illness as a result of drinking Perrier water. Perrier's handling of the crisis may have cost them an estimated £2 million in terms of managing the crisis, product recall and lost market share. Contrast this experience with Johnson & Johnson's when their painkilling drug Tylenol was maliciously laced with cyanide in two separate incidents, two years apart. A total of eleven people died in the two incidents. The threat might have been averted had Johnson & Johnson switched from a capsule to a contamination proof tablet form sooner – they did so immediately after the second incident. The impact for Johnson & Johnson was far less severe than for Perrier, with little impact on the company's market share and retention of the product's position as market leader. In these two instances, the impact of the post-crisis phase was vastly different – the apparently more threatening crisis (which involved deaths to customers) did not significantly threaten the position of the company affected.

Why the different experiences? A large part of the explanation concerns the pre-crisis preparations of the two companies. Where the media found Perrier to be aloof and secretive, Johnson & Johnson had an open approach with good media relations. Where Perrier seemed slow to respond to their crisis Johnson & Johnson responded quickly and positively. Their strong and popular public image allowed them a third chance when Perrier was denied a second. Our conclusions are that the outcomes of the crises were determined by these companies' preparations for crisis and their ability to respond quickly and positively. Johnson & Johnson had healthy relations with the media, a good understanding of their customers and as a result recovered quickly. The unhealthy relations between Perrier and the media acted as a powerful force that prevented Perrier from mounting an effective response to their crisis.

Summary

Having examined the regulatory and legal pressures which increase the need for organizations to introduce or improve continuity management, this chapter introduced a BCM process which is comprised of four stages – initiation, planning, implementation and operational management. The chapter continued by focusing upon the first stage, initiation.

Three basic strategies underlying business continuity provision have been introduced. These suggest differing approaches and attitudes toward the way in which an organization can influence and be influenced by its environment in the event of a crisis or interruption. The recognition of which strategy an organization has adopted, or should adopt, will influence the resource requirements and investments necessary to improve the protection against crises and the effectiveness of recovery activities.

Initiation comprises seven steps. It begins with the need to set the scope and policy of continuity management. Without this, there is the danger that the organization may be too ambitious in attempting to introduce continuity management. Once the remit of BCM has been established, organizations need to decide how the continuity activities will be integrated into the prevailing structure. The formal coordination of business continuity is vital, since, if it is to be more than merely IT disaster recovery, it may be advisable to position the activity as a general business function. As the chapter noted early on, it is only with the wide and full participation of employees that continuity management can achieve its full potential.

Once structural issues have been resolved, clearly defined resources, projects and responsibilities need to be attached to BC activities. The latter is often achieved through monitoring and communication mechanisms such as project teams and coordinators. Once established, the preliminary steps toward planning can be undertaken.

The preliminary steps for planning include the development of a draft business continuity policy and the wide communication of its existence and content to employees. Once this is in place, one final step is required – a shift in the mindset.

We ended the chapter by 'shifting the mindset' that we may have of crises and disasters by examining a three-stage process of crisis. By adopting a crisis management perspective on business continuity, a greater acceptance of the role of prevention in addition to recovery will likely arise.

Having completed an examination of how planning for business continuity is initiated, the next chapter introduces the second stage of the BCM process – planning for business continuity.

References

Carrington, D. (2000) *Virgin on a Disaster*, [on-line] http://www.news.bbc.co.uk/hi/english/sci/tech/, accessed 18/01/01.

CCTA (1995) *A Guide to Business Continuity Management*, London: HMSO.

Chandler, A.D. (1962) *Strategy and Structure: Chapters in the History of the Industrial Enterprise*, Cambridge, MA: MIT Press.

Chattopadhyay, P., Glick, W.H., Chet Miller, C. and Huber, G.P. (1999) 'Determinants of executive beliefs: comparing functional conditioning and social influence', *Strategic Management Journal* 20: 763–89.

Day, D.V. and Lord, R.G. (1992) 'Expertise and problem categorization – the role of expert processing in organizational sense making', *Journal of Management Studies* 29: 35–47.

Dutton, J.E. and Dukerich, J.K. (1991) 'Keeping an eye on the mirror: the role of image and identity in organization adaptation', *Academy of Management Journal* 34: 517–54.

Eisenhardt, K.M. and Zbaracki, M.J. (1992) 'Strategic decision-making', *Strategic Management Journal* 13: 17–37.

Elliott, D., Swartz, E. and Herbane, B. (1996) 'Business continuity planning in the finance sector', *Proceedings of the British Academy of Management Conference: 30 years on . . . . What have we learned?*, Aston, 16–18 September.

Elliott, D., Swartz, E. and Herbane, B. (1999a) *Business Continuity Management – Preparing for the Worst*, London: Incomes Data Services.

Elliott, D., Swartz, E. and Herbane, B. (1999b) 'Just waiting for the next big bang: business continuity planning in the UK finance sector', *Journal of Applied Management Studies* 8(1): 43–60.

Facer, D. (1999) 'Rethinking business continuity', *Risk Management* October (Suppl.): 17–18.

Feldman, P. (1998) 'Surviving Internet disasters', *Risk Management* 45(2): 56.

Finkelstein, S. and Hambrick, D. (1988) 'Chief executive compensation: a synthesis and reconciliation', *Strategic Management Journal* 9: 543–58.

Fitzgerald, K.J. (1995) 'Establishing an effective continuity strategy', *Information Management and Computer Security* 3(3): 20–4.

Greiner, L.E. (1972) 'Evolution and revolution as organizations grow', *Harvard Business Review* July–August: 37–46.

Hammer, M. (1990) 'Re-engineering work: don't automate, obliterate', *Harvard Business Review* July–August: 104–12.

Heng, G.M. (1996) 'Developing a suitable business continuity planning methodology', *Information Management and Computer Security* 4(2): 11–13.

Herbane, B. (1997) 'Business continuity: facts and effects', in B. Herbane (ed.) *Centre for Business Continuity Planning; Proceedings of the Launch Symposium*, London, Institute of Directors, 16 April, pp. 79–88.

Herbane, B. and Rouse, M.J. (2000) *Strategic Management: An Active Learning Approach*, 1st edn, Oxford: Blackwell.

Herbane, B., Swartz, E. and Elliott, D. (1997) 'Contingency and continua: achieving excellence through business continuity planning', *Business Horizons* November–December: 19–25.

Hirschheim, R.A. and Verrijn-Stuart, A.A. (1996) *Office Systems*, London: Elsevier-North Holland.

Janis, I.L. (1983), *Victims of Groupthink*, 2nd edn, Boston, MA: Houghton Mifflin.

King, J. (1997) 'Business continuity is focus of disaster recovery', *Computerworld* 31(35): 17.

Kumar, N., Scheer, L. and Kotler, P. (2000) 'From market driven to market driving', *European Management Journal* 18(2): 129–42.

Locke, E.A. (1968) 'Toward a theory of task motivation and incentives', *Organizational Behaviour and Performance* 3: 157–89.

Mintzberg, H. (1994) *The Rise and Fall of Strategic Planning*, London: Prentice Hall.

Moss-Kanter, R. (2001) *E-volve!: Succeeding in the Digital Culture of Tomorrow*, Cambridge, MA: Harvard University Press.

Mumford, E. and Hendricks, R. (1996) 'Business process re-engineering RIP', *People Management*, 2 May: 22–9.

Parris, D. (1999) 'Image conscious', *Survive* August: 11–15.

Pauchant, T. and Mitroff, I. (1992) *Transforming the Crisis-prone Organisation*, San Francisco, CA: Jossey-Bass.

Perrow, C. (1984) *Normal Accidents*, New York: Basic Books.

Petroni, A. (1999) 'Managing information systems' contingencies in banks: a case study', *Disaster Prevention and Management* 8(2): 101–10.

Power, P. (1999) *Business Continuity Management – Preventing Chaos in a Crisis*, management Action Notes, London: Department of Trade and Industry.

Schein, E.H. (1992) *Organizational Culture and Leadership: A Dynamic View*, Oxford: Jossey-Bass.

Schneider, R.O. (2000) 'Knowledge and ethical responsibility in industrial disasters', *Disaster Prevention and Management* 9(2): 98–104.

Shrivastava, P. (1987) *Bhopal*, London: Ballinger.

Simon, H.A. (1957) *Administrative Behaviour*, 2nd edn, New York: Macmillan.

Smith, D. (1990) 'Beyond contingency planning: towards a model of crisis management', *Industrial Crisis Quarterly* 4(4): 263–75.

Snyder, A.V. and Ebeling Jr, H.W. (1992) 'Targeting a company's real core competencies', *Journal of Business Strategy* 13(6): 26–32.

Thomas, J.B., Clark, S.M. and Gioia, D.A. (1993) 'Strategic sense-making and organizational performance – linkages among scanning, interpretation, action and outcomes', *Academy of Management Journal* 36: 239–70.

UK Online for Business (2000) 'Business in the information age', London: Department of Trade and Industry.

Further reading

Barton, L. (1993) 'Terrorism as an international business crisis', *Management Decision* 31(1): 22–5.

Clair, J.A. (1998) 'Reframing crisis management', *Academy of Management Review* 23(1): 59–76.

Mitroff, I., Pauchant, T., Finney, M. and Pearson, C. (1989) 'Do some organisations cause their own crises? The cultural profiles of crisis-prone vs crisis-prepared organisations', *Industrial Crisis Quarterly* 3(4): 269–83.

Smith, M. and Sherwood, J. (1995) 'Business continuity planning', *Computers and Security*, 14(1): 14–23.

Study questions

1 How would you encourage a small business owner to introduce continuity management?

2 Using the Internet, look at how the mineral water market has changed since the Perrier crisis. How is market share distributed?

3   Find an example of a crisis which has occurred recently. You may wish to use electronic databases to search for information using keywords such as 'crisis', 'strike', 'product recall', 'interruption', etc.

   (i) What evidence can you find to support Smith's three-stage model of crisis?

   (ii) What was the outcome of the crisis for the organization concerned? You should try to look for financial performance and stock price changes, and changes to the senior management team.

4 Continuity analysis and planning

Introduction

In Chapter 1, the necessity for organizations to absorb business continuity management into underpinning practices was asserted. Without such management, organizations are not only exposed to a wide range of interruptions, they also face problems with their compliance with a burgeoning variety of regulatory requirements and stakeholder expectations (Chapter 2). In the previous chapter, we examined the necessary steps to initiate the process of continuity management. In this chapter we focus on planning for business continuity.

From the outset it is worth noting that the keys to successful business continuity planning are *understanding* and *thinking*. Understanding in this context represents the attempt to recognize the caricatures and subtleties of an organization and its environment. Thinking implies and necessitates the application of understanding to develop effective and efficient solutions to potential interruption scenarios.

Moreover, business continuity *management* (as opposed to business continuity *planning*) implies an ongoing and iterative business and human process (Chapter 3). Indeed, Chapters 5 and 6 examine the maintenance of business continuity provisions through testing and maintenance procedures. The implications of such activities is that many of the issues addressed in this chapter are continuously undertaken. The objective of this chapter is to examine the wide variety of methods which organizations can use to arrive at a business continuity plan. As a starting point for the planning process it is important to consider a business continuity plan as a guide for action in the event of an interruption to an organization's operations. We will elaborate on the content of BC plans later in this chapter. From the outset, therefore, planners should be cognizant of the fact that the plan they intend to produce may not lie dormant in an office drawer. Upon invocation, its value will be determined by the manner in which it guides staff (and in some cases third parties) through the recovery process to the most effective restoration of pre-interruption activities.

Consider a plan to be like a pet – both start with a 'P' and both need to be fed to be kept alive! Thus we begin the chapter with a consideration of some of the necessary steps in the planning process, whereupon we examine each stage in greater detail.

Planning within the business continuity management process

Figure 4.1 portrays the BCM process introduced in Chapter 3. Since this chapter is concerned with planning for business continuity, you will observe a planning flowchart connected to the second step, showing the sequence of activities that are typically used to generate a business continuity plan (Figure 4.2). The value of the activities is often determined by the degree to which planners think about what is the most appropriate method of analysis. Thus, whilst a wide variety of frameworks and models exist for this purpose, our objective is to identify and explore the key steps required to generate business continuity plans. Central to the process is a business impact evaluation which draws together the analysis of the organization and its environment. From this analysis a risk assessment profile can be developed which, combined with scenario planning, leads to the generation of the plan.

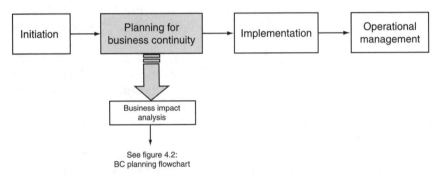

Figure 4.1 The business continuity management process

Source: Adapted from Elliott *et al.* (1999a).

Framework for identifying crisis types

Preparing and planning for the unexpected in a constantly changing world offers one of the primary difficulties facing the planner (or planning team). The desire to arrive at a 'definitive' list of crises which the organization might face could prove to be counterproductive. Why? The natural question of 'What interruptions or crises could we face?' may lead to an unstructured list similar to that shown in Figure 4.3.

The most logical next step is to attempt to deal with each one and have specific recovery provisions for each. However, this could lead to planning in perpetuity, whereby planning is determined by the length of the list of crises, rather than the needs and priorities of the organization. Shrivastava and

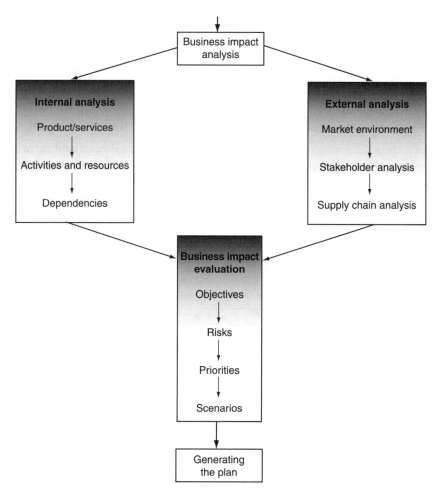

Figure 4.2 BC planning flowchart
Source: Adapted from Elliott *et al.* (1999).

Adverse weather	Hostile takeover	Product injuries
Computer breakdown	Illegal activities	Product tampering
Computer 'bugs'	Industrial action	Sabotage by outsiders
Computer failures	Kidnapping	Sabotage by staff
Currency fluctuations	Loss of important staff	Societal crisis
Disease/epidemic	Major industrial accidents	Supplier crisis
Fire	Media crisis	Telecommunications failure
Floods	Nature disasters	Terrorism

Figure 4.3 An unstructured list of crises

Mitroff (1987) have developed a framework for classifying types of resources according to *where* the crisis is generated and *which* systems are the primary cause (Figure 4.4).

The benefits of using such a matrix is that it can act as the starting point for a brainstorming session for any organization that wishes to identify the range of interruptions that it might experience. Developing contingency plans for every eventuality may be impractical, given the wide variety of potential failures. This matrix provides the basis for clustering 'families' of crises together and preparing for these rather than for each individual incident. Planners are limited in terms of time and resources and cannot account for all eventualities. So, for example, the consequences of fire, flood, earthquake and bomb are likely to be similar and may require one type of preparation. The example shown in Figure 4.4 is a generic model prepared by Shrivastava and Mitroff (1987).

The categories and crisis types identified in the generic model could relate to any industry. While it may be useful for managers or those involved in identifying the range of potential threats facing an organization to examine this framework, it is important that a new matrix is created that is directly relevant to each organization and industry. Below are shown examples from a travel agency and a university.

From the travel agent example (Figure 4.5) it is evident that some types of crisis are common to all organizations for example, computer viruses, strikes and loss of key staff. However, others are specific or more relevant to some industries than others, such as a coach crash or the kidnap of customers for some travel companies. Third-party failure refers to the dependence that all travel companies usually have on other organizations to supply, in part, the final service, ranging from hoteliers and air carriers to coach excursion companies. In this example, the matrix builds on the categories identified in the generic model and produces crises relevant to the travel industry.

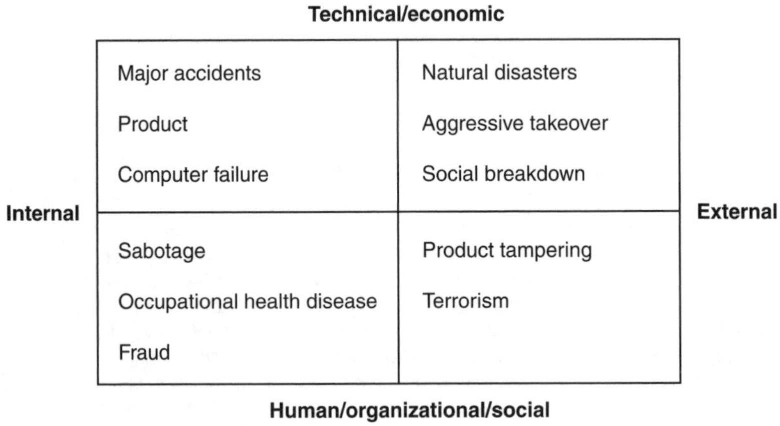

Technical/economic

	Major accidents	Natural disasters
	Product	Aggressive takeover
Internal	Computer failure	Social breakdown	**External**
	Sabotage	Product tampering
	Occupational health disease	Terrorism
	Fraud	

Human/organizational/social

Figure 4.4 Generic crisis typology

Source: Adapted from Shrivastava and Mitroff (1988).

Technical/economic

Computer breakdown Computer virus	Floods, heatwave Bad weather Fluctuating rates
Strike Sabotage Lose key staff	Travel accidents Customers held hostage Terrorism Third-party failure

Internal (left) **External** (right)

Human/organizational/social

Figure 4.5 Crisis typology: travel agent example

Source: Adapted from Mitroff *et al*. (1988) and Elliott *et al*. (1999a).

Technical/economic

Computer failures Fire Computer virus Hazardous leak from labs	Flood Telecommunications failure System failure
Strike Legionnaire's disease/RSI Series of suicides Drugs problem	Major public event Adverse media Poor public image

Internal (left) **External** (right)

Human/organizational/social

Figure 4.6 Crisis typology: university example

Source: Adapted from Mitroff *et al*. (1988) and Elliott *et al*. (1999a).

The university example (Figure 4.6) highlights, again, that certain crisis causes are common to many industries. Timing may also play an important part in the impact of a crisis. Organizations may be more vulnerable at certain times than at others. For example, one university experienced a telecommunications failure during 'clearing', the weekend following the release of A-level results and a prime recruitment time.

The matrix may be used as a framework from which potential crisis triggers and their consequences are considered. A word of caution should be noted at this juncture. As with all models and frameworks, they are merely tools with which to think about situations and problems. Many such models are, by their very nature, one-dimensional, and may not reflect the impact of time and the subtle relationship between two or more factors. The external/economic crisis that is a natural disaster may be difficult (if not impossible) to prevent. However, such an event could be exacerbated by human and organizational factors. For instance, the impact upon humans of the flood in Mozambique in early 2000 was compounded by a lack of available rescue resources and the decision of neighbouring governments to reduce the threat of flooding by manipulating the relief flow of water through their hydroelectric resources. Nevertheless, Shrivastava and Mitroff's framework offers a useful starting point.

An important component of crisis which has received little explicit attention in the models examined thus far is that of intention – that is the degree to which an individual or group sought to generate an interruption for an organization. Karakasidis (1997) addresses this issue by suggesting that not only should the cause–effect relationship be examined, but also intention. This is shown in Table 4.1.

Table 4.1 Intention and crisis types

Cause	Effect
Intentional crises	
Bomb	Building evacuation, search, defusing of device, declaration of safety, return to normal
Data disclosure/corruption	Deliberate theft or disclosure, programme code manipulation, virus
Extortion	Hostage-taking, ransom demands, product-tampering.
Industrial action	Lockouts, go-slow, work to rule, processing delays
Vandalism	Loss of equipment and ability to process customer orders
Unintentional crises	
Communication service loss	Failure of phone network and exchange, possible damage to equipment
Disease/epidemic	Closure of company facilities, quarantine, staff/customer contamination
Fire	Internal/external cause leading to fire damage, and secondary damage due to water and smoke
Power failure and electrical faults	Power surges, sags, spikes, loss of voltage, insufficient power to back up systems

Source: Adapted from Karakasidis (1997).

In identifying the causes of crises, organizations should seek to understand how they may make themselves more vulnerable to external events. Despite the fatalistic connotations of the term disaster, such incidents are rarely unpredictable or unavoidable. There is much that organizations can do to reduce their exposure to crises. However, while a focus upon prevention makes sense, it will never be a completely successful approach, so identifying the range of crisis types facing an organization represents an important step in the process of business continuity management. The major objective of the analysis stage is to identify the potential risks that the organization is exposed to and to consider strategies for reducing those risks as part of a BCM process.

Business impact analysis

The business impact analysis (BIA) is a critical part of the planning for business continuity. Meredith (1999: 139) refers to this analysis as forming the 'backbone of the entire business continuity exercise'. This will determine priorities which in turn influence many of the financial commitments to business continuity provisions. The BIA involves assessing the likely financial and operational consequences of a crisis. The focus of the BIA should always be upon a specific business process, which might be defined as a group of business activities undertaken within an organization. Such activities may occur within or between departments. Such business processes might be function-based (e.g. marketing or personnel) or not (e.g. quality management which often spans more than one function). The CCTA (1995) recommends using strategic planning or business process re-engineering documents to identify such business processes. A further alternative is value chain analysis (Porter, 1985).

Widely acknowledged as the originators of business impact analysis, Strohl Systems recommend that the BIA process should involve the following nine steps:

1 Define assumptions and scope of project for which BIA is being conducted
2 Develop a survey or questionnaire to gather necessary information
3 Identify and notify the appropriate survey recipients
4 Distribute the survey and collect responses
5 Review completed surveys and conduct follow-up interviews with respondents as needed
6 Modify survey responses based on follow-up interviews
7 Analyse survey data
8 Verify results with respondents
9 Prepare report and findings to senior management
(Strohl Systems, 1995: 2–11)

The content of the interview schedule or questionnaire will differ for each organization and each business process. The objective of such interviews is for the BCM team to gather data from line managers and other informative participants. The content should cover the generic categories outlined below:

- range of potential crises
- business unit objectives
- descriptions of key processes (flowcharts, etc.)
- resource needs
- linkages and dependencies with other business units
- linkages and dependencies with suppliers, customers and other agencies
- legal issues
- consequences of being out of action for different time periods (e.g. 1 hour, 8 hours, 24 hours, 1 week, etc.)
- prioritization of core and other activities
- minimum resources required to restore key activities
- seasonal trends or critical timing issues

These headings (which lead to related questions) should be adapted to meet the needs of the organization – be it public or private. The objective of such questions is to stimulate the interviewee to think about risk and how change in any of these broad categories might affect business processes. Proformas similar to that shown in Figure 4.7 provide a helpful way of ensuring consistency of data collection. Hence, each of these categories should be used to define situations which could have business impact for specific periods of time. The analysis should concentrate on those impacts most likely to occur and where the potential for damage is greatest. Managers should be encouraged to quantify impacts as far as is possible – this may involve financial impact or less easily quantifiable impacts such as loss of credibility, loss of quality of service or product, etc. A critical consideration is the duration of impact. How long could the interruption last? To ensure an effective BIA organizations should consider the full range of internal and external factors.

The approach suggested here is but one way to use BIA. In contrast, Gluckman (2000) suggests that BIA should be the foremost analysis which leads to the final generation of the business continuity plan(s). However, the position and role of BIA in our process echoes the view of Lee and Harrald (1999: 188), reached from their research into the use of the technique, that 'in order to carry out the [BIA] efficiently, it is first necessary to identify business functions/processes'.

The BIA offers a preliminary analysis of some of the idiosyncrasies of every organization's resources, systems and operations. The next step is to build on this through a systematic analysis of the organization's operating environment and a detailed examination of its outputs, activities and dependencies. The final three aspects come to form the internal analysis.

BIA Proforma

Date:	Role of function/department:
Time:	
Interviewee:	
Position:	

Links to other departments:

Systems/resource usage and dependency:

System/resource (name, etc.)	Purpose of system/resource (relationship to dept)	Usage (how often and by whom?)	Impact of loss (what could we not do?)	Degree of loss (halt or slow down the process) 1, 2, 5 days

- range of potential crises
- business unit objectives
- descriptions of key processes
- resource needs
- linkages and dependencies with other business units
- linkages and dependencies with suppliers, customers and other agencies
- legal issues
- consequences of being out of action for different time periods (e.g. 1 hour, 8 hours, 24 hours, 1 week, etc.)
- prioritization of core and other activities
- minimum resources required to restore key activities
- seasonal trends or critical timing issues

Figure 4.7 Business impact analysis proforma

Internal analysis

Internal analysis is needed to understand the nature of an organization's operations and how these influence the recovery priorities that will be a central part of business continuity plans. This analysis should be undertaken in three ways and in the following order:

- products and services
- activities and resources
- linkages and dependencies

The rationale behind this is to begin the analysis at the level of the product or service, the most direct contact with the customer. From this, the concern is with how a company's products or services share resources, since an interruption may have far more insidious effects due to such sharing. In so doing, the analysis should answer three important questions:

- What does the organization do?
- Who and what is involved in the creation of products and services?
- How are our activities linked?

Products and services

Since BCM is concerned with the organization's survival and the protection of its strategic objectives, the first stage of the internal analysis involves the identification of its products or services. In the case of a public sector organization, an analysis of the major (often statutory) responsibilities of the organization should be identified. This starting point indicates what is likely to be affected by a business interruption (products and services) and who will be affected (customers).

The portfolio of products or services produced by an organization is a further consideration. Key issues to identify are:

- the number and variety of products and services
- the market shares of individual products and services (where appropriate)
- the revenues and profits of individual products and services (where appropriate)
- temporal issues (e.g. seasonality, daily, weekly sales patterns, etc.)

This information helps to identify those products and services which, in the event of a crisis, would have the greatest impact on organizational performance and survival.

Consider the example of two well-known companies, the Coca-Cola Company and PepsiCo International. The former is reliant upon the carbonated drinks market to a greater degree than PepsiCo which has diversified into restaurants and snacks. A threat to the carbonated drinks market would have a greater impact upon Coca-Cola than PepsiCo.

Whilst it is important to consider current products, it is equally prudent to include within the same analysis the impact of new product introductions and strategies that involve a move into new product or geographical markets. Such changes in the future may significantly alter an organization's dependence on current products and markets, thereby reducing the salience and relevance of current continuity provisions. By considering such issues, continuity planning provides a contingency for the future.

Rover's 75 model was designed using a new process named 'e-build'. Part of this innovation was to extend car design using computers towards the simulation of the actual assembly of the vehicle on a virtual assembly line (Kochan, 1999). One clear outcome has been to reduce the likelihood of assembly problems and errors which could lead to a costly product recall. Here we can observe a new technology development which could not only improve product quality but also mitigate against the threat of costly litigation that may follow a product recall (Chapter 2).

Analysis of the organization's portfolio is only a starting point. It is insufficient information to evaluate the impact of an interruption. Products may be very similar or share resources. They may equally be dependent upon each other in ways that are not immediately evident. This understanding is achieved by looking at activities and resources.

Activities and resources

Once the profile of products and services is known, the analysis should progress to an identification of all resources which contribute to the product. These include those activities and resources which lead to the development, manufacture and sale of the product. By working back from the final product or service, all key resources leading to the final output should be identified. The types of resources that should be considered include:

- physical manufacturing equipment
- information technology
- transportation, storage and logistics assets
- telecommunications systems
- financial resources
- intellectual property
- employees
- buildings
- subsidiaries or divisions which produce components, parts or materials

The contribution of each of these resources will vary according to the nature of the organization's business. For instance, a direct insurance company will rely to a far greater extend upon IT and communications (telephones) than a manufacturer of electronic goods. Similarly, a physical goods manufacturer would be affected by petrol shortages, port blockades and haulage company interruptions. The degree to which these resources contribute to the final product or service will determine the provisions that are chosen for their continuity.

One way in which to assist this activity is to look at which business units are involved in creating a product or service. In addition, the role of outside suppliers should be examined. The greater the number of in-house departments and/or suppliers that are used in a product or service, the wider the scope for an interruption to occur. This does not necessarily mean a greater likelihood of interruption, simply that there are more links in the chain that could fail.

Dependencies

Whereas the previous components of the internal analysis deal with individual links, the final stage is to consider the whole chain together. The purpose of identifying the dependencies is to determine how an interruption in one part of an organization could affect the ability to supply goods and services (see Box 4.1). Dependencies are important linkages in which one activity must be preceded by another. If one activity fails, all other activities that are dependent upon it will fail. For example, the provision of consumer goods on supermarket shelves requires the production and transportation of each unit from a factory to the supermarket. Within this process there are many dependencies and potential points of failure. Thus the process is dependent upon the availability of raw materials, processing equipment and lorries to transport the finished goods.

Within this stage of the internal analysis it is important to develop links with operational planning in order to ensure that future operational investments are examined. For instance, new investment in IT or automation may radically alter employee skills requirements, training, supervision and functional structures.

Some of this analysis may have already been carried out in business process re-engineering and Y2K projects. Indeed, where organizations have a clear structure and system for strategic analysis, it is likely that much data will already be available. This applies equally to the next stage, external analysis.

External analysis

Without reference to the external environment, business continuity planning will be limited to an internal focus which does not make provision for the market, stakeholders and the supply chain. By understanding how these groups interact with an organization, tangible improvements can be made to BC provisions. Indeed, you will recall that Shrivastava and Mitroff's (1987)

Box 4.1 Functional dependencies

Dependencies	Examples
Operations management and production	Production of components must precede assembly of finished product
Information and communication technologies (ICT)	Growing use of direct financial services (PC and Internet banking and insurance)
	Growing use of call centres and automated help-lines in many sectors (e.g. Cable and satellite companies, Hewlett Packard)
	Relocation of call centres overseas (e.g. BA customers directed to call centres in India)
Marketing (shared brands, marketing and promotion)	Coca-Cola perceived to be contaminated leads to fears that other soft drinks may also be harmful to consumer
	Mercedes A-Class fails elk test with resultant threat to corporate reputation
Distribution channels (type, number and mix of wholesalers/ retailers)	Increasing concentration of power in large retailers in many European markets (e.g. Wal-Mart, Carrefour, Tesco, Aldi, J Sainsbury)
Purchasing and procurement (raw materials and components from suppliers)	Carrefour review purchasing guidelines for genetically modified foods
	Peugeot compelled to halt production following industrial action at suppliers
Logistics (whether in-house or otherwise)	Strike by Royal Mail prevents delivery of Internet purchases.
	Toyota requires suppliers to use helicopter delivery to maintain JIT schedules
Organizational support activities (such as legal, finance, etc.)	Increased regulation of financial services requires regular and ongoing review of day-to-day activities or else face punitive fines

typology of crises explicitly recognizes the external environment as a potential cause of crises. Moreover, Smith's (1990) crisis of legitimitation implies the response of an organization facing an interruption and the way that it is seen (or otherwise) to act appropriately by rivals, customers, regulators and other observing parties.

The market environment

The position of a company's product or service in a market will influence the impact of an interruption. A product with a low market share and few dependencies will suffer a lesser impact from a crisis than one with a high market share and high degree of dependency. Market position may also contrive to alter the level of impact that an organization suffers. Market position, relative to rivals, can be considered in two ways:

- actual market share, and/or
- image

In the case of Perrier (Chapter 3), the dominant position of the company as market leader in the mineral water market was irrevocably damaged. In terms of image, Mercedes-Benz recalled its all-new A-Class vehicle in 1997, shortly after its launch, and suspended deliveries for three months at an estimated cost of £100 million (Prowse, 1998). This blow to the company's image arose from a product that had yet to establish any market share. Ironically, the company had recalled a far larger number of their existing luxury car models for component replacements. Moreover, the A-Class recall highlights the effects of a crisis across an entire organization. In a two-month period as the crisis unfolded, Mercedes-Benz's parent company (Daimler-Benz) saw its share price fall by 32 per cent (Olins and Lynn, 1997).

Next, those involved in the planning process should consider how the market position (market share and image) could be affected by the onset of a disaster. Could it delay a new product launch, erode the company's market position or adversely change the company's image? In terms of the effect on company performance, these products/services and their dependencies should be a priority for business continuity protection.

A commonly used tool for analysing an organization's environment is the so-called PEST analysis, an acronym that has been stretched in Table 4.2 to include the physical environment and geographical themes, and competitors' activity. Used primarily as a tool in the process of strategic management it provides a checklist of potential environmental forces. The purpose is to identify those factors that might increase the potential for crisis or hinder an effective response.

Stakeholder analysis

The concept of stakeholders acknowledges that no business is an island and that business interacts with society in a number of different ways. This notion is not new. Dill (1958) noted the manner in which outside parties could bring their interests to bear upon an organization's managers and vice versa. It makes good business sense for organizations to be aware of their stakeholders as their interests and the satisfaction of their needs may determine business

Table 4.2 PEST applied in a business continuity context

Category	Examples
Political	Environmental policy, training provision, ICT initiatives, food hygiene regulations, industry watchdogs
Legal	Regulation/legislation relating to: Health and safety Product liability Negligence Hazardous substances Security and information Food-processing Building and construction Intellectual property
Economic	Fiscal and monetary policy
Environmental and geographical	Floods, pollution, drought, earthquakes
Social	Pressure group activities Consumer watchdogs Cultural and social changes (religious observance, ethnicity, etc.)
Commercial	Actions of competitors – legal or illegal
Technological	New products (recall of faulty products) New processes (moves toward paperless office environments)

success. The objectives of an organization will be circumscribed by the extent to which relationships with stakeholders such as suppliers, bankers, shareholders, customers are successfully managed. Nowhere is this more important than in BCM, since their response to the organization in the post-crisis phase will have an impact on the success of recovery efforts and, ultimately, survival of the company (see Box 4.2).

Stakeholders are those individuals, groups or organizations who have an interest in the success or otherwise of an organization. More importantly, stakeholders possess power that can be wielded to support or to thwart organizational change. An organization's stakeholders may be divided into 'primary' and 'secondary' groups.

Primary stakeholders are those who enable the organization to produce its goods and services. The involvement with primary stakeholders usually involves a transaction of resources, finances or services. Figure 4.8 illustrates the range of different stakeholder groups that constitute primary stakeholders. These groups will fundamentally affect the strategic objectives and

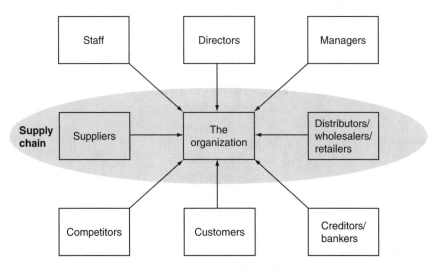

Figure 4.8 The organization and its primary stakeholders

policies of the organization. Alternatively, other primary stakeholders are typically those organizations that form part of the organization's supply chain or its value system – key suppliers, distributors or retailers and wholesalers.

Secondary stakeholders include those organizations or individuals that are affected indirectly by the activities of the organization. Figure 4.9 represents these. Professional bodies, competitors, pressure groups, local authorities all form part of this group of stakeholders. Clearly, they all have very diverse objectives and their influence over the organization will also differ greatly. The use of the term 'secondary' is not meant to indicate that these groups have a lesser impact on organizations. Far from it. Local authorities wield a great deal of power over where businesses might be sited and in recent years the Green movement has been very successful in getting corporations to consider environmental issues.

Internal stakeholders

Equally, the crucial role of internal stakeholders in implementation of a BCM process is being recognized. At a broad level, employees or managers form one category of direct stakeholder. However, rarely do they form a monolithic whole in terms of aims and objectives. Organizations are political in nature and different departments or functions will regard continuity management differently. Board members and other senior managers are regarded as much more important than they might have been in the past. The company board and other directors have a legal responsibility to ensure the survival of the organization. This is often one mechanism that might be used in support

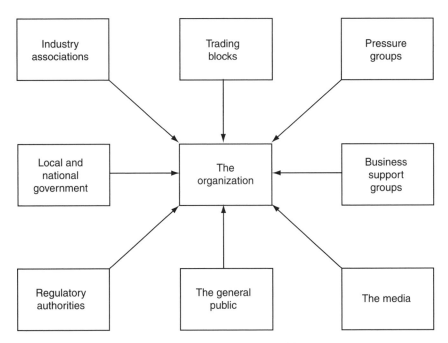

Figure 4.9 The organization and its secondary stakeholders

of continuity management where resistance to implementation is encountered. Such recourse to power clearly has to be used sparingly and wisely. But in those organizations where the culture is not supportive of planning for preparedness, it is often well nigh impossible to implement BCM programmes effectively without the support of an internal coalition – be it the board or other groups that carry power.

The planning team should conduct a thorough stakeholder analysis of the organization, similar to that used by Thames Water. This can then form the basis of a discussion between business units and the BCM team of potential strategies that might be used to manage key relationships. Indeed, Ramprasad *et al.* (1998) argue that a systematic stakeholder analysis can help to ascertain the organization's recovery priorities and can also act as a valuable tool for communicating the importance of business continuity and for re-educating sceptical managers and functions. A framework for stakeholder analysis, should consider:

- who the organization's stakeholders are
- the goals of stakeholders with regard to the organization
- the likely reaction to the types of interruption that could be encountered
- ways in which stakeholder relationships can be managed during an interruption

---

Box 4.2 Stakeholder analysis and continuity planning

Thames Water in the UK has used stakeholder analysis to enhance the understanding of how an incident will have different repercussions upon different groups. In the past, a burst water main was seen as a question of identifying the fault and repairing or replacing it, whereas now, the company has invested time and effort in identifying different types of stakeholders and their needs. For example, a detailed database will inform Thames Water quickly whether vulnerable groups (such as an elderly persons' residential home) are affected by a burst water main pipe, or whether a business customer operates processes requiring large volumes of water. The database provides the central point for the collection of information that relates to the different needs of users and the likely impact of a failure on them and Thames Water. Internally, the development of staff training in handling events has distinguished between the needs of line managers and operational staff. Stakeholder analysis has been used in an analytical way to discover the range of needs of the different groups of people that surround it. By identifying groups (such as pressure groups) that have no direct stake in the organization, potential problems can be anticipated and possibly avoided.

Based on Elliott *et al.* (1999a)

In one local authority, involvement in planning new facilities highlighted to the BCP team the importance of planning officers. They had not previously specifically considered this group as necessarily constituting an important stakeholder, but realized that a cooperative relationship might be advantageous should they require planning or siting permission in the future. The professional body for this group is one that is now consciously targeted as a networking organization.

The concept of stakeholders and its value for BCM is not a distant and abstract one. No organization is self-sufficient and each organization will depend to a greater or lesser extent upon a range of different stakeholder groups. The key is to identify the key relationships, especially those which might not immediately be apparent. As Shell discovered when they sought to dispose of the Brent Spar oil rig in the North Sea, it may be the least obvious stakeholder groups that can exert tremendous power. Greenpeace, through clever use of media images and an essentially emotional argument, forced the giant Shell and the UK government to back down over the issue of oil rig disposal. An environmental activist now advises the Shell board on environmental matters.

Without due regard for the role that stakeholders play in enabling companies to carry out their activities, crises can be exacerbated. When, in early 2000, it was discovered that staff working at the Sellafield reprocessing plant owned by British Nuclear Fuel Ltd (BNFL) had falsified safety records, the company faced public humiliation, internal and external inquiries, a damaged reputation and the loss of future business, including £4 billion from Japan's Kansai Electric alone (Jones *et al.*, 2000). Following the immediate crisis arising from falsification activities, the company announced that it would compensate Kansei Electric with a payment of £40 million and would re-take possession of the controversial shipment of mixed oxide. Seemingly near to the conclusion of the crisis, the re-possession of the shipment would itself widen the membership of the stakeholder group pertinent to the crisis, as concerns were raised by the USA and Pacific, central and south American states over the dangerous cargo which could pass through or near their territorial waters. To compound the situation, the Japanese government has moved its energy policy toward 'greener' sources following the BNFL incident, local opposition and a nuclear accident at Tokaimura in September 1999 (Rahman, 2000).

Despite the dynamic and unexpected manner in which stakeholder relationships develop, it is important for organizations to keep their attention on the day-to-day relationships between themselves and their direct stakeholders. For example, stakeholder relationships are a constant reality within an organization's supply chain (Bursa *et al.*, 1997).

Planning for supply chain interruptions

Supply chain issues, such as purchasing and product development have traditionally fallen under the remit of purchasing and procurement departments. Increasingly, the role of the supply chain in business continuity has grown given that the tight integration of companies along a supply chain often comes to form a source of competitive advantage (Chadwick and Rajagopal, 1995). A stark illustration of this can be seen in the events following a fire at a natural gas processing plant in Australia. The 1998 incident cut supplies for over a week and restrictions lasted for several months. As a consequence, both Toyota and Ford were forced to close their plants with Toyota estimating losses of AUS$10 million for each day of non-production (Tilley, 1998). In addition, we have previously noted that, as stakeholders, suppliers are clearly influential to the degree to which they can exert their bargaining power over customers downstream in the supply chain (Porter, 1980). Thus, planners' attention should also be directed to the potential risks that their organizations face from its suppliers, in spite of having well-developed internal business continuity management.

In business continuity planning, there are two types of suppliers – *operational* suppliers, those day-to-day companies which supply goods or services for production or service provision activities, and *recovery* suppliers, which are companies whose services are used in the event of business interruption. These services include hot sites (buildings furnished with hardware, software, data and telecommunications specific to a company's requirements), data mirroring (the real-time off-site storage of important computer data), salvage (physical building search and recovery), and telecommunications (for alternative phone and data lines, and emergency call centres). You will recall that the assessment of third-party requirements offered by recovery suppliers formed part of the purpose of the business impact analysis seen earlier in this chapter.

Returning to our focus on operational suppliers, the planner should be cognizant of the analogy of a chain being only as strong as its weakest link, which is valid in the context of the supply chain and business continuity. Operational suppliers could cause a business interruption in several ways:

- industrial action halting production
- faulty components are supplied which lead to a product recall
- cessation of trading (bankruptcy and receivership)
- fire or flooding in the supplier's premises
- failure of computer systems

For instance, in mid-1997 a strike at the largest of the US delivery services, United Postal Service (UPS), brought the company's deliveries of domestic and commercial parcels in the USA to a halt. The industrial action severely affected mail-order companies' ability to deliver products on time to customers. In particular, Gateway, a personal computer manufacturer that sells directly to customers, suffered substantial disruption to its business during the lengthy duration of the strike, as around half of its shipments were made by UPS.

As Gateway's sole distribution channel had been interrupted, a tangible impact was seen on its mid-year earnings at a time when it was seeking to consolidate its European expansion strategy. When the company's third quarter earnings did not meet stock market analyst's forecasts, the company's share price fell by 8 per cent. Dell, Gateway's major rival, had only 20 per cent of its deliveries made by UPS and reported revenue growth in line with expectations. Many other PC mail-order rivals used Federal Express as a delivery partner and, consequently, were less affected (CNN, 1997).

Many organizations, through projects to deal with the Year 2000 computer problem, have turned to the supply chain to identify further possible sources of interruption. Increasingly, organizations have introduced sophisticated links through technology for ordering, payment and information interchange that are vital to the logistics and production process, such as electronic data interchange (Kcrmar *et al.*, 1995) and, more recently, the Internet. Weiner (1995) highlights some of the major risks associated with the interruption of systems shared with suppliers (Table 4.3)

Although the term 'supply chain' suggests suppliers only, it includes all organizations that participate in value creation from the extraction of primary materials through to the end consumer. To a greater or lesser degree, mutual dependence will exist between the members of a supply chain. With large stocks and cancelled deliveries from a major customer, a supplier could easily find its own production halted quickly.

Table 4.3 The impact of interrupted suppliers

Type of impact	Reason for impact
Loss of independence	The company is unable to fulfil its customers' orders
Loss of confidential/sensitive information	Proprietary information could fall into the wrong hands
Increased exposure to fraud	Unauthorized transactions/invoices could arise following the loss of data
Loss of audit trail	Particularly where no paper copies of document exist
Software failure	Purchasing and scheduling systems which rely on EDI information could subsequently fail
Legal liability	Due to an inability to fulfil contractual obligations with trading partners

Source: Based on Weiner (1995: 56).

Auditing the supply chain for business continuity

The audit of the supply chain comprises two steps. The first involves the identification of supplier and buyers, highlighting those which are most important. Several factors will provide a suitable indication. For buyers, this includes what is bought from the organization, the value of output sold to the buyer and the proportion of output sold to the buyer. In addition, any collaboration with buyers in terms of distribution, retail and marketing should be considered. Furthermore, through the purchasing department, it should be known whether there are alternative buyers that could be used in the event of a lengthy (or permanent) interruption, in the case of a retailer going bankrupt, etc. These issues should also be considered in the context of the suppliers used by the organization.

Second, an evaluation should be made of the provisions which these organizations (buyers and suppliers) have in place in the event of a disruption. These will include:

- the level of interaction between the organizations (IT, staff, resources)
- whether they have BC plans in place
- the nature of recovery contingencies that may be in place, if no formal BC plans exist
- how long plans have been in place
- who are the main business continuity contacts in the organization
- whether reference is made to the organization by its buyers'/suppliers' BC plans
- how often plans are tested and revised
- whether the buyer or supplier evaluates its buyers'/suppliers' BC plans

The selection and evaluation of recovery suppliers should be treated with equal rigour, although, given the specific nature of the service provided, certain issues should receive a higher priority. There could be nothing worse than for a recovery supplier to be unable to offer its full service to an affected company (which is contractually agreed in advance) in the event of an interruption.

Business impact evaluation

The final steps in the planning process involve drawing together the preceding analyses into a cohesive whole in order to begin the process of drafting the actual business continuity plan The business impact evaluation re-evaluates the initial objectives, set at the outset of the BCP process, and assesses the risk against those objectives. It determines the priorities for business resumption and BC investments. Thus it should incorporate an assessment of the resources that each business unit and function requires to resume at an appropriate time. Of course, such analysis may provide many alternative 'resumption scenarios' and the business impact evalaution concerns the stage at which these are identified and considered. The BIE comprises four analyses. First, the business continuity objectives are refined. Second, risks are evaluated. Third, priorities for business recovery are established and, fourth, business interuption scenarios are developed.

Objectives

In order to have feasible and testable objectives, those which have been identified prior to the BIA should be refined in order to elucidate the minimum required level at which each function or business process can operate. These revised objectives may include reference to time. For example:

- Customer contact must be re-established within 2 hours
- Invoicing must be resumed within one week for major customers and return to normal within two weeks
- Delivery from suppliers must recommence within 4 hours
- Telephones must be operational within 30 minutes

Through the incorporation of greater detail into these objectives, a further sequence of events and timings can be devised and incorporated into the draft business continuity plan.

Risk assessment

Risk assessment is the term used to describe the process of gauging the most likely outcomes of a set of events and the consequences of those outcomes. At a personal level, informal assessments of risk are a more or less continual mental process, from crossing the road and judging when to contribute to a meeting, to buying goods and so forth. The risk management discipline has sought to formalize risk assessment in an attempt to reduce the effects of personal bias. A limitation is that, where complex systems are concerned, identifying all possible outcomes and consequences is extremely difficult. It has been argued that any attempt to quantify risk will fail because, no matter how sophisticated the mathematics are, all risk assessment is inherently value laden. Nevertheless, a structured approach to risk assessment is better than none (see Box 4.3). But a good understanding of the aims and objectives of such a process is more important than a detailed statistical knowledge.

A simple matrix is commonly used to categorize risks and hence to priori- tize remedial actions (Figure 4.10). Although providing a useful rule of thumb, it does not take into account the extent to which an organization has the potential to control an incident, nor for any asessment of the extent to

---

Box 4.3   Risk assessment questions

- What hazards, potential failures or interruptions face the organization?
- What would be the effects of particular failures on the organization? Our business partners? Our customers? The local community? Our staff? And so forth.
- What is the likelihood of each failure or hazard occurring?
- Do we do enough currently to identify and prepare for such events?
- Is the risk acceptable? To the organization? Our business partners? Our customers? The local community? Our staff? And so forth.
- What could be done to control the level of risk or to prepare for a failure?
- What should the organization do?
- What constraints are there?

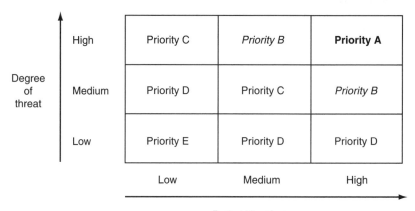

Figure 4.10 Risk assessment matrix

which certain 'risks' might be deemed acceptable to an organization or to other stakeholders. For example, Johnson and Johnson might have deemed that the public would treat them sympathetically if they suffered from a repeat malicious product-tampering episode. In many instances the trade-offs will not be as extreme as in the case of the Tylenol poisonings and organizations must themselves balance investment in preparations against what the public or other groups may consider that they should do.

Priorities and scenario planning

The determination of resumption priorities is not an exact science. Far from it. In many cases, particularly where there is a lack of historical data to draw on, BCM managers find that they have to base their analysis on past experience and judgement. However, a systematic BIA and BIE will offer a clear understanding of the most effective way to implement the necessary steps to undertake recovery activities.

Companies often find that, where leading-edge technology is used, due to the lack of appropriate data to draw on, they have to make use of what historical data they have, together with the experience of highly skilled functional experts and BCP managers.

The involvement of experienced BCM personnel is particularly important to facilitate a realistic determination of priorities. Elliott *et al.* (1999a) recount how, at a UK bank, the BCM team was actively involved in this part of the planning process. The company also instituted a structure that enabled BCP managers to appeal to higher authorities should individual functions not arrive at sensible priorities. This acts as further evidence to highlight the need to have an effective structure to enable implementation of the BCP (Chapters 5 and 6).

Conducted well, the BIA and the subsequent BIE allow the development of plans that reflect the best and most sensible balance between BCM investment and the exposure to risk. The resulting strategies should be based upon the information generated by the BIA

Scenario planning

Whilst BC planning is an activity undertaken for the present, its value will generally only be realized in the future when a plan is invoked and an organization is able to recover more swiftly and easily than might previously have been the case. Nonetheless, without an understanding of how the organization and its markets, stakeholders and supply chains may change, the assumptions that are made today may not be valid tomorrow. Whilst the BC planning process has, so far, focused on the past and present, it is equally important to address these future changes. The problem that arises, however, is finding a way to look at the future analytically. To do otherwise would make such efforts purely speculative. Scenario planning is an approach that can be usefully employed for this purpose. It has its origins in wider business planning (Leemhuis, 1985; Kassler, 1995; Moyer, 1996) but it has been shown to generate further value in the context of BCP (Herbane and Rouse, 2000).

Scenario planning recognizes the uncertainty that faces organizations. It has developed as an alternative method of planning in circumstances where predominantly quantitative analysis cannot adequately deal with high levels of uncertainty. Its value in business continuity planning cannot be under-estimated. In essence, a scenario is a story of a major event in the future, its implications for an organization and an understanding of the major changes that are needed for managers to confront the future. What differentiates scenarios from speculation is that they are carefully considered, internally consistent and are based on knowledge, expertise and experience (see Box 4.4).

The key to successful scenario planning is participation. Without it, the scenarios will not benefit from a wide variety of experience from contribu-tors. In the context of business continuity planning, the following questions could be used in scenario planning:

- How would a change in government in a major overseas market affect business continuity?
- How would business continuity change if a supplier is acquired by another company?
- How would a major product recall affect the company?
- How would a change in government affect the funding of an organiza-tion in the public sector?

In each of these cases, there is a great deal of uncertainty and variety in the outcome. For example, a change in the governing political party could lead to a major swing in policy. Equally, only minor changes may occur.

The scenario planning process for BCP comprises of six stages. First, the identification of participants is undertaken. These might include employees throughout an organization, suppliers, buyers, industry experts, trade associ-ations and government agencies. Second, data is collected from participants in the form of a questionnaire or interview. Participants are asked to consider the central question and related themes such as:

- how quickly changes are expected to happen
- the impact of the changes on the organization
- the impact of changes on similar organizations/rivals
- steps that can be taken to prevent or reduce the impact of the scenario arising

The answers are normally structured in the form of a questionnaire to ensure comparability of the (often large) number of responses.

The third stage entails the analysis of responses. The planner should then aggregate the responses in order to identify common themes and issues in the

Box 4.4   Scenario planning at Artem Plc

Artem Plc (a fictional company) is a manufacturer of plastic packaging used by the manufacturers of cleaning products (bleach etc.). Currently its markets are UK and EU based, although it intends to enter the US and South-East Asia markets in the next five years. With a presence in these new markets, Artem will be in position to provide higher returns to shareholders and achieve growth through strategic alliances and takeovers of smaller companies in the industry. Artem is uncertain how a product recall could affect the organization. Scenario planning has led to two main scenarios.

The first scenario occurs prior to the company moving into the new markets. The company's plastic bottles are recalled from customers (cleaning product producers) due to an anomaly in the manufacturing process. In order to recover from this crisis the company has to re-deploy substantial resources to deal with enquiries from customers, identify the cause of the product defect, improve processes and compensate customers which have to find alternative suppliers. Consequent to the immediate crisis, Artem has to pay heavy fines levied by Health and Safety bodies in the UK and EU countries and pay for increased insurance premiums. Furthermore, with a tarnished reputation, the company encounters major difficulties in establishing local distribution and sales agreements with third parties in the new markets. The loss of sales and the fall in reputation leads to the abandonment of the market entry strategy. Artem Plc's share value falls substantially and the company becomes the target for a hostile takeover.

The second scenario occurs having entered the US market. The company's products are affected by one of its customers recalling its bleach products after a split in the bottles causes bleach to spray onto customers' hands leading to several injuries. The reaction of the bleach manufacturer is to (erroneously and publicly) blame the packaging producer (Artem Plc) for the split in the plastic bottle. The attention of the public and the regulatory authorities turns immediately to Artem Plc, which finds itself the subject of several lawsuits. In addition, several other buyers in the US market have suspended orders pending an official enquiry into the incident. The incident leaves the company with rapidly falling sales, a tarnished reputation and facing several lawsuits which it must set out to defend (although it is clearly not culpable). A year later, the bleach manufacturer finally admits that the bleach contained in the damaged bottles was the result of faulty production which made the bleach far more corrosive than normal, although it still claims that the plastic bottles should have been more resilient. Artem Plc now decides that the only way in which it can restore its image and lost sales is through litigation against the bleach manufacturer for lost revenue and libel. Some eight years after the initial incident, the company successfully concludes litigation and receives substantial compensation. However, Artem's intended strategy of growth through alliances and acquisitions has been severely impeded.

Whilst both scenarios are quite different, the common themes are BCM related. The product recall exposes the organization to a wide variety of risks which cannot be foreseen precisely.

responses, and identify variations in the responses. Once the analysis is complete, scenario planning marks the fourth stage. From the responses, scenarios should be written in the form of a narrative, starting from the precursors to the scenario event (i.e. what are the signs that it may happen?), the event itself and the aftermath and implications for the organization. In many instances, more than one scenario may be written, reflecting the degree of uncertainty.

The scenarios that have been developed require validation to ensure that they reflect the views of participants and contain a logical and feasible narrative. Hence, the penultimate stage normally involves group seminars charged with scrutiny of the scenarios which have been devised. This scrutiny serves to evaluate whether the assumptions underpinning the scenarios are correct, raise awareness of the impact of the scenarios arising, and stimulate discussion of the ways in which the organization should have provisions in place to deal with the scenario(s). Finally, the scenarios should be integrated into the business continuity plan. Many organizations' business continuity plans will contain a section labelled 'scenarios'. In other cases, rather than provide the lengthy detail of the scenario, a short summary is provided (see Box 4.5).

Box 4.5   An example of a summarized scenario

Access to Yorkshire building is lost due to:

- building collapse in vicinity
- utility leak (gas/water)
- anti-capitalist demonstrations
- closure of vicinity by police
- malicious hoax

Outcomes of the scenario:

Computer and telecommunications systems are available but activities need to be located to the hot site (invoke part 2 of the plan).

Or . . .

All resources within the building are not available/damaged (invoke part 3 of the plan).

Summary of the planning process

Scenario planning is the penultimate stage of the planning process. Each of the preceding stages has been designed to gather information systematically and develop knowledge about the nature of the organization and its business continuity requirements. These are summarized in Table 4.4.

The final stage is the development of the plan itself – the document (s) to be used in the event of a crisis.

Table 4.4 Summary of the planning process

Stage of planning process	Purpose
Identifying objectives and scope	*Recognize* why and where BC is needed
Identifying the causes of crisis	*Anticipate* and evaluate a range of interruptions
Business impact analysis	*Assess* the balance between investment and exposure
	Evaluate outputs, resources, linkages and dependencies
	Understand the external influences on BCM
Business impact evaluation	*Balance* internal and external analyses
	Consider the likelihood and consequence of crises
	Incorporate future changes into today's plans

Generating the business continuity plan

The development of a business continuity plan does not mark the end of the BCM process. It marks only a small part of it. The emphasis of BCM is upon management. However much attention is placed on plans, they can often lead to the mis-belief that an organization has good business continuity practices in place. It is the improvements provoked by the plans for business resumption that are the real indicators of their worth. Any plan that arises from the planning stage of the BCM process is a reflection of the quality of input.

Plans do not exist to show the merit and exactitude of the planning process from which it was born. Plans exist to:

- help to establish the severity of an incident
- coordinate human resource requirements
- guide people in a systematic way through the recovery process
- to demonstrate to stakeholders that an organization's business recovery arrangements are suitable, and
- to guide the process of testing (Chapter 6)

However many plans are in place within an organization, they must be *achievable*, *testable* and *cost-effective*, in order for them to be effective.

Organizations can generally determine the content of plans in two ways. The first is to use specialist software that provides a template (often adapted). This provides a comprehensive and consistent structure with which to work. The second is an organic approach developed in-house. In these cases the BC manager devises a structure developed from the internal and external analyses and may be influenced by a variety of publicly available sources. Every organization has a different style of plan. Some organizations tend to combine several documents together whilst others retain the documents as separate (but related documents).

In addition to how well-developed BCM is, factors such as organizational structure and size, geographical location, the number of departments and the variety of products sold will determine whether an organization has many or few plans. The term 'plan' in a business continuity context often refers to a series of interrelated documents which are broadly found within the following categories:

1   the 'general' BC plan
2   the call-out lists
3   the time-line of recovery
4   functional business continuity plans

Whichever combination of documents an organization chooses to devise, they must be considered to be 'live'. Without regular maintenance and testing, their usefulness in a real crisis may be severely limited.

The general BC plan

Effectively the reference work for BCP within an organization or large function, and the size and use of the general BC plan will vary between organizations. In some organizations, the general BC plan will effectively be the document to which reference is made during an interruption. In others, factors such as size and structure will lead to the development of functional/departmental sub-plans which are implemented by smaller groups. However, as Smith (1996: 27) notes: 'Sub-plans for individual departments . . . need a coordinating "top" plan to prevent conflict of interest and misuse of resources. The priority should be to incorporate measures to contain the crisis, ensuring continuity of function and a speedy return to normality.' Given that sub-plans will be derived from the general plan, the latter will use the analysis derived from the process outlined in this chapter. Table 4.5 shows the relationships between the planning activities and specific sections of the plan.

The general plan forms the basis from which call out lists, time-lines of recovery and functional policies are devised. Figures 4.11 and 4.12 show some of the structures that plans may adopt.

In the first example (Figure 4.11), the document structure serves as a broader reference 'manual' for the business continuity procedures that the organization has in place. Reference is made to the general objectives of the business continuity plan and to the ongoing testing and auditing (which we consider in Chapter 6). In addition, the plan details the types of equipment that are necessary to carry out recovery activities (Section 2) and contractual relationships that the company has with recovery suppliers (Section 5). The second example (Figure 4.12) is focused more toward the activities and organization involved in practical recovery efforts. Issues such as objectives, testing

Table 4.5 General plan content and relationship with the planning process

'General BC plan' Section name	Source of information: Analysis/planning activity
The organization's goals and objectives	Objectives and scope
BCM policies	BIE – objectives
Identification of which business areas have BC plans	BIE – risk assessment
Terms of reference, i.e. what constitutes a crisis that would lead to invocation of plans	Frameworks of crisis types and scenario planning
Priorities of business operations	BIE
Immediate resumption	BIA, BIE and priorities
Intermediate resumption	BIA, BIE and priorities
Late resumption	BIA, BIE and priorities
Scenarios (including the 'worst case')	Scenario planning
How simultaneous interruptions are dealt with	Scenario planning
Resources and deployment	BIA
Off-site facilities	BIA and supply chain analysis
Composition and structure of the crisis management team	Objectives and scope
General recovery procedures	BIE
Plan maintenance and testing	Discussed in chapter 5
Contracts and agreements with third-party suppliers	BIA and supply chain analysis

and third-party relationships are not included. This does not mean that the company has chosen not to include these within the plan. Instead, it recognizes that much of this information may not immediately be required in the event of an interruption. Accordingly, rather than having one single 'plan' which documents all aspects of business continuity management, this plan is focused on the structure and organization of recovery activities following invocation.

Their differences are, *prima facie*, that of focus. Ultimately, however, it is the testing process that will determine the usability of the plan under circumstances of an interruption. Elements which are common to both plans and all practical plans are call-out procedures (which systematically call staff to the recovery location) and time-lines of recovery (which direct the recovery process). We now turn to each of these important elements, starting with the call-out procedure.

Call-out procedures

Often found as an appendix of departmental or functional plans, the call-out procedure provides a systematic way in which to call out employees in the event of a business interruption outside office hours. Also known as a

	Investment operations: ********* Bank plc
Section number and title	**Contents**
Section 1 **Overview**	Objectives Terms of reference BCM policies Identification of critical tasks Continuity of management Resumption of normal operations

Section 2
Recovery procedures
	Declaring the 'zero hour'
	Initiating call tree/cascade call: criteria and report of unreachables
	Arrangements for transport to alternate facilities
	Establishing emergency command centre
	Inventory of equipment and matched against requirements:
	    Office equipment
	    Telecommunications
	    Vital records and supplies
	    Terminal hardware
	    Computer equipment
	    Software
	Set-up and testing of equipment
	Establishing telecommunications

Section 3 **Operating requirements and reference**	Call tree, initiator and recovery team details Alternative location specification (workspaces) Proximity requirements Dependencies on other groups

Section 4
Plan maintenance and testing
	Identifying changes to plans
	    Amending current 'live' plan
	    Authorization of changes
	Testing
	    Pre-defined scenarios
	    Frequency and type
	        Announced
	        Unannounced
	        Walk-through
	        Live
	Evaluation
	    Measurement criteria
	Procedures and review

Section 5 **Forms, logs and general reference**	Restoration logs General supply requests Contacts Telecommunications Service agreements PR guides
Appendices	BC plans for departments and functions Call-out lists Time-lines of recovery Functional policies

Figure 4.11 Sample BC plan structure (A)

Source: Based on Elliott *et al.* (1999a).

International operations: ********* Bank plc	
Section number and title	**Contents**
Section 1 **Introduction**	1.1 Control levels and escalation 1.2 Incident response 1.2.1 Duty emergency team 1.2.2 Incident response group 1.2.3 Emergency management board 1.2.4 Business continuity team 1.2.5 Front-line team 1.3 Command-and-control system 1.3.1 Gold, silver, bronze hierarchy 1.4 Associated documents
Section 2 **Definition of terms used in this document**	Explains the terms used in Section 1 of the plan and other relevant terminologies
Section 3 **Plan index**	Index to general BC plan and functional plans
Section 4 **Plan detail**	Time-lines of recovery
Appendix 1	Emergency services incident information
Appendix 2	Duty emergency team membership
Appendix 3	Incident response group membership
Appendix 4	Emergency management board membership
Appendix 5	Procedure for call-out of incident response group Call-out script
Appendix 6	Evacuation Inside the building Leaving the building At the assembly points
Appendix 7	Maps and plans
Appendix 8	Local and national government contacts

Figure 4.12 Sample BC plan structure (B)

'cascade call', the objective is to call out essential personnel in the most efficient manner possible. Any variation to the contrary will affect the ability of recovery efforts to take place effectively. Such lists have to be revised constantly to incorporate changes to personnel, changes to roles and responsibilities and home telephone numbers. The call-out should be designed to bring the appropriate employees to work on business recovery at the appropriate time. Plans can stand or fall by virtue of call-out procedures. If too many staff are called out, valuable time is wasted in deciding which staff to retain, and which to send home to await further instructions. Equally, too few may be available for call-out due to personal details being out of date or incorrect, incorrect feedback as to who and how may people have been called, and a lack of arrangements for staff transportation and childcare.

Good links between BC managers and human resource departments are essential to the success of call-out lists. Perhaps the most critical relationship however, is between the BC department and line managers who should be responsible for ensuring that cascade lists are kept up to date. Call-out lists have to reflect the dynamics of the organization's human resources through arrivals, departures, promotions and restructuring, etc.

Time-lines of recovery

The general plan identifies the priorities of business operations which are incorporated into a chronology of events from the time that an incident takes place (known as the 'zero hour'). Listed in sequence are the activities required to resume normal operations. The business impact evaluation provides the list of priority tasks which should be completed as quickly as possible. The levels of recovery for prioritized tasks are known as 'recovery time objectives' or 'recovery milestones'. The timing of an activity's recovery is determined by the strategic importance of the activity to the organization. Often, these priorities are agreed at board level to ensure that resumption is truly based upon a highest priority first. Those which require immediate resumption are critical to the survival of the organization. Next, those which could affect the position of the organization are resumed. Following these are activities which could have an effect upon the longer-term position of the organization. Following the resumption of these priority tasks, activities which restrict customer service or hamper administration should be recovered. The approach taken will vary according to the organization and the type of interruption. For example, Lee and Russo (1996) suggest that the response to an interruption has two phases. The response phase deals with bringing the situation under control (such as stabilizing a leak, restoring power, recalling products) and the recovery stage which follows deals with returning operations to normality (repairing and preventing the leak, upgrading/introducing back-up power systems, rectifying the recalled product's design). Recovery time objectives should be incorporated where such a two-phase plan is put in place.

Clearly, each crisis will have different effects, but the time-line will clarify the priority and timing of critical activities. An example can be seen in Figure 4.13. There are two critical features – the chronological order of activities from the time of the incident (spanning from 1 to 24 hours), and the sequence of activities which should be undertaken within each time period. For example, within the first hour of the incident, there is little to be gained if

Tick when completed	1	2	3	4	5	6	7	8	24
RTO to be achieved within time after invocation (hours)	✓	✓	✓	✓	✓	✓	✓	✓	✓
Inform BC manager	☐								
Establish staff help-line	☐								
Inform staff of incident	☐								
Inform staff of incident and tell them to be on stand-by	☐								
Await Recovery Team (RT) approval to invoke plan		☐							
Establish customer/supplier help-line		☐							
Conduct preliminary assessment of damage		☐							
RT go-ahead to invoke functional plans if needed		☐							
Identify staff requirements		☐							
Inform senior management of incident		☐							
Invoke contingency service agreements			☐						
Attend recovery site			☐						
Request critical staff to attend site			☐						
Inform non-critical staff to remain at home and await further instructions				☐					
Hold situational report meeting				☐					
Set team objectives				☐					
Assess state of work in progress				☐					
Call up back-up tapes or records				☐					
Inform linked departments					☐				
Inform linked departments of new arrangements					☐				
Inform customers and external suppliers					☐				
Initiate delivery of contingency agreements:						☐			
Equipment						☐			
Stationery						☐			
Telecommunications						☐			
Mail service						☐			
Prioritize new work						☐			
Test new equipment							☐		
Resume critical activities								☐	
Inform non-critical staff of progress								☐	
Prepare schedule for return to full capacity (including the clearance of any backlog)									☐

Figure 4.13 Example structure of time-lines of recovery

staff are informed (and subsequently called out or otherwise) and the staff help-line is not available. Equally, within three hours of the incident, recovery suppliers are informed that their services will be required and therefore the recovery team is expected to arrive. Then, staff called to the recovery site can be managed and directed upon their arrival.

Organizations can use alternatives to the method shown in Figure 4.13, for instance by using flowcharts. However the sequence of events is organized, employees involved in recovery should be aware of what they ought and ought not be doing. This can be communicated to employees through awareness raising, meetings, testing and documentation. A free phone number, with a changing message, may also provide a means of easily communicating with staff during and after a crisis.

Functional business continuity plans

At a functional or departmental level, organizations may choose to develop individual continuity plans. For instance, the time-lines of recovery for an IT department could differ widely from those of a production department. It is therefore prudent to develop recovery-time objectives (RTOs) and recovery milestones for each. Such department-specific RTO grids (similar to Figure 4.13) will be found in the general plan, but the department's business continuity plan will contain a greater level of specific detail on how the department will recover its operations. Functional business continuity plans may take another form, which recognizes the specialist assistance that it can provide in the event of an interruption elsewhere in the organization.

The human resources/personnel department may be deployed in an interruption situation to liase with employees who are not immediately required, ensuring that employees are paid, that overtime payments are promptly processed and that extra expenses (for transportation and food) incurred are dealt with promptly. It may also provide counselling facilities or coordinate contact between staff and third parties in this regard. A further role may involve managing the release of confidential employee information via the PR department to the media (in the event of fatalities or injuries) and to provide continuance in its obligation in relations to the availability of documents required by law (e.g. for industrial tribunals, etc).

The public relations function will adopt the role of interface between the organization and the public. Its functional BC plan will pay particular attention to protocols for the release of authorized verbal, printed or electronic information to the media, organization of PR briefings and dealing with unsolicited media enquiries. Moreover, a crisis media centre will also require advance planning and organization, the detail of which should be explicit within both the functional BC plan and the general BC plan.

In the event of an interruption which does not directly affect the sales department, the sales function BC plan should aim to ensure that existing and future sales are not jeopardized. Therefore, the critical activities are to maintain contact with customers, establishing a customer database in alternative locations (if necessary), to provide and resource a help desk for customers, to ensure the continuity of sales in progress and payments, and to ensure the availability of documents required by law (e.g contracts, etc.).

Similarly, the purchasing/procurement/logistics functions focus on parties in the supply chain, but, in this instance, those from which deliveries of goods and services are required. Important activities in the functional BC plan will typically involve contact procedures with suppliers in order to divert or suspend deliveries, the redirection of deliveries to alternative premises, business continuity of electronic ordering/payment systems (EDI) and the provision of documents required by law (e.g vehicle licensing, etc.).

The health and safety department has an obvious role in the management of an incident which involves hazards, accidents and evacuations. In addition, where the recovery process moves to another location, the department will be involved in ensuring the compliance of alternative premises with due regard to statutory provisions. Similar to sales and personnel functions, documents required by law will have to be made available and post-incident reporting will often represent the mainstay of the department's activities.

The facilities (or property/premises) function will play an important role in providing an emergency centre (food, drink, toilets, etc.), ensuring security, and liasing with emergency services and local authorities.

The functional BC plan associated with legal departments will include provision for activities such as the preparation of insurance claims, liaison protocols with other functions to determine the scope for litigation, preparation for product or company liability litigation and the ongoing pursuance of industry and regulatory requirements. Often, it is the legal department which has the longest role in the post-recovery phase, often due to the initiation of legislation against the organization in the aftermath of a crisis.

The development and implementation of functional BC plans recognizes that a 'one-size fits all approach' may lead to less clarity in the event of a crisis. As we pointed out earlier, whilst plans are a tangible output of the BC planning process, they are only as useful as their relevance in the event of a crisis.

Summary

Planning for the future is well established. Indeed, the twentieth century marked the birth, adolescence and maturity of many planning techniques which have influenced the BC planning process. There is a critical difference however. General business planning (strategic, operational or marketing) is underpinned by the expectation – indeed the hope that – the scenarios (the future) contained within the plan will arise. In contrast, the BC planning process differs in its expectation and its hope – that the plan will not be used.

This is not a mandate to disregard the importance of the plan, but rather to consider the impact of not having a well-formulated business continuity plan in place.

In this chapter we have explored the individual stages of the planning process. The planning process is derivative of organizations' widely differing approaches and should be tailored to meet the idiosyncrasies of an organization's structure, processes, people, industry and stakeholders. Without this, the likelihood of poor planning and poor plans is heightened.

Critical to the planning process are knowledge and participation. Without the two, those who are best served to inform the plan and its procedures will remain under-utilized, and those who will be required to implement the plan in the event of an interruption will have little ownership of the processes which they are to follow.

As we made clear early in this chapter, planning and plans do not mark the end of business continuity activities. They are the pivot between planning and the ongoing management of increased resilience from and response to business interruptions. In the next chapter, we address how such management is enacted in organizations, and specifically how the changes which necessarily accompany business continuity are implemented, both strategically and operationally.

References

Bursa, M., Hunston, H., Lewis, A. and Wright, C. (1997) *The Automotive Supply Chain – New Strategies for a New World Order*, London: Informa Publishing Group.

CCTA (1995) *A Guide to Business Continuity Management*, London: HMSO.

Chadwick, T. and Rajagopal, S. (1995) *Strategic Supply Management*, London: Butterworth-Heinemann.

CNN (1997) 'Computer maker says $194 million purchase allows it to grow server line', *CNNfn* 19 June.

Dill, W. (1958) 'Environment as an influence on managerial autonomy', *Administrative Science Quarterly* 2(4): 409–43.

Elliott, D., Swartz, E. and Herbane, B. (1999a) *Business Continuity Management – Preparing for the Worst*, London: Incomes Data Services.

Elliott, D., Swartz, E. and Herbane, B. (1999b), 'Just waiting for the next big bang: business continuity planning in the UK finance sector', *Journal of Applied Management Studies* 8(1): 43–60.

Gluckman, D. (2000) 'Continuity . . . recovery', *Risk Management* 47(3): 45.

Herbane, B. and Rouse, M.J. (2000) *Strategic Management: An Active Learning Approach*, 1st edn, Oxford: Blackwell.

Jones, M., Rahman, B. and Newman, C. (2000) 'Dismay as BNFL agrees to take back Japanese fuel', *Financial Times* 12 July: 2.

Karakasidis, R. (1997) 'A project planning process for business continuity', *Information Management and Computer Security* 5(2): 72–8.

Kassler, P. (1995) 'Scenarios for world energy: *Barricades* or *New Frontiers*?', *Long-Range Planning* 28(6): 38–47.

Kochan, A. (1999) 'Rover's E-Build process assembles cars in the virtual world', *Assembly Automation* 19(2): 118–20.

Krcmar, H., Bjorn-Andersen, N. and O'Callaghan, R. (1995) *EDI in Europe*, Chichester: John Wiley.

Lee, Y.J. and Harrald, J.R. (1999) 'Critical issue for business area impact analysis in business crisis management: analytical capability', *Disaster Prevention and Management* 8(3): 184–9.

Lee, R.G. and Russo, R.J. (1996) 'Dealing with disasters takes careful planning ahead of time', *Building Design and Construction* 37(9): f37–8.

Leemhuis, J.P. (1985) 'Using scenarios to develop strategies', *Long-Range Planning* 18(2): 30–7.

Meredith, W. (1999) 'Business impact analysis', in A. Hiles and P. Barnes (eds) *The Definitive Handbook of Business Continuity Management*, Chichester: John Wiley.

Mitroff, I., Pauchant, T. and Shrivastava, P. (1988) 'The structure of man-made organisational crisis', *Technological Forecasting and Social Change* 33: 83–107.

Moyer, K. (1996) 'Scenario planning at British Airways – a case study', *Long-Range Planning* 29(2): 172–81.

Olins, R. and Lynn, M. (1997) 'A class disaster', *Sunday Times* (London) 16 November: 14.

Porter, M.E. (1980) *Competitive Strategy* , New York: The Free Press.

Porter, M.E. (1985) *Competitive Advantage*, New York: The Free Press.

Prowse, R. (1998) 'A legal moose on the loose?', *Motor Industry Management* October: 18.

Rahman, B. (2000) 'Nuclear hopes dashed by furore', *Financial Times* 12 July: 2.

Ramprasad, A., Ambrose, P. and Komarov, M. (1998) 'The power of stakeholders in continuity', *Disaster Recovery Journal* 11(4): 11–13.

Shrivastava, P. and Mitroff, I. (1987) 'Strategic management of corporate crises', *Columbia Journal of World Business* 22(1): 5–11.

Smith, D. (1990) 'Beyond contingency planning: towards a model of crisis management', *Industrial Crisis Quarterly* 4(4): 263–75.

Smith, R. (1996) 'Planning for contingencies', *Industrial Management and Data Systems* 96(6): 27–8.

Strohl Systems (1995) *The Business Continuity Planning Guide*, King of Prussia, PA: Strohl Systems.

Tilley, K. (1998) 'Fire shows disaster plans wanting', *Business Insurance* 32(40): 57.

Weiner, S. (1995) 'Business risk, internal control and audit implications of EDI', *The CPA Journal* November: 56–8.

Further reading

Alexander, D. (2000) 'Scenario methodology for teaching principles of emergency management', *Disaster Prevention and Management* 9(2): 89–97.

Keown-McMullan, C. (1997) 'Crisis: when does a molehill become a mountain?', *Disaster Prevention and Management* 6(1): 4–10.

Morwood, G. (1998) 'Business continuity: awareness and training programmes', *Information Management and Computer Security* 6(1): 28–32.

Smallman, C. and Weir, D. (1999) 'Communication and cultural distortion during crises', *Disaster Prevention and Management* 8(1): 33–41.

Study questions

1 Visit the websites of BNFL and Shell to follow up the incidents that they have experienced above (www.shell.com and www.bnfl.co.uk). You will find that Shell has an extensive section about 'Issues and dilemmas' and BNFL has a web area entitled 'Impact on society'.

   What do these companies have to say about their stakeholders?

2 What are the problems associated with the methodology of risk assessment?

3 Write down some examples of resources that are shared widely across organizations.

4 Identify a small number of examples of how the PEST factors could increase the potential for crisis.

5 Management of change

Embedding business continuity management

Introduction

Investment of time and capital in using business continuity tools and techniques is of little value without a fully embedded management process. Where previous chapters have presented and examined tools and techniques this chapter is primarily concerned with the issues of change management and, in particular, with considering how business continuity processes may be embedded throughout an organization, the third stage of our model of effective BCM, shown in Figure 5.1.

Two elements provide the key to securing effective implementation. First is the organizational structure required to ensure clear lines of authority, control and communication. The second element is the creation of the organizational conditions for effective implementation (communications, culture, and control and reward systems and training). The first part of this chapter places the discussion within the wider context of organization studies, with a brief review of the literature associated with change management and organizational culture. The second part reviews a number of practical issues associated with building a flourishing BCM process. While 'audit'-driven

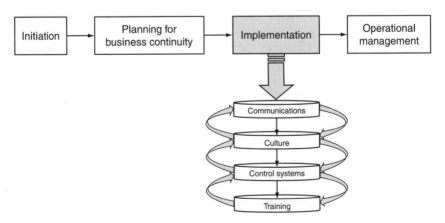

Figure 5.1 BCM as a business process

approaches (see for example the Government Centre for Information Systems, 1995a, 1995b) provide a useful checklist of 'things to do' the logical and sequential approach that it suggests is rarely possible. Such approaches fail to capture the messy complexity of organizational life, which arises from a diversity of factors including changing contexts, internal politics, faulty assumptions and the bounded rationality of managers. Successful business continuity management requires effective change management.

Change management

Two fundamental theoretical perspectives to change management may be identified (Clegg, 1992; Wilson, 1992;[1] Collins, 1998). The first places great emphasis on structural approaches to change and includes concern with organizational design and organization–environment linkages. This perspective places less emphasis upon human activity and how individuals make sense of the world. Instead it emphasizes the importance of *getting* the logic of the change strategy right, persuading people of that logic and designing appropriate structures and control systems for the next steps. Such an approach involves a minimum of three stages:

* analysis
* choice
* action

Such an approach suggests that the management of change may be dealt with in a logical, rational manner. Once a chosen change strategy emerges from the analysis and selection process, the central task for the 'change agent' is to convince individuals and groups affected of the need for change.

The second approach combines behavioural studies derived from interpersonal and social psychology and cultural studies, which regard organizational climate, ideologies and beliefs as pre-eminent (see, for example, Deal and Kennedy, 1982). As Johnson and Scholes (1997) have argued, ultimately the success of strategic change depends upon the extent to which people change their behaviour. Change is thus concerned with their beliefs and assumptions and the processes in their organizational lives. In some instances, managers are perceived as possessing superhuman qualities that enable them to alter the thinking of colleagues, subordinates and customers. While not dismissing the need for planning, proponents of this view emphasize the importance of securing the commitment of individuals to change.

These two perspectives are not mutually exclusive but reflect trends within the study of change management. Indeed, following an examination of these two dominant approaches a hybrid model is suggested, one that seeks to combine the rationality of planning approaches with the 'humanistic emphasis' of behavioural approaches.

Wilson (1992) provides a four-celled matrix characterizing approaches to change management (see Figure 5.2). The matrix is founded upon two dimensions, planned–emergent change and process–implementation of change. Models of change which assume that it can be planned for in advance will differ radically from those which have been developed from the premise that change emerges from the interplay between a myriad of variables. While much can be gleaned from pursuing a logical process of analysis there are dangers that the difficulties of achieving change will be underestimated. The process–implementation dimension is less clear as represented by Pettigrew *et al.*'s (1989) attempt to span the two in their work. For Wilson (1992) the distinction between process and implementation is that the latter focuses on the management of individuals while 'process' is concerned with the critical examination of the context, history, motivations and movement of change. For our current purposes it is sufficient to note these contributions and move on to consider using the change management literature from a practical perspective. More detailed reviews of the change management literature can be found in Wilson (1992) and Collins (1998).

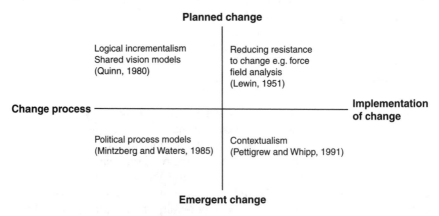

Figure 5.2 Approaches to organizational change

Source: Adapted from Wilson (1992).

Planned change

Planned approaches follow a predetermined path through analysis of change, identifying likely consequences and developing the means to overcome resistance. Forces for and against change can be shown in terms of a force field analysis. Lewin (1951) held that organizations existed in a state of equilibrium created by the interplay between opposing forces. This results in a state not conducive to change. Change, argued Lewin, required the 'unfreezing' of the existing state of affairs, the intended change to be enacted, and then the new *status quo* to be refrozen (as shown in Figure 5.3).

The concept of force-field analysis underlies many planned change

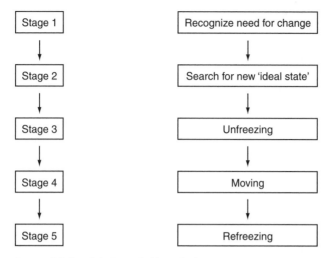

Figure 5.3 Lewin's force-field analysis

approaches (see for example, Kotter and Schlesinger, 1979; Dunphy and Stace 1987; Plant, 1987) and its use is widely advocated in strategic management textbooks. Table 5.1 shows an example of force-field analysis applied to an organization implementing a business continuity process. The forces for change include external and internal pressures. These may represent forces specific to an organization (e.g. experience of a crisis) as well as generic stimuli such as industry or national and international standards of expectation. Forces acting against change are usually concerned with the individual organization, including its belief systems, operating norms, reward and control systems (see Table 5.1). A later section of this chapter examines Johnson and Scholes's (1997) cultural web and it is suggested that elements of these two tools may be combined to provide an insightful analysis.

The success of planned approaches to change depends on accurate identification of the best way forward and anticipating barriers to change. In their adaptation of a force-field analysis Kotter and Schlesinger (1979) identified self-interest, misunderstanding, lack of trust, different assessments of the need for change and low tolerance as the most common reasons for resistance to change. All may be present, to differing degrees, within one organization or even within an individual. For example, misunderstanding or different assessments of the need for change may be reinforced by self-interest.

Selecting the means for overcoming resistance will depend on a correct diagnosis of the cause(s). Dealing with resistance can encompass at one extreme, coercion; although inevitable when managing change that is urgent and important (for example, during a turnaround situation) it may encourage resistance where urgency does not provide much needed legitimacy. Elliott *et al.* (1999a) have argued that the successful embedding of a BCM process

Table 5.1 Example of force-field analysis for business continuity management

Forces for change	Forces acting against change
Customer–supplier relationships (mutual dependencies in supply chain)	Partner intransigence
Growing reliance upon technology	BCM a non-core activity: other priorities
Customer expectations: client focus	Too little time
Experience of interruption	Individual not team incentives
Corporate Governance, BS7799	Complacency about change
Board commitment	BCM not my job
Insurer requirement	BCM an expense not an investment
Change normal	No reward for BCM success

requires line managers to assume responsibility for the process. As Kotter and Schlesinger (1979) noted, coercion is not effective as a means of securing a long-term change in beliefs.

Change management's relationship with business continuity is not simply with managing interruptions, but also with enhancing an organization's capabilities for preventing and responding to potential crises.

In summary, the advice emanating from planned approaches is that successful change efforts will be those where choices are internally consistent and fit the key situational variables. Table 5.2 combines a traditional force-field analysis with a range of options for overcoming resistance. Burnes (1996: 342), drawing upon extensive empirical data, argued that, in spite of the prescriptive planning approaches offered by the gurus, 'most managers are driven by expediency and operate in a responsive mode'. Whatever the appeal of planned approaches, and it is our view that they may provide a valuable source of data and a process to aid reflection, they do not act as a mirror of practice. The management of change within organizations is more complex and messier than is often suggested in textbooks. Although Burnes (1996: 322) proceeds to critique emergent approaches to change management, it appears from a close reading of his work that he is dealing with a simplistic view of the emergent nature of change.

In our usage of the term, the emergent properties of change refer to their human and organizational behavioural origins. In other words, successful change management depends on changing the values, beliefs, attitudes and thus actions of individuals and groups. Planned approaches may assist in determining the nature and extent of required change. Emergent approaches emphasize the important human element that will determine the success of any change management programme and it is to this that we now turn.

Table 5.2 Planned change

Forces for change	Forces against change (Kotter and Schlesinger)	Strategies for overcoming resistance (Kotter and Schlesinger)
External • economic • political • social • competitive • legal Internal • experience • board • strategic decision	• differing perceptions • self-interest • misunderstanding • mistrust • different assessments • low tolerance for change	• education • communication • participation and involvement • facilitation and support • negotiation • manipulation • coercion

---

Box 5.1

Some organizations delegate responsibility for business continuity from a dedicated team to line managers. A common pattern emerged from these organizations. Education and communication played an important role in raising the profile of business continuity and informing managers of why they should take it seriously. Thus, short training programmes, regular newsletters and ongoing informal contact created the platform from which effective BCM was implemented. Potential resistance to change was further reduced by encouraging participation and involvement. For example, the Royal Bank of Scotland and J Sainsbury included staff from a range of business areas within their business continuity teams. Such secondees contributed to the process by bringing in differing perspectives and by acting as ambassadors for business continuity when their period of secondment ended. A further source of resistance to change concerned a possible lack of expertise in the area of BCM. While secondees provided one means of spreading expertise, business continuity teams provided ongoing support, coordination and encouragement. In one USA-based bank, the business continuity team possessed an almost evangelical zeal in terms of combining education, communication, encouragement and, as a last resort, cajolement, to ensure that line managers treated continuity seriously. In some other banks the individual reward systems appeared to act against the taking of continuity seriously. For the successful dealer, like the top football player, if the team fails they can simply transfer to a new one and possibly earn even higher rewards.

Source: Herbane *et al.* (1997), Elliott *et al.* (1999a)

Emergent change management: creating a vision for change

Approaches to change management, which emphasize its emergent nature, are particularly concerned with managing the process and less concerned with implementing a detailed plan. Key issues concern organizational politics, culture and setting a sense of vision. As many authors have noted, change management is all about modifying individual and organizational behaviour. This section draws on a strategic management literature and considers how managers might manage the change process.

Effective change management requires a clear sense of purpose well communicated throughout an organization. Many successful organizations have a clearly expressed sense of vision. For Komatsu, the Japanese bulldozer manufacturer, the sense of vision was to encircle Caterpillar, symbolized as ©. Komatsu's strategy was to build market share slowly by targeting small customer segments, not fully satisfied by Caterpillar, and to build market share incrementally, thereby avoiding a head-on clash that would have been too risky for Komatsu. For Microsoft 'Windows software on every desk' proved irresistible until it was observed that this suggested office workers and computers, it is now 'Windows everywhere' reflecting a drive towards any viable technical platform. In Figure 5.4 the vision may be seen as setting the parameters for the stream of decisions in an emergent strategy.

With regard to BCM, preparing a vision statement may fulfil two important roles:

- First, the very process of formulating a short, sharp statement of intent should help clarify for the BCM manager, other line managers and senior executives, the essence of continuity management. For some, business

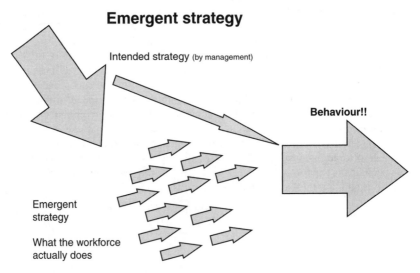

Figure 5.4 Deliberate and emergent strategies

Source: adapted from Mintzberg and Waters (1985).

continuity may concern only technical or IS problems, for others it may include many forms of operational risk. The speedy refund and compensation paid to passengers on the cruise ship *Aurora* in April 2000 may be seen as a consumer-oriented approach to business continuity.

- Second, such a statement should provide a valuable communication tool for raising awareness across an organization and to staff at all levels. To be effective it must not only be easily understood but also must combine relevance with simplicity and thus impact upon an organization's culture. All staff should be made aware that, even where a dedicated business continuity team exists, it forms a part of everyone's job.

An apocryphal story tells of an international bank invoking its business continuity plan and assembling its senior management team. Unfortunately none had the necessary skills to access the relevant databases; this was a task usually delegated to a secretary who was not included within the continuity plan. Continuity management is not the preserve either of senior managers nor of a dedicated team; effective continuity depends on successfully harnessing the energy and interest of staff at all levels. The role of the vision statement is to communicate clearly to all staff.

From our earlier discussion it will be clear that organizational culture has tremendous influence over organizational, and thus individual behaviour. The long-term success of organizations such as British Airways, Hewlett Packard, GE, Marks & Spencer and Disney has been explained in terms of their distinct cultures. For some, the customer service ethos has been key, for others innovation. Whichever, long-term success has been achieved by the development and ongoing support of what Peters and Waterman (1982) described as shared values and which we define as culture.

Culture

Culture, stated Hofstede (1990), has acquired a status similar to strategy and structure within the management literature. Pauchant and Mitroff (1988) suggested that culture is to the organization as personality is to the individual. Many models of culture (see Table 5.3) agree that it may be thought of as combining a number of distinct layers, some hidden, including individual beliefs and assumptions coming together in the form of shared values and operating norms and, ultimately, consistent patterns of behaviour. More specifically, Mitroff *et al.* (1989) suggest that:

> The culture of an organization may be defined as the set of rarely articulated, largely unconscious beliefs, values, norms and fundamental assumptions that the organization makes about itself, the nature of people in general and its environment. In effect, culture is the set of

'unwritten rules' that govern 'acceptable behaviour' within and outside the organization.

(1989: 271)

Table 5.3 Alternative models of organizational culture

	Schein (1992)	*Pauchant and Mitroff (1988)*	*Williams et al. (1989)*	*Hofstede (1990)*	*Trompenaars (1993)*
Description	Multi-layered	Onion	Lily pond	Onion	Onion
Surface level	Artefacts, creations, structures and processes	Plans	Behaviours	Symbols	Observable reality in language, etc.
		Organization structure		Heroes	
				Rituals	
Partly visible level	Espoused values strategies, goals, philosophies	Assumptions and beliefs	Attitudes and values (reportable)	Values	Norms and values
Invisible level	Basic underlying assumptions	Individual beliefs	Unconscious beliefs		Core assumptions about existence

Culture provides an important element of the context in which change occurs. Effective change requires that new behaviours be learnt. Learning occurs within a 'structure of meaning' that is broadly shared, and Levitt and March (1988) suggested that such structures need to be sufficiently flexible to permit some change in operational procedures, although in practice:

> participants collude in support of interpretations that sustain the [organizational] myths. As a result stories, paradigms and beliefs are conserved in the face of considerable disconfirmation and what is learned appears to be influenced less by history than by the frames applied to that history.
>
> (1988: 324)

Similarly, Starbuck *et al.* (1978) observed that organizations sought to 'routinize' the means by which they had become successful and in so doing became internally focused and concerned with efficiency. In an analysis of man-made disasters, Turner (1976, 1978; Turner and Pidgeon, 1997) argued that all organizations developed a continuous culture closely related to their tasks and environment, and that there was a developmental tendency for a 'collective blindness' to important issues:

> This is the danger, that some vital factors have been left outside the framework of bounded rationality. When a pervasive and long-established set of beliefs exists within an organization, these beliefs influence the attitudes of men and women inside the organization. They affect decision-making procedures and mould organizational arrangements and provisions so that there is the possibility of a vicious self-reinforcing circle growing up.
>
> (1976: 388)

A basic barrier to embedding business continuity processes concerns cultures, which, it is argued, are resistant to change. The rhetoric of continuity may be spoken but either this falls on stony ground or it slowly percolates to the substrata of the organization. Culture represents the ground and provides the context for change. As with change there are different views about the concept 'culture'. Two alternative perspectives are put forward in the next two sections.

The first, drawing from a psychoanalytical base, explores in greater detail Pauchant and Mitroff's (1988, 1992) crisis-prone to resistant continuum. The second section presents a normative model of culture. Although its theoretical grounding is limited, it is argued that it can provide useful insights into the many facets of an organization's culture.

Crisis-prone or resistant: onion model of culture

People and groups within organizations may employ a range of reasons and strategies to resist change, even when events highlight inadequacies in systems, procedures and beliefs. The failure to invest in railway infrastructure during the 1990s created a dangerous context as indicated by the accidents at Paddington in 1999 and Hatfield in 2000.[2]

Whilst many of these reasons may differ in their detail, Pauchant and Mitroff (1992) suggest that individuals, alone and collectively, employ a range of defence mechanisms or faulty rationalizations that support resistance to change. The greater the use of such defence mechanisms the more prone to crisis an organization will be. Pauchant and Mitroff (1988, 1992) concluded that organizations might be placed on a continuum from crisis-prone to crisis-prepared according to the prevalence of defence mechanisms. The place of an organization upon such a continuum would be determined by assessing a combination of factors:

- organizational plans and behaviour
- organizational structures
- collective beliefs and assumptions
- individual beliefs

Box 5.2

The UK railway industry had undergone dramatic change during the 1990s but it might be argued that little progress had been made. There is evidence that faulty organizational communications hindered the transmission of warnings to key executives; that Railtrack and the rail companies were focused on improving efficiency and their utilization of resources. A culture focused on economic efficiency and faulty organizational communications combined to provide the underlying causes of the crash. They were manifest in greater debate about the precise nature of improvements to be made to track infrastructure; disagreements regarding the sources of investment; difficulties in prioritizing investment; the fragmentation of control over repair and maintenance through growing use of subcontractors.

At Paddington, concerns over the position of signal 109, partly obscured by other fixtures and bright sunlight at certain times of the year, were not heeded. At Hatfield, plans to replace faulty tracks had been made but not acted upon.

Before the Paddington and Hatfield crashes, 'cost-benefit analysis' indicated that sophisticated train warning systems were too costly. The deaths of 34 people in the two incidents altered the statistics and provided the political will for change.

These four groups of factors were depicted as an onion model of crisis management (see Figure 5.5).

This model provides a framework for considering discrete areas requiring management attention during a programme of change. The inner layers refer to individual and group beliefs and assumptions, the focus of behavioural studies of change management. The outer two layers refer to structures, plans and actual behaviour, and provide the focus for the advocates of a planned approach to change management. These tangible elements reflect the beliefs, values and assumptions of the core. The onion model suggests that the effective management of change requires attention to both elements. Mitroff *et al.* (1989: 273) suggest that there is: 'extreme overlap and interpenetration between the various factors that compose the levels such that it is extremely difficult to say at times which circles are true subsets of which.'

Core beliefs

At the heart of the onion model lie core beliefs. For Pauchant and Mitroff (1988, 1992) three key factors provide a basis for an organization's crisis proneness:

- the degree of self-centredness

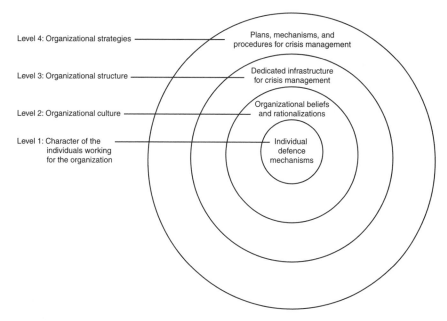

Figure 5.5 Onion model of crisis management
Source: Pauchant and Mitroff (1992).

- the degree of fatalism
- the nature of defence mechanisms

The degree of self-centredness is closely related to an organization's ability to consider a range of points of view. A stakeholder perspective is akin to a system's perspective; it acknowledges the importance of other groups and their viewpoints, providing a greater basis for understanding. An outer orientation, associated with crisis resistance, may be expressed in terms of seeing beyond traditional organizational boundaries, thereby facilitating a greater understanding of the environment. Crisis-prone organizations had a narrower view of stakeholders, failing to see that they were part of a wider system. An example might be a travel company that perceives of a faulty aircraft as a technical problem rather than as an interruption to its customers. When travellers are delayed for lengthy periods, a customer-oriented airline will provide refreshments, telephone facilities and accommodation.

Fatalism, observed Mitroff *et al.* (1989), reduces guilt and responsibility and acts as a justification for doing nothing. At its most basic, the view that disasters are freak accidents or caused by some other external agency reduces the perceived control that any organization has over them. Such a view will have a strong influence on the amount of time and resources that are invested in crisis prevention and preparation. The President of Exxon insisted that the Valdez accident was an 'act of God that could not have been prevented'; he failed to acknowledge twenty-nine previous oil spills that shared many similarities (Pauchant and Mitroff, 1992).

Defence mechanisms, argued Pauchant and Mitroff (1992), are employed to 'distort external reality' to such an extent that individuals can avoid having to deal with complicated, potentially threatening situations (see Table 5.4). Crisis-prone organizations were approximately seven times as likely to use these devices as crisis-prepared ones. Fixation, the unquestioning pursuit of a particular course of action represents an almost complete absence of double-loop learning.

> Single-loop learning asks one-dimensional questions to elicit a one-dimensional answer. For example, a thermostat which measures ambient temperature against a standard setting and turns the heat source on or off accordingly. Double-loop learning takes an additional step, or more often than not, several additional steps. It turns the question back on the questioner. . . . In the case of the thermostat for example, double-loop learning would wonder whether the current setting was actually the most effective temperature at which to keep the room and, if so, whether the present heat source was the most effective means of achieving it. A

Table 5.4 Defence mechanisms

Level 1: Defence mechanisms	Explanation
Denial	Expressed refusal to acknowledge a threatening reality or realities
Disavowal	Acknowledge a threatening reality but downplay its importance
Fixation	Rigid commitment to a particular course of action or attitude in dealing with a threatening situation
Grandiosity	The feeling of omnipotence. 'We're so big and powerful that nothing bad can happen to us' (Mitroff and Pauchant, 1990)
Idealization	Ascribing omnipotence to another person
Intellectualization	The elaboration of an action or thought. Pauchant and Mitroff (1992) argue that intellectualizations frequently involve distorted schemes of reasoning to justify a particular course of action
Projection	Attributing unacceptable actions or thoughts to others
Splitting	The extreme isolation of different elements, extreme dichotomization or fragmentation

Source: Adapted from Pauchant and Mitroff (1988).

double-loop process might also ask why the current setting was chosen in the first place.

(Argyris, 1994: 78–9)

For BCM the over-emphasis upon IT interruptions might provide one example of single-loop learning. Similarly, denial and disavowal provide some justification for executives doing nothing – the 'it couldn't happen here syndrome', or if it does, 'it won't be very serious'. Grandiosity and idealization reflect a view that someone (us or another agency) will be sufficiently powerful to deal with all eventualities. In the case of Y2K many small businesses, in particular, assumed that government would resolve any serious problems. The blockade of UK oil refineries during September 2000 demonstrated the impotence of government to act when a vital resource is removed from circulation. Individually and together, the presence of these defence mechanisms provides a strong indication of the effectiveness of organizational learning.

Defence mechanisms may lead to the distortion and manipulation of information as individuals acting in groups make use of vagueness, ambiguity, inconsistency and withholding data to obscure errors and make them uncorrectable. Hirokawa's (1988) analysis of the Challenger disaster described how defence mechanisms acted as powerful blockers to the collection, analysis, discussion and exchange of information between engineers employed by the designers of the Space Shuttle and NASA representatives. Crisis management teams are considered in detail in Chapter 6.

In summary, defence mechanisms act as powerful barriers to change. At their most extreme (denial) they block out any attempt to collect information. More subtly, they permit the distortion and misinterpretation of information and reduce the effectiveness of learning. Denial and disavowal may be employed by organizations to ignore potential environmental threats. Pauchant and Mitroff (1992) argue that inner-oriented organizations were more likely to ignore external threats. More significantly, their lack of environmental awareness was reflected structurally and procedurally in the lack of any mechanisms for scanning the environment. This may raise the probability that warning signals are not interpreted accurately and this inner orientation may also act as a barrier to learning from the experience of other organizations.

From a change management perspective, assumptions regarding these issues will create not only ideological barriers to change, but will also influence the transfer of knowledge into action by determining the allocation of resources in the form of time and money devoted to a particular area. Thus, assumptions about the nature of the organization will play an important role in determining the importance given to issues such as business continuity. An organization that believes itself 'omnipotent' will not devote time or money to business continuity. Change may be constrained through lack of time to consider the relevant issues and through the lowly status of its champions.

Cultural web analysis

Cultural web analysis (Johnson and Scholes 1997) provides a simple tool for painting a rich picture and thereby gaining some insight into the nature of culture within a particular organization. An example of a cultural web for a university is shown in Figure 5.6. Such analysis, if it is to be meaningful, requires input from many members of staff, indeed, a useful way of using the tool is to use it as the focus for discussion so that differences and similarities in perception may be examined.

The *stories* told in organizations help shape behaviour by communicating the unwritten values. They indicate what is important. An apocryphal story told at Disney Corporation is of a car park attendant who checks the temperatures of the car engines of senior executives at 7.15 a.m. each day. If the engine is too warm the executive is fired; because it means that the executive has recently arrived – the story is told to reinforce the view that to get on at Disney you have to work hard and get in early. Staff at IBM claim that the initials stand for 'I've been moved' or 'I've been married'; success at IBM means giving your all to the company. *Symbols* are a powerful communications tool. The old Woolworth's company removed the pockets from staff overalls to prevent pilfering. When Kingfisher acquired the retailer the pockets were sewn back on, a powerful symbol of trust. In many Japanese companies all staff (including executives) wear the same type of overall to symbolize the importance of teamwork. *Rituals and routines* provide a powerful, socializing influence. Routines may include never leaving before the boss; everything stopping for the doctor's walk around the ward in a hospital.

Stories	Power structures
Remote Vice-Chancellor communicates via annual video Win major research or consultancy funds Eccentric staff	Extreme centralism (tail wags the dog) Hidden power of technical support Rivalry in fight for resources between departments
Symbols	**Control and reward systems**
Professorships, PhDs, MSc's, etc. Jargon Parking space Expensive equipment	Research success Tight budgetary controls Avoid complaints in teaching
Rituals and routines	**Structures**
Teaching comes first Complicated bids for funding Work alone, little team spirit	Vertical hierarchy Little inter-school communication
Paradigm Low-cost educational provider Maximize non-teaching income Excellent external programmes, poor internal ones	

Figure 5.6 Cultural web of a university

Power is located throughout the organization, and not just at the pinnacle of the hierarchy. A school's lunchtime supervisor can go on strike; an aggrieved technician can sabotage essential laboratory equipment; an IT technician can plant a virus-bomb – each can disrupt the smooth running of an organization. Power is not always in the most obvious place. Changes in the funding of universities led to changes in *reward systems*. Where once administration was highly prized and rewarded, research is apparently the main objective. When rewards switched to researchers academics paid less attention to administration (including course management and recruitment) to pursue research, which would lead to promotion. Of course this left a gap in a key area of activity. Finally, *structure* may act as a facilitator or as a constraint.

The framework can be used to assess where an organization is and where it wishes to be. It identifies a number of the softer issues that must be managed if change management is to be effective.

Applying cultural analysis to organizational change

Cultural web analysis provides an opportunity for those involved in continuity planning to identify barriers and aids to change. A number of stages may be envisaged (shown in Table 5.5). The first stage refers to a state in which it is perceived that there is no need for change and that there is a high degree of fit between an organization and its environment. Within studies of crisis (see Turner, 1976, 1978, for example) a significant happening is usually required to create the recognition that change is necessary. For IBM, Marks & Spencer and C&A major losses forced a strategic review and refocus. The scale of these losses and the obligation to report them publicly required these companies to change their strategies. C&A chose to withdraw whilst IBM and Marks & Spencer sought changes in style, process and market focus. Triggers may arise from the environment too. Bombs at the World Trade Centre and in London highlighted vulnerabilities, as did the love letter virus which demonstrated the growing reliance of international business on e-mail communications.

The second stage occurs as pressures for change build. Where companies report significant losses within one year it is usual to find a longer, underlying trend of falling profitability that was ignored or played down. Warning signs might include changing customer preferences, new product or process developments. With regard to BCM, warning signs might include ongoing difficulties with a group of suppliers, low staff morale with high absenteeism, problems experienced by competitors, intermittent failures or difficulties experienced by suppliers and competitors, unrest in the Middle East, etc.

Stage 3 is the trigger, a turning point at which it is recognized that change is needed. The nature of this event will depend upon the sensitivity of each particular organization. For example, some bottled mineral water producers have yet to introduce a despatch control system that would enable them to identify stocks on supermarket shelves quickly in case of a product recall.

The estimated $2 billion cost of Perrier's 1990 recall was clearly not seen as providing sufficient warning. Responding to a spate of product tamperings, Heinz have 'tamper-indicating' bottle tops on their baby food ranges.

Depending upon its severity, an incident will trigger a state of organizational flux as alternative models of response are examined. This is stage 4 and fits closely with Lewin's unfreezing stages. The degree of search will depend upon the perceived importance of the imbalance between the current state

Table 5.5 Cultural readjustment

Stage	Description
1 Initial beliefs and norms	Perceived harmony between organization–environment
2 Incubation period	Events indicating need for change unnoticed or misunderstood because of: • erroneous assumptions • rigidities of beliefs • perceptions • a reluctance to fear the worst outcome • difficulties of handling information in complex situations
3 Trigger	Felt need for change
4 Flux and unfreezing	Information collected and interpreted within managerial mindset
	Political testing of support for options
5 Cultural readjustment	Definition of new well-structured problems and appropriate changes in light of newly acquired knowledge
	Stories shape attitudes and beliefs
	BCM seen as an integral part of sound business
6 Active learning and refreezing	Communication of knowledge and of new expectations to target personnel and/or organizations
	Knowledge filtered through culture, communications and structures of organizational personnel. New symbols reflect change
	Questioning of organizational norms and operating procedures
	Organizational cultural readjustment occurs
	Cultural readjustment process triggered by perceptions regarding the symbolic importance of 'precipitating event'
	Propensity of an organization to learn determines effectiveness of learning process

Source: Adapted from Lewin (1951), Turner (1976), Elliott and Smith (2001).

and the desired state. This stage of analysis will be influenced by the interplay between different interest groups, each with its own peculiar view of the need for change whether founded upon self-interest or upon a different assessment. Identification of these differing interpretations is vital to securing the success of the change management process.

From this flux will emerge a growing consensus on the nature of change required. This fits closely with Turner's (1976, 1978; Turner and Pidgeon, 1997) cultural readjustment. Active learning (Toft and Reynolds, 1997) refers to the effective translation of change into new operating norms and practices. This fits with Lewin's notion of refreezing, although the growing literature concerned with learning organizations may argue that refreezing is an outdated notion in a constantly changing world. Refreezing, to be effective, requires communication of how and why change must occur; the processing of this knowledge by groups and individuals; and finally, the absorption of the new knowledge through its translation into new or adapted behaviour.

Cultural web analysis has been identified as a tool which may assist in the change process. It may be used to identify a current profile, including barriers to change, with a desired profile to aim at. Figure 5.7 depicts an 'ideal' cultural web for effective BCM.

As the Government Centre for Information Systems (CCTA) (1995)

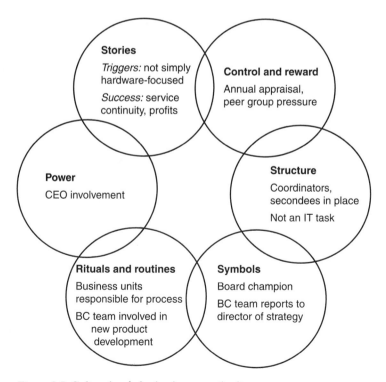

Figure 5.7 Cultural web for business continuity

Box 5.3   Cultural web

The stories reported by business continuity managers often included events that had initially triggered the continuity process. For some it was a personal experience of the Severn floods, the bombings of the City of London or the World Trade Centre in New York that had caused the senior management to consider continuity management. In South Africa, a history of political tension was key. In the travel industry, kidnapping and incidents at Luxor triggered interest in BCM in smaller and medium-sized travel organizations.

The symbols associated with BCM also provide indicators of its status. For example, who does the Business Continuity Manager report to? Is it to the Head of IT, Audit or to the Director with responsibility for strategy? The reporting structure will not only make more or less difficult the task of communications but symbolize whether or not BCM is seen as an IT or a strategic issue. A direct or easy link to the board will indicate real board interest, as will the presence of a board-level champion.

Rituals and routines may be concerned with the extent to which BCM forms a part of the day-to-day management of an organization. Is continuity routinely considered in the design stages of new products and services, as is increasingly the case with Japanese car manufacturers Toyota and Nissan? Do discussions of strategy routinely include a business continuity perspective? Are line managers responsible and resourced for the BCM process or is it left to a specialist team? In short, is BCM seen as an extension of sound management practice or is it a bolted-on process that touches the organization only partially?

Power and control are closely linked with the preceding two categories. The hierarchical structure provides the formal context in which the BC manager operates. If formally a part of the IT department, then barriers may be created between the BC manager and other parts of the organization. In some organizations, the lead BC coordinator is viewed as a 'special projects officer'; a well-liked member of staff who had provided good service to the company but not been seen as sufficiently dynamic for other more demanding tasks. We saw the contrary too. The selection of a manager for business continuity planning sends out powerful signals regarding its perceived importance and thus influences the likely support or interest of line managers who have many tasks to occupy their time.

Reward and control systems influence organizational behaviour. To ensure that business continuity receives adequate middle management attention requires that it form a formal component in their appraisal. The nature of the measurement will also be important. For example, is performance measured on the readily observed production of new plan documents or on the less tangible measures of effectiveness, of gaining real commitment from line managers and enhancing organizational resilience to interruption? The latter is clearly more difficult to measure but arguably more important. Better an approximate answer to the right question than an accurate answer to the wrong question.

Structure provides the means by which individual efforts are coordinated and orchestrated into an organizational whole. It provides the conduit along which formal communications run. The range of communication tools includes formal meetings, interviews, training, newsletters, short presentations, testing and informal links. Effective communication in support of BCM requires a combination of these that is appropriate to each organization at different stages of development.

> We look at the types of people we are dealing with and we will tackle them depending on what they are, so we study them for a while. We learn what their life is like, what they do, what their role is in the organization and what kind of skills and what type of people are doing this job. You therefore cannot come up with a standard 'stand up and tell them that this is the way in which you are going to do contingency' because it won't work like that. You have to look at them and understand what they are like and hit them with the right kind of story. We've become very inventive, haven't we? (both respondents laugh).

> (BC managers quoted in Elliott *et al.*, 1999a: 52)

Further means of communication might include the recruitment or secondment of staff from the business to work within the BC team. This ensures input from the business and, after the secondment, it secures continuity ambassadors around the organization. Staff recruited to BC might be usefully drawn from general business or professional backgrounds to ensure a rich combination of skills and knowledge that can be vital to a creative team.

---

handbook emphasizes, the establishment of a successful business continuity initiative requires the awareness of the board of directors and senior managers and then the real and physical acceptance of key managers and staff. In preceding chapters we have identified the important role played by external factors in triggering an organization's interest in BCM in the first place. Bombs, viruses, floods and fires come to mind as obvious examples. These triggers may play an important role in raising the profile of business continuity.

However, as the Home Office (1997a, 1997b) handbook, *Bombs: Protecting People and Property*, indicates, terrorist incidents are few and far between in the UK. When they occur they attract considerable interest and possibly they divert attention away from the routine interruptions that have a higher probability of occurring. Effective BCM should be concerned with anticipating and preparing for internal and external, technical and human threats. Despite its focus upon facilities-type interruptions, the CCTA handbook recognizes the threat inherent in the failure of key suppliers. BCM is thus about maintaining competitiveness, not the physical infrastructure that supports a firm. As such, it needs to be embedded through all the activities of an organization, if resilience is to be real.

Awareness without commitment is meaningless. This is highlighted by the broad awareness of the so-called Millennium Bug or Year 2000 problem.

Despite the offer of free government training, the take-up rate of SME's was minimal (Williams, 2001). The first step in extending BCM beyond the bounds of a dedicated team is to secure the commitment of key personnel. We have discussed above the reasons why resistance to change may be present, and we have considered alternative means by which these may be overcome. From the evidence collected it appears that participative approaches combining communication, education, support, encouragement and finally cajolement have proved to be the most effective. Any successful change strategy must meet the complexity of organizational behaviour that it seeks to influence.

We have also considered cultural approaches to change management. It is our opinion that the issues covered support the continuance of BCM as a discipline once the initial launch is completed. As with Human Resource Management, a specialist department may exist to provide specialist support, but it is our view that BCM is the responsibility of line managers and their staff. For its ongoing consideration requires that it forms a part of the organization's culture in the forms of values, beliefs and operating norms. To further reinforce this type of behaviour requires that control and reward systems support efforts in this area, otherwise it will quickly be relegated to the group of 'should do, but don't have time for' duties.

Finally, for change to be managed effectively a number of key issues need to be addressed. First, it is important that a clear view exists within an organization regarding the desired changes. Second, change requires both awareness and commitment from key personnel. Third, contextual issues must be identified and addressed. Each organization will require its own pattern of change management, possibly following similar designs to other organizations, but the fine detail must match organizational idiosyncrasies. Fourth, cultural constraints, although often hidden, must be uncovered and addressed. Failure to do so is the equivalent of papering over the cracks. How do organizations create the preconditions for effective BCM?

Creating the preconditions for effective BCM implementation

Overcoming resistance and securing commitment to BCM are key to the success of the implementation process. The importance and influence of middle managers in determining the successful implementation of business continuity cannot be overestimated. The four vital components from which to develop effective business continuity management include communications, culture, control and reward systems, and training, and the cooperation of middle managers is required to ensure that these four components are put in place.

Communications

Middle managers play a key role in shaping communications; they are often the main conduit for information within an organization. The mechanism used by many companies to ensure that information about BCM does not get 'stuck' at this level is a system of 'departmental' coordinators who work with the business continuity management team. These coordinators may act as champions of BCM within front-line departments, or they may simply provide a formal day-to-day point of contact between the business continuity team and line managers. Swartz *et al.* (1995) identified that the role of the coordinator was often imprecisely defined, with real responsibility remaining with the business continuity manager. Many respondents reported difficulties in securing the full commitment of line managers, citing in particular the higher priority given to achieving business objectives. Within many organizations, preparing for a business interruption was seen as a luxury, unless there was an obvious motive such as the threat of terrorism or the expectation of 'Y2K' difficulties (Elliott *et al.*, 1999b).

In 'better-practice' organizations (Herbane *et al.*, 1997) the business continuity team typically consisted of a small, multi-disciplinary group which reported good relations and regular contact with a group of coordinators drawn from all levels of their business. For instance, at the Royal Bank of Scotland, close contact and a reported high regard for one another enabled the business continuity team to work with different business units in the development and implementation of new products. The Royal Bank of Scotland business continuity manager emphasized that his team always sought to persuade and negotiate with managers should they have very pressing business objectives at a particular moment in time. 'Better-practice' organizations utilized a combination of methods, carefully targeted to communicate the relevance of business continuity throughout their organizations (see Table 5.6). These methods included formal reporting requirements as well as the development of informal peer pressure and company Intranet sites. The range of media, as well as the deliberate search for new and better ways to communicate the importance of business continuity, distinguished better from mediocre or poor practice.

Communication plays a number of roles in developing an effective business continuity process. At one level it raises awareness and informs staff of the need for crisis preparation. At J Sainsbury, an in-house journal article depicted an office complex destroyed by a bomb. The picture was accompanied by a short statement that summarized the aims of the new business continuity team as:

> to develop a business continuity plan to form part of an ongoing management discipline to ensure that if a similar fate befell J Sainsbury that the impact to the business would be minimised.

This combination of words and picture helped raise the profile of business continuity and demonstrate its value. That message was continually repeated through a variety of media to staff and through the induction process to new appointees.

Table 5.6 Communications methods used to support implementation

Organization	Communications mechanisms
Automobile Association	Coordinators play key role in transmitting information BCM policy document and guide circulated to all staff Presentations by BCM manager to board and business continuity forum
British Telecom	Intranet and emergency planning quality council Peer pressure as BCM is regarded as 'part of the job'; coordinators
Calor Gas	Board briefed every three months Company magazine used to communicate progress Ongoing communications with business units via coordinators
Royal Bank of Scotland	BCM structure ensures close contact with strategy development Quarterly report to board Liaison meetings with project members BCM policy statement Company video on corporate security issues BCM quality assurance manager feedback to line managers Video and 'roadshows' organized by BCM team Peer group pressure
Health Trust A (teaching hospital included)	Business continuity plans prepared by dedicated team in liaison with line departments Briefing seminars Deliberately selected team members with strong communication skills
Health Trust B	Business continuity plans prepared by dedicated team in liaison with line departments. Briefing seminars
J Sainsbury	BCM is developed from clearly identified objectives for each business unit. BCM planning and preparation process includes regular meetings of the steering group with each director signing off the review and plans for her/his own section BCM and emergency procedures forms part of induction process for all new staff Regular articles within in-house journal publicize the work of the BCM team Staff credit card-sized emergency instruction sheet J Sainsbury Intranet bulletin board Regular tests Awareness-raising seminars for all head office staff Videos of tests are circulated
Sunderland	Each department has a nominated officer with responsibility for risk management. The process of identifying and preparing for risk is fed back to the relevant committee and departmental management team Emergency plan documents are distributed to key officers in an accessible format The success of the authority in a number of risk management areas has created a number of success stories
Thames Water	New event management procedures form a part of standard practice for Thames Water. The risk identification and management process is regularly reported to the board Event management card is distributed to all operational staff to clarify emergency procedures and philosophy; regular seminars

Source: Adapted from Elliott *et al.* (1999b).

A second key role for communications is continually to remind staff of the ongoing relevance and value of business continuity management. J Sainsbury regularly provides progress reports through Intranet sites, seminars and in-house journal articles. A permanent reminder of emergency procedures is carried by all staff in a credit card-sized leaflet. The Royal Bank of Scotland employed regular liaison meetings to update project members who communicate with staff within their own business units.

A third role for effective communications concerned the process of collecting and disseminating data during the analysis stages. Line departments and managers know most about their business, the business continuity team knows most about continuity processes. Good communication is essential if the parties are to work well together. The clarity of data collection forms and questionnaires is one aspect of good communication. Another is a clear sense of the purpose and scope of the process, which helps line managers to identify the information required from them quickly. Similarly, good processes for monitoring and updating staff contact lists will also ease the business continuity process. The approach to communications is clearly linked to the issue of organizational culture.

Culture

Organizational culture, as discussed earlier, refers to the deep-seated values and beliefs members of an organization hold about their approach to business continuity. In a number of organizations that had prepared business continuity plans, whilst there was evidence of new structures, there was little evidence of any change in the core organizational assumptions, even though some new structures had been put in place. In 'better-practice' organizations the development of business continuity had led to a deeper re-evaluation of core assumptions. This had resulted in a process that not only sought to protect the integrity of their systems but also extended to a concern for protecting their customers and other stakeholders. In a number of other organizations, line managers saw business continuity as someone else's problem and expected that someone else (e.g. the business continuity team) would rescue them should an incident directly affect their area. This view seemed to be typical where the focus of business continuity was internal and upon hardware.

The recognition of internal and external dimensions to the business continuity planning process was also characteristic of 'better-practice' organizations (Herbane *et al.*, 1997; Elliott *et al.*, 1999a, 1999b); here there was evidence that plans were developed in partnership between the business continuity team and front-line operatives. As a result, business units, rather than the business continuity team, appeared to 'own' the planning process. Thus, at BT, sales staff who interfaced with government and corporate clients saw the value of business continuity: 'We have good plans and processes that have been tested and they [sales staff] can utilise this in talking to customers . . . use it as a differentiator to point to things we do.'

At Thames Water, a database was used to identify vulnerable residents and businesses in order that the full implications of a service interruption could be identified quickly. In one case, a burst water main flooded a large garden two days before it was to be used for a wedding reception. Thames Water called in a contract team that restored the garden and ensured that the reception was not spoilt. Although not an everyday event, this was held to typify the growing customer orientation of Thames Water's preparation for emergencies. Indeed, Thames had not publicized the incident because they thought that others might see it as a cynical public relations exercise. The story, however, is repeated within Thames as a symbol of its growing customer orientation and to reinforce the view that events are not just technical in nature. Instead, an interruption's severity is measured by the impact upon customers. Thames Water now uses the term 'service continuity' to emphasize a customer-first philosophy.

In the examples given above, of BT and Thames Water, the so-called business continuity approach was adopted by operational staff and became, quite simply, 'the way in which they do things'. It had entered their culture.

Achieving cultural change

Achieving desired cultural change is a difficult and lengthy process requiring education, communication, participation and leading by example to effect change. In particular, an approach to changing organizational culture to incorporate a new priority for business continuity management might include:

- the development of a clear business continuity purpose or vision
- communication of this and a published action plan
- visual depiction of the relevance of business continuity
- awareness-raising newsletters
- ongoing seminar programme
- supporting and guiding people towards the acquisition of knowledge and confidence
- business continuity team members working alongside operational staff and line managers
- begin with people in key positions (opinion formers)
- Chief Executive or other champion to provide symbolic support
- and finally by providing effective leadership

Lou Gerstner, Chief Executive of IBM, decided that all directors, including himself, would spend 50 per cent of working time with customers to demonstrate IBM's new customer orientation. The visible commitment of the CEO and/or a senior board member as champions of business continuity at organizations such as Sunderland City Council and the Royal Bank of Scotland was highly effective. J Sainsbury employs a system of clearly stated objectives for all business units, including the BCM team, as a means of communicating to team members and internal customers the aims of each unit. The regular review of these objectives encourages staff frequently to think about why they do what they do. Business continuity at J Sainsbury is thereby clearly focused upon business objectives and priorities.

Previous research indicates that effective business continuity requires the specialist team to play a leading, guiding and supportive role while operational units take responsibility for the business continuity plan itself. Thus, although business continuity skills are clearly essential for members of the specialist team, change management skills are also required.

Control and reward systems

Adjusting control and reward systems can lead to changes in individual and organizational behaviour. The persistent abuse of pensions-selling reflects the difficulty in changing the behaviour of financial services sales representatives when a large proportion of their salary is commission-based. Control and reward systems are the mechanisms by which an organization makes its requirements of employees explicit. Such systems reinforce operating norms and practices and culture. A performance management system, which cascades an organization's top level objectives down through successive layers of managers and front-line staff, may be one useful method of communicating goals, such as the need for effective business continuity management.

If business continuity is to receive adequate middle management attention, the individual's performance in this area should be regularly reviewed, as part of their normal performance appraisal. The results of such an appraisal may, formally or informally, feed into pay decisions. Evidence indicates that those organizations which use business continuity to add value, use business continuity management objectives in performance appraisal.

The way in which performance in business continuity is measured is also important. On the one hand, the production of new plan documents is readily observed and easily measured. Alternatively, less tangible measures of effectiveness – gaining real commitment from line managers and enhancing organizational resilience to interruption – are more difficult to measure yet arguably more important.

Where business continuity forms a component of the appraisal system for line managers and operational staff, it indicates that business continuity is an important part of day-to-day practice and not a separate activity. Business continuity management becomes, not simply a technique to be applied to particular functions, but consonant with the business approach.

Comparing two approaches to quality management illustrates the differences between standard and better practice. Quality control inspections are an after-the-event, weeding exercise that seeks to prevent faulty goods from reaching customers. It is expensive because it can lead to high wastage levels and requires expenditure on an inspection team. A Total Quality Management

(TQM) approach works from the starting point that quality is everyone's job and sets a target of zero defects throughout the value chain. This reduces wastage and eliminates the need for an inspection team. Quality inspection is bolted on whilst TQM is embedded within the organization. A range of tactics employed by organizations in promoting BCM is shown in Table 5.7.

Table 5.7 Control and reward systems used to support BCM implementation

Organization	Formal mechanisms
Automobile Association	Ownership placed with business unit managers
British Telecom	Appraisal system used for all management staff involved
Calor Gas	No formal mechanisms – rewards are intrinsic rather than extrinsic
Royal Bank of Scotland	Formal appraisal system not used but de facto use of BCM as a key result are for business unit coordinators
	Quality manager recognizes coordinator contribution through formal letter to line manager
	Peer group pressure
Health Trust A (teaching hospital included)	Business continuity (millennium bug project) a key element of the appraisal for key administrative staff
Health Trust B	No formal mechanisms
J Sainsbury	BCM policy explained via company newsletter
	BCM formally part of induction process; Intranet site
	'Buddy' scheme between head office and store managers to be used to improve communications regarding BCM
Sunderland	Formal appraisal of staff with responsibility for risk management. Forms an element of Chief Officer performance measurement
Thames Water	Appraisal planned. Performance indirectly assessed through review of event handling; peer recognition of contribution of new event management procedures

Source: Adapted from Elliott *et al.* (1999b).

Training

As a new and evolving discipline business continuity training provides an essential source of up-to-date knowledge and skills. The training needs of business continuity managers and operational staff differ. It appears that business continuity teams appear to acquire skills and knowledge in the following ways (Elliott *et al.*, 1999b):

- as a result of internal training by business continuity management consultants – in particular the process of acquiring skills by working alongside such consultants
- through external business continuity training delivered by external business continuity consultants

Training seeks to develop relevant skill sets covering such areas as those identified within the Business Continuity Institute's ten standards (BCI, 2001). Although these standards reflect the 'hardware focus' origins of the Institute, they identify a key part of the range of activities that a business continuity team may be expected to undertake. Thus research has indicated that business continuity practitioners consider that expertise in areas such as strategic analysis is essential preparation to their work. This reflected a concern that business continuity could become both insular and too technical in its focus. A sound grasp of strategy would encourage the practitioner to consider the role of business continuity activity within the broader objectives of an organization. For example, the Royal Bank Scotland used tools and frameworks covered on conventional Master of Business Administration courses in its business continuity planning processes. The use of such general business tools supports a broad view of business continuity and helps to ensure that preparations are not simply restricted to hardware and facilities. Effective business continuity management also requires training in the relevant tools and frameworks, outlined in Chapters 3 and 4.

Operationalizing business continuity also requires skills in corporate communications, change management, business process understanding, to name but a few. Effective BCM is a way of thinking as much as a set of tools. The good driver will have a good understanding of the highway code and know what each pedal and lever does. But on its own this understanding does not make a good driver; competent and excellent driving reflect an attitude of mind. This is based on sound principles, of course, but it is the way in which the skills and knowledge are put into practice that distinguishes the good from the mediocre and bad driver.

In terms of training for other staff, a range of practices currently used are shown in Table 5.8. These range from formal skills training in aspects of managing specific technology, to more informal, on-the-job training which is, in the main, provided by the BCM team.

Whilst some of these organizations do not directly engage in providing training, they are often invaluable sources of information. For instance, these bodies might have special interest groups, which focus on specific aspects of BCM that would enable practitioners to share experiences and knowledge in a safe and knowledgeable environment. Such groups also share information more directly through members presenting on practice in their companies. Much learning can transpire in this way. Other forms of more direct collaboration are clearly feasible. For example, there is evidence that, within specific sectors, organizations are starting to engage in a sharing of very expensive

Table 5.8 Training practices supportive of BCM

Company	Practices
Automobile Association	In-house training in use of software and data collection
	Post-test evaluations
British Telecom	Live exercises (major 'lift and shift' exercises)
	Desk check testing
Calor	Training of steering group and continuity manager by external consultants
Royal Bank of Scotland	Desk check testing
	On-the-job training for coordinators
	Consultants train continuity team
Health Trust A (teaching hospital included)	Desk checks with external suppliers
	Business continuity team 'downsized' 31/03/2000
Health Trust B	Not tested, disbanded 01/01/2000
J Sainsbury	Plan-testing for each business unit
	High-profile media handling training event
	Desk check exercises
	New staff briefed on BCM as a part of induction
Sunderland	Officers with risk management responsibility sent on relevant external courses
Thames Water	Desk check exercises
	Continuity team members attend university conferences and higher education courses

Source: Adapted from Elliott *et al.* (1999b).

physical resources. For instance, two organizations requiring a hot or cold site to be available might collaborate to share the facility and hence reduce costs.

Summary

This chapter has identified those elements that, when successfully managed, will aid the development of effective business continuity processes. Our concern has been to argue that effective BCM requires a cultural change. Effective continuity management is not a bolt-on process but an integral part of sound management. As human resource managers should aim to facilitate the day-to-day efforts of line managers and their staff, the effective business continuity team should play the role of championing and communicating good practice, providing expert support and ultimately working through line managers. There is no simple recipe but this section has identified the importance of:

- alternative communications strategies
- suggestions on cultural change
- control and reward systems used by organizations
- sources of training
- providing a clear structure for business continuity

It is evident that generic change management strategies may be employed to ensure the effective implementation of business continuity. Where this has been recognized, 'better practice' has emerged as a consequence. We finished the chapter with brief reference to user groups, forums in which business continuity practitioners can meet to exchange views and ideas. The value of such mechanisms cannot be underestimated as the cross-fertilization of ideas should propel practice forward.

Notes

1 Wilson (1992) identifies three approaches. However, two of these fall within the 'cultural/behavioural' category.
2 Thirty people died when a train crashed leaving Paddington station in October 1999. Four people died in a train accident near Hatfield in October 2000.

References

Argyris, C. (1994) 'Good communication that blocks learning', *Harvard Business Review* July–August: 77–85.
BCI (2001) 10 Standards [on-line] available at: www.thebci.org
Burnes, B. (1996) *Managing Change: A Strategic Approach to Organizational Dynamics*, London: Pitman.
Clegg, S. (1992) *Modern Organisations: Organisation Studies in the Postmodern World*, London: Sage.
Collins, D. (1998) *Organisational Change: Sociological Perspectives*, London: Routledge.
Deal, T.E. and Kennedy, A.A. (1982) *Corporate Cultures: The Rites and Rituals of Corporate Llife*, Reading, MA: Addison Wesley.
Dunphy, D.C. and Stace, D.A. (1987) 'Transformational and coercive strategies for planned organizational change', *Organisational Studies* 9 (3): 317–34.
Elliott, D. and Smith, D. (2001) *Learning from Crisis*, Leicester: Perpetuity Press.
Elliott, D., Swartz, E. and Herbane, B. (1999a) 'Just waiting for the next big bang: business continuity management in the UK finance sector, *Journal of Applied Management Studies*, 8 (1): 43–50.
Elliott, D., Swartz, E. and Herbane, B. (1999b) *Business Continuity Management*, Report for Income Data Services (IDS), London.
Government Centre for Information Systems (CCTA) (1995a) *An Introduction to Business Continuity Management*, London: HMSO.
Government Centre for Information Systems (CCTA) (1995b) *A Guide to Business Continuity Management*, London: HMSO.
Herbane, B., Elliott, D. and Swartz, E. (1997) 'Contingency and continua: achieving

excellence through business continuity planning', *Business Horizons* November–December: 19–25.

Hirokawa, R. (1988) 'Understanding the sources of faulty decision making', *Small Group Behaviour* 19: 411–33.

Hofstede, E. (1990) 'Measuring organisational cultures: a qualitative and quantitative study across twenty cases', *Administrative Science Quarterly* June: 286–316.

Home Office (1997a) *Business as Usual: Maximising Business Resilience to Terrorist Bombings*, London: Home Office.

Home Office (1997b) *Bombs, Protecting People and Property*, 3rd edn, London: Home Office.

Johnson, G. and Scholes, K. (1997) *Exploring Corporate Strategy: Text and Cases*, 3rd edn, London: Prentice Hall.

Kotter, J.P. and Schlesinger L.A. (1979) 'Choosing strategies for change', *Harvard Business Review* March/April: 123–36.

Levitt, B. and March, J.G. (1988) 'Organisational learning', *Annual Review of Sociology* 14: 319–40.

Lewin, K. (1951) *Field Theory in Social Science*, New York: Harper & Row

Mintzberg, H. (1983) *The Structuring of Organisations*, Englewood Cliffs, NJ: Prentice Hall.

Mintzberg, H. and Waters J. (1985) 'Of strategies, deliberate and emergent', *Strategic Management Journal* 6: 257–72.

Mitroff, I., Pauchant, T., Finney, M. and Pearson, C. (1989) 'Do (some) organizations cause their own crises? Culture profiles of crisis-prone versus crisis-repared organizations', *Industrial Crisis Quarterly* 3: 269–83.

Pauchant, T. and Mitroff, I. (1988) 'Crisis-prone versus crisis-avoiding organizations: is your company's culture its own worst enemy in creating crises?', *Industrial Crisis Quarterly* 2: 53–63.

Pauchant, T. and Mitroff I. (1992) *Transforming the Crisis-prone Organization*, San Francisco: Jossey-Bass.

Peters, T.J. and Waterman, R.H. (1982) *In Search of Excellence*, New York: Harper & Row

Pettigrew, A.M. and Whipp, R. (1991) *Managing Change for Competitive Success*, Oxford: Basil Blackwell.

Pettigrew, A.M., Whipp, R. and Rosenfeld, R.H. (1989) 'Competitiveness and the management of strategic change processes, in A. Francis and P. Tharakan (eds) *The Competitiveness of European Industry*, London: Routledge.

Plant, R. (1987) *Managing Change and Making it Stick*, London: Fontana.

Quinn, J.B. (1980) *Strategies for Change*, New York: Irwin.

Schein, E. (1992) *Organisational Culture and Leadership*, 2nd edn, San Francisco, CA: Jossey-Bass.

Starbuck, W., Greve, A. and Hedberg, B. (1978) 'Responding to crisis', *Journal of Business Administration*, spring. Reprinted in J. Quinn and H. Mintzberg (eds, 1992) *The Strategy Process*, Englewood Cliffs, NJ: Prentice Hall.

Swartz, E., Elliott, D. and Herbane, B. (1995) 'Out of sight, out of mind: the limitations of traditional information systems planning', *Facilities* 13 (9/10): 15–21.

Toft, B. and Reynolds, S. (1997) *Learning from Disasters*, Leicester: Perpetuity Press.

Trompenaars, F. (1993) *Riding the Waves of Culture*, London: Nicholas Brearley Publishing.

Turner, B. (1976) 'The organisational and interorganisational development of disasters', *Administrative Science Quarterly*, 21: 378–97 .

Turner, B. (1978) *Man-made Disasters*, London: Wykeham.

Turner, B. and Pidgeon, N. (1997) *Man-made Disasters*, 2nd edn, London: Butterworth-Heinemann.

Williams, A., Dobson, P. and Walters, M. (1989) *Changing Culture*, 2nd edn, London: Institute of Personnel Management.

Williams, D.M. (2001) private communication with the authors.

Wilson, D.C. (1992) *A Strategy of Change*, London: Routledge.

Further reading

Barney, J. (1986) 'Organisational culture: can it be a source of sustained competitive advantage?', *Academy of Management Review*, 11: 656–65.

Bryman, A. (1989) 'Leadership and culture in organisations', *Public Money and Management* autumn: 35–8.

Casse, P. (1991) 'Deciding on change: what and how?', *European Management Journal* 9(1): 18–20.

Hassard, J. and Sharifi, S. (1989) 'Corporate culture and strategic change', *Journal of General Management* 15(2): 4–19.

Study questions

1 Draw up a cultural web analysis of two organizations with which you are familiar. What are the key differences between them? How would these differences influence the development of business continuity management?
2 Identify five successful organizations. How clearly do they articulate their vision?
3 What are the key issues for a large organization introducing business continuity management to consider with regard to creating the effective preconditions for successful implementation?

6   Operational management

From testing to incidents

Box 6.1   A tale of two crises

'Don't make a drama out of a crisis'

(Commercial Union, 1992)

Late one Friday evening Commercial Union's Chairman, Peter Ward, was alerted to a bomb explosion in the vicinity of his company's St Mary's Axe headquarters in the City of London. An emergency crisis management team meeting was convened at 7.30 the following morning.

Some years earlier, Commercial Union had prepared detailed disaster plans for computer installations, datacom systems, hardware, software and telecommunications, with general plans for premises. After all, its advertising catchphrase was 'Don't make a drama out of a crisis.'

The headquarters was badly damaged. Three people had died and another sixty-seven were injured. Had the bomb exploded earlier, the casualty list would have much longer. Commercial Union staff could not gain access to the building for some days as the emergency services sought to make the premises safe and, where appropriate, collect forensic evidence.

The bomb had badly damaged the headquarters and the network nodes and telephone switchboard contained within it. This loss affected other Commercial Union sites and initially the crisis management team were unable to make outgoing calls nor receive incoming ones. The establishment of new communication facilities was a top priority.

The senior management team was divided into two, one to deal with ongoing business issues, the other to deal with the incident. The business team advised key staff that they intended to have business as usual by Monday.

Outlining their response afterwards, Peter Ward reported that during the early stages it was martial law 'We couldn't afford to have a committee meeting to decide who should go where and who didn't like going there. It was a question of allocating space and telling people where they were going.' The intense time pressures required decisions to be made quickly regardless of cost. Replacing the switchboard and network nodes was simply too important to be hindered by an extensive tendering process. Commercial Union was anxious to live up to its catchphrase and not to make a drama out of a crisis.

Source: Commercial Union Video (1995)

Customers first: Aurora

In May 2000 P&O's £200 million cruise ship *Aurora* sailed out of Southampton on its maiden voyage; 1,800 passengers were aboard the luxury cruiser. Within 24 hours the cruise was over and the *Aurora* was heading back to port. It had simply broken down.

The *Aurora's* passengers were described by P&O as 'bitterly disappointed'. Anxious to compensate passengers and to avoid extensive negative publicity P&O quickly offered a generous compensation package, including a full refund and the offer of a free cruise of an equivalent value. The compensation package cost P&O's insurers an estimated £6 million but was successful in controlling negative publicity. Jill Turner, 37, from Bishop Auckland, Co. Durham, said: 'There was a general feeling that there should have been more rigorous sea trials before the voyage. People are disappointed but the compensation package is very generous.' The quick and generous response removed uncertainty, pacified customers and prevented greater harm to P&O's reputation. Indeed, the speed of response may have enhanced it.

Source: Perry (2000)

Introduction

Previous chapters have considered business continuity in terms of its evolution, scope and frameworks for analysis. Concern for continuity has emerged from the recognition that things can go wrong and that the prudent organization will seek to anticipate these and make effective preparation for them. Commercial Union's experience highlights the importance of having continuity plans if organizations are to recover quickly. P&O's rapid response indicates how a quick response, focused upon key stakeholders can limit the impact of an interruption.

More attention has been given to the planning dimension of the BCM process than that of implementation, both in practice and in publications (see, for example, Ginn, 1989; Strohl Systems, 1995; Hiles and Barnes, 1999). The aim of this chapter is to provide an overview of the key issues associated with incident management. Successful management of an incident is the decisive test of the efficacy of the business continuity process (see Figure 6.1.) It represents the culmination of the organizational pre-crisis efforts.

Effective incident management can be summed up in a two-page article, if you believe some authors. It is our view that there is no simple, quick fix or prescription. Effective management of an incident is dependent on sound preparation, correct data in contact lists and a flexible plan and attitude. Earlier chapters have dealt with analysis, planning and testing which may provide a sound platform from which to manage an incident. Pauchant and Mitroff's (1988, 1992) seminal work has indicated that while some organizations are prone to crises, others are more resistant to interruptions. Resistance may be developed through the identification and examination of potential

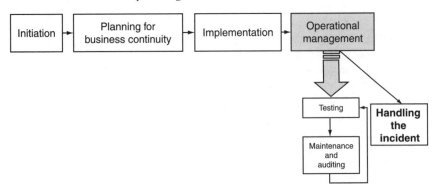

Figure 6.1 BCM as a business process

failures, their implications and the detection of potential remedies. Our concern in this chapter is to consider key issues pertaining to incident management.

Handling events

There is a growing public expectation that organizations should develop the capability to manage major incidents (Cameron, 1994). Within the United Kingdom, the loss of the Piper Alpha oil rig provided an important stimulus for the development of crisis management teams, as it highlighted the limitations of much that had passed as accepted practice (Smith, 2000). Whilst agencies such as the Home Office 1997a, 1997b and the Government Centre for Information Systems (1995a, 1995b) have published guidelines, Smart and Vertinsky's (1977) seminal work also remains highly relevant. Handling major incidents places specific demands upon an organization. Such incidents are likely to be characterized by complexity and dynamism, requiring organizational and communications structures to fit. Time is likely to be of the essence, a view reflected in ten Berge's (1990) 'The first 24 hours', which seeks to provide advice on how to manage the first elements of a crisis. Whilst there is some truth in ten Berge's (1990) assessment, particularly with regard to the shaping of perceptions and the commonsense observation that, where there are multiple fatalities or injuries to people, then urgent rescue is essential, the first twenty-four hours are not always the most salient. In the case of the 1990 contamination of Perrier water, the crisis spread over a number of weeks; in this example the ten days before the full-blown crisis might be seen as the critical period. Crisis management teams are not required simply for twenty-four hours but for the entire lifetime of an incident.

Turner (1976; Turner and Pidgeon, 1997) argued that organizations incubate the potential for major interruptions themselves. Although particularly concerned with major disasters investigated through the public inquiry process, Turner's model (see Table 6.1) has a broader applicability for business interruptions of all types.

Table 6.1 Turner's model of crisis

Crisis stage	Description
Initial beliefs and norms	Notional starting point
Incubation period	Ignore warnings and complaints
Trigger incident	Precipitating event
Onset	Focal crisis
Rescue and salvage	Immediate response
Cultural readjustment	Organizational learning

Source: Adapted from Turner (1976).

Box 6.2   Missing the warning signals

For example, a car manufacturer seeks to employ a minimal stock system, a variant of just in time. A contract to provide good quality components at a competitive price is agreed with relevant suppliers. Initial beliefs and norms refer to the stage at which the contract is agreed and seen to work. However, imagine a scenario in which the supplier of a key component begins to miss supply deadlines or provides sub-standard parts. At first, the car manufacturer's buffer stocks disguise the problem and, whilst managers are aware of difficulties, they take no action. They ignore the warning signs because they have many other demands on their time. Then, a significant supply shortfall occurs. Fortunately, the car manufacturer is able to bring forward some planned maintenance and avoids a major problem. Somehow, over a period of a few years many potential minor interruptions are dealt with or avoided by 'muddling through'. The difficulties are never significant enough to warrant a questioning of the supplier contract. Partial unreliability is excused because of a long-term business relationship and competitive price.

Then the motor industry enters the growth part of its economic cycle leading to increased demands. The supplier that had been unable to deal with demand properly at its previous level is faced with a sudden surge in demand for the components that it supplies. Despite having given assurances to its customers of its ability to increase production quickly, it is unable to do so. All the warning signs had been there before. Its difficulties had been caused by obsolete production processes, lack of investment in new technology and a demoralized work force looking for employment elsewhere. Entry into the growth stage of the business cycle placed more pressure on the production process at a time when employees could find employment elsewhere more easily. This is the trigger that causes a crisis for both supplier and car manufacturing customer. The success of rescue and salvage will be dependent, in large measure, on the quality of continuity plans prepared prior to the 'incident'; the identification of alternative sources of supply or components, for example. Cultural readjustment refers to a post-incident stage in which the car manufacturer might reconsider its methods of supplier recruitment, monitoring, discipline and management.

An incident of the type depicted in Box 6.2 was chosen to emphasize that the methodologies discussed in this chapter are not solely concerned with major accidents involving fire, death and explosion. It is possible that the shortage of a key component might have damaged, significantly, the competitiveness of a large car manufacturer which would have required a coordinated response to manage an interruption to production, distributors, other suppliers and, ultimately, to customers. Increasingly, BCM is gaining a customer focus as organizations provide means to an end.

In this chapter we consider, first, crisis management teams, building on the seminal work of Smart and Vertinsky (1977). The chapter then progresses to an examination of major incident management structures chosen by some organizations. A natural progression is to consider, albeit briefly, the nature of stress and its potential for hindering an organization's response to crisis. As stress arises from a perceived imbalance between an individual's capabilities and demands, we consider how organizations may test and maintain plans and processes whilst building individual capabilities. We conclude with a consideration of the communication aspects of major incident management.

Crisis management teams

Teams are important because, generally, they outperform individuals although, as Janis's groundbreaking work identified, teams are still fallible. Smart and Vertinsky (1977) have argued that 'crisis decision units' may be particularly vulnerable to malfunctions affecting the quality of decisions. Raiffa (1968) identified four types of decision error:

- rejecting a correct course of action
- accepting a wrong solution to a problem
- solving the wrong problem
- solving the right problem, correctly, but too late

Errors may arise from the poor quality of information available, the cognitive abilities of the group and the 'fidelity of objective articulation and trade-off evaluation'. These will manifest themselves in the emergence of groupthink, rigidity in problem-solving, the distortion of information, and a reluctance to adapt to new circumstances or to implement solutions quickly. Such errors rarely occur in isolation and some authors have identified organizational cultures according to the way in which they deal with safety information (see Table 6.2). A practical question for organizations to consider is, to what extent do we possess a pathological culture? The characteristics of a pathological culture will include the employment of the defence mechanisms identified in the last chapter. Such organizations make themselves more prone to crisis. With hindsight, it is possible, usually, to pick out warning signals of impending failure. Union Carbide not rectifying a number of safety

Table 6.2 How different organizational cultures handle safety information

Pathological culture	Bureaucratic culture	Generative culture
• Don't want to know • Whistleblowers are 'shot' • Responsibility is avoided • Failure is punished or hidden • New ideas are discouraged	• May not find out • Messengers listened to if they arrive • Responsibility is compartmentalized • Failures lead to local repairs • New ideas often present problems	• Actively seek it • Messengers are trained and rewarded • Responsibility is shared • Failures lead to far reaching reforms • New ideas are welcomed

Source: Reason (1997).

difficulties at their Bhopal plant in the years preceding the 1984 disaster; Barings had identified deficiencies in their risk control procedures following a 1994 fraud but, as their treasurer observed, regarding the implementation of remedies, 'There was always something else that seemed more pressing' (quoted in Reason, 1997: 39).

A summary of the remedies to these potential difficulties includes:

- encouraging alternative viewpoints through creative problem-solving techniques
- rotating team members
- including outside experts
- protecting minority points of view
- developing better information collection techniques
- formally creating a devil's advocate role
- encouraging expression of concerns or doubts
- developing flexible operating procedures
- establishing contingency plans
- holding crisis simulations
- building network of trusted, potential coordinators in line departments

(adapted from Smart and Vertinsky, 1977)

Implicit in Smart and Vertinsky's analysis is the development of the critical team. A recurring theme within the literature (with regard to teams in general and crisis management teams in particular) concerns variety and balance. For example, Belbin (1981) suggested nine key roles for individuals within teams, arguing that a balance between these roles is key to ensuring team success. For crisis management teams, Carley (1991) argued that personnel should be recruited from a range of backgrounds and knowledge bases. The effective crisis management team, it is suggested, incorporates processes and people for continually questioning decisions and information, and has in place the mechanisms, personnel and communication channels to support quick and effective implementation. The nature of criticism is not that of the awkward individual but that of devil's advocate. In practice, a careful balance must be maintained between an open mind and procrastination. Structure can play a vital role in determining an organization's propensity for either haste or procrastination.

Configuration

Not all structures are as effective in providing the context for the emergence of the characteristics of the effective crisis management team. Mintzberg (1983) argued that organizational success required a fit between structure and environment. From his analysis, Mintzberg identified a range of organizational structure types, five of which are shown in Figure 6.2.

A simple and stable environment provides the right conditions for an organizational programme, the so-called 'machine bureaucracy'. Lack of change and simplicity of environmental demands permits control through strict procedures. Within this predictable context, nothing new happens so the workforce are not permitted to deviate from plan; they have no need as all has been anticipated and all eventualities prepared for. Organizational success follows the ruthless pursuit of efficiency. Examples include large manufacturing plants, IBM's focus upon sales in the 1980s and British banks during the 1960s and 1970s. All activities, in these examples, were tightly controlled. Arguably, these mechanistic approaches, and the insularity associated with them, played a major part in a failure to read the warning signs of environmental change. IBM placed too much emphasis on the mainframe to the detriment of the personal computer; British banks were slow to innovate in terms of customer service and in their use of new technology; flexible manufacturing units threatened large manufacturing plants. The machine

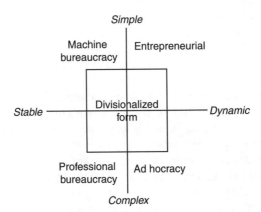

Figure 6.2 Configuration–environment–organizational fit
Source: Mintzberg (1983).

bureaucracy is not well suited to crisis management as its structures and procedures are likely to slow down and confuse any response to a dynamic and complex situation. There will not be time to work through an organization's usual processes. An effective crisis management team is unlikely to flourish within a bureaucratic context.

The entrepreneur flourishes in a context combining simplicity and dynamism. With no need to consult, he or she can respond quickly to change. The small firm is the typical example of this organizational form. Many entrepreneurs describe their work as fire-fighting. They have the advantage of being able to respond quickly should they need to. Typically, one person can make a decision. However, the individual cannot hope to deal with the same degree of complexity as an effective group. There is also the danger that, within the entrepreneurial context, there will be insufficient scope for the leader to be questioned, preventing the development of the 'critical team'.

The professional bureaucracy occupies a context combining complexity with relative stability. Complexity is dealt with by professionals who receive extensive training before commencing employment. Health, education, public service professionals, engineers, etc. provide examples. These professionals are sheltered within a bureaucracy that provides the organizational means by which stability is managed. Inevitably, professional associations may play a major part in regulating behaviour and influencing operating norms as may be seen in the case of the medical profession. Thus, internal procedures and external pressures may slow down decision-making, undermining any effective crisis response.

A further organizational type, Mintzberg labels the adhocracy; small groups of highly trained individuals working together (for example, a research and development team or management consultancy). A collection of highly skilled people enable it to deal with complexity, whilst its small size and network structure permit rapid decision-making, facilitating a quick response to environmental change. Smart and Vertinsky's (1977) model crisis management team fits closely with Mintzberg's adhocracy.

The final pure type is the divisionalized form in which Mintzberg recognized that the large size of firms often meant that one company might incorporate a number of these types. Of course, each of the five is a pure type and, in practice, it is likely that an organization will show a tendency towards a particular type rather than adopt it as a pure structure.

What is the relevance of structure to continuity? Structure will condition the types of response to the environment that an organization can make. In times of rapid change, bureaucracy tends to stifle change causing the structure to be out of fit with its environment and thereby limiting effectiveness.

It is not suggested that organizations configure themselves as an adhocracy, just in case. Managers, however, must be aware of their usual configuration and the difficulties that may be posed when dealing with a major interruption. A critical question concerns how personnel, used to tight order and prescription, may be encouraged and empowered to deviate and

Box 6.3   Machine bureaucracy

An extreme example concerns the fire service. Although dealing with our day-to-day crises and what we would consider to be the complexities and dynamism of house fires and road traffic accidents, the fire service has developed a drilled response to such incidents. That is, when it arrives at an incident each fire fighter knows exactly his or her specific task. Deviation from the drilled response requires authority from a supervising officer, who retains a note of all such deviations in order that the lives of other fire-fighters are not placed in jeopardy. Put another way, the fire service operates in a very machine bureaucracy manner. For a large proportion of incidents, such a style works well. However, when faced with a major incident that bears little resemblance to those practised by fire-fighters in training, deviation from the plan is required. The supervisor will be inundated with requests for permission to deviate from the plan and will become overloaded with information. Effective emergency response is in danger of breakdown at this point, as the structure fails to cope with the demands of the environment. Such a breakdown affected the fire service at Kegworth in 1989 and the police at Hillsborough in the same year (see Elliott and Smith, 1993). Structure provides the context in which strategy is implemented. If it does not fit with its environment then the strategy will at best be hindered, at worst fail.

use their initiative in the event of a major interruption. This is the purpose of command-and-control structures, which should incorporate a clear sense of ultimate objective with flexibility in how that may be achieved.

Command-and-control structures

In addition to the day-to-day structures required to implement BCM, a command-and-control structure for managing major events is needed. Many companies utilize a three-tier structure as advocated by the Home Office (1997a, 1997b) and the Government Centre for Information Systems (1995b). This mimics the structure used by the British police service, who label the three levels bronze, silver and gold system (respectively tactical, operational and strategic). This structure emerged from an attempt to encourage consistency between the emergency services and thereby minimize confusion when dealing with an incident (Flin, 1996).

The purpose of the three levels is to ensure that an organization's response to an incident is effectively coordinated. Bronze (operational) corresponds to the normal operational response provided by the emergency services where the management is of routine tasks. The immediate response to an incident is likely to be managed at this level. When the emergency services deal with a major incident, the 'bronze commander' is likely to lead a front-line team. Silver (tactical) refers to the command level, which seeks to identify priorities and allocate resources accordingly. During a major incident, it is likely that

Box 6.4 World Trade Center, 1993

The New York World Trade Center (WTC) was one of the tallest buildings in the world with twin towers, each with 110 storeys. The WTC was a major commercial building with over 1,000 businesses employing more than 50,000 staff.

McFadden (1993), reporting for the *New York Times*, recorded that the bomb blast 'knocked out the police command and operations centers for the towers, which rendered the office complex's evacuation plans useless'. Many of those who walked down scores of flights from the upper reaches of the trade centre towers said there had been no alarm bells and no instructions from building personnel or emergency workers. While little panic was reported, witnesses said confusion reigned in the darkness of crowded stairwells, where smoke billowed and unknown dangers lurked below.

The immediate impact of the explosion was to leave an estimated 50,000 people in a building, parts of which were burning, with little power for light and with none of the 250 elevators working. The scale of the interruption had taken the WTC's management team by surprise. A knock-on effect was that, with so many firms experiencing an interruption, there was a surge in demand for disaster recovery services, a surge that could not be readily met by supply.

Dean Witter, which employed 5,000 staff in the WTC, invoked contingency plans and made use of access to alternative office space in New York.

Source: McFadden (1993), Hiles and Barnes (1999)

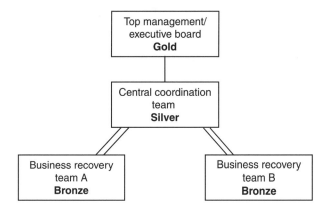

Figure 6.3 Three-tier command-and-control system

the silver commander will take charge of managing the incident itself. The role of the gold (strategic) group and commander is to take an overview, to arbitrate between any conflicts at silver level and to assume responsibility for liaising with the media and key stakeholder groups. The 'gold commander' is not expected to participate in the detailed management of an incident (adapted from the Home Office, 1997a, 1997b).

The applicability of such a framework to the emergency services is relatively clear. However, its suitability for a wider range of organizations is less obvious. For this reason we devote the remainder of this section to an examination of how this framework was adapted to meet the requirements of an international bank (see Figure 6.4). The key word is 'adapted'; all organizations are unique in terms of structures, cultures, personnel and location to name four factors. Any contingency plans should be developed with that uniqueness in mind.

The three levels identify a minimum of three roles to be undertaken when managing an incident. In smaller organizations one team or individual may perform these distinct roles. Two further roles have been added to the framework for the international bank. The first is the 'ongoing support box', which identifies the activities that deal with the day-to-day interruptions that face organizations of all types. For example, most organizations have systems in place to deal with maintenance and routine problem-solving; invoking a full emergency response every time a computer fails or another problem occurs would be both time-consuming and expensive. Many types of interruption may be initially logged as minor difficulties and it is likely that internal help desks will be called upon to deal with them first.

The second additional tier is the 'incident assessment team', which consists of business managers, both those affected by an interruption and managers drawn from the relevant support services from IT and facilities through to personnel. In the event of an interruption this team should undertake an initial assessment and determine the most suitable response for an organization. Determining when a minor interruption requires the activation of a

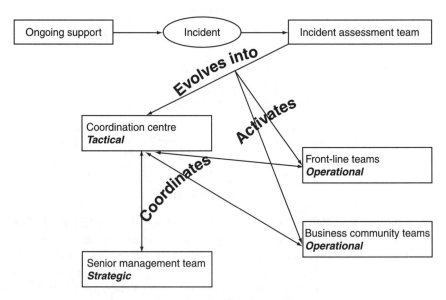

Figure 6.4 Incident management

full-blown incident response is not always straightforward. A major fire or systems failure may be obviously serious, but often the significance of an interruption may not be immediately evident.

Figure 6.5 represents a matrix that can be used to assess the severity of an incident. It is not intended to provide a quantitative tool but rather a checklist of key issues. This particular example was developed for a large financial sector organization and should be adapted to meet the needs and priorities of a particular organization. System rating refers to the importance of a particular IT system. Tier 1 systems are business-critical, essential for trading and for regulatory compliance. Tier 3 might include stand-alone packages whose loss poses no more than an inconvenience. Regulatory impact was a key criterion for the bank, given the increasing requirements for financial sector organizations to demonstrate probity. Recovery time-line refers to the predicted length of the interruption. Where expense concerns the tangible cost of dealing with an interruption, financial impact deals with the consequences of an interruption. For example, the failure to respond to an incident quickly may lead to the loss of key customers who move their business elsewhere. Deadline impact identifies the vagaries of the calendar for all businesses. There are in most industries busy and lean times. Interruptions at critical times may have a dramatic effect. For example, one British university experienced a breakdown in its telephone systems in the period following the publication of A-level results, its busiest recruitment time. A toy retailer may experience the loss of critical systems during the six weeks before Christmas.

The final row indicates the type of response required by an incident. Few incidents warrant the active and ongoing attention of a senior management team. Working processes already exist to deal with these. Every organization can determine the most appropriate level of response to an incident. Following its evaluation the incident assessment team will activate bronze, silver and gold teams to meet the needs of the organization. The tool is best used as an aid to decision-making rather than in a simple quantitative way.

	Interruption	Incident	Major incident
System rating	Tier 3	Tier 2	Tier 1
Regulatory impact	No regulatory issues	Minimal regulatory issues	Significant regulatory matter
Recovery time-line	Up to 2 hours	Between 2 and 24 hours	1 day or more
Expense	£10k	£100k	£1m
Financial impact	Potential loss of £x	Potential loss of £x	Potential loss of £x
Deadline impact	Routine	Regular milestone approaching	Key deadline approaching
Appropriate recovery mechanism	Normal procedures	Normal procedures I	Major incident plan

Figure 6.5 Incident severity assessment matrix

Bronze tactical

Business recovery teams include specialist support teams (for example, IT, premises, personnel) and business unit teams (that is, those performing primary activities). To use a military metaphor these are the troops on the ground combining the sappers and engineers with the fighting platoons. Following an interruption, it is likely that support teams will seek to prepare suitable accommodation, information systems, and transport and subsistence arrangements. Business units will seek to establish agreed levels of service in key activities to important customer and stakeholder groups. Financial organizations may focus upon 'triple A rated clients', utilities might concentrate upon vulnerable groups or vital industrial plants; such priorities having been identified during the stages of analysis.

In summary, business continuity plans exist at business unit and team level, identifying what is to be done in the event of short, long and uncertain interruptions. These might include, for a large investment bank, switching to manual systems, reducing levels of trading to key customer accounts or ceasing trade completely.

Silver operational

Within Figure 6.4 the role of the 'coordination centre' is to coordinate the business continuity teams from both primary and secondary teams. Members of the silver team, although dependent upon the demands of a particular event, are drawn from a pool of senior operational managers. Its primary task is to ensure that the bank's response to an incident is effectively coordinated and that the bronze support and business teams are deployed in the sequence most appropriate to the needs of the bank. For example, if an organization is forced to relocate to an emergency site with accommodation for fewer staff than the regular building, decisions will need to be made about which staff will be relocated and in what priority order. At this level, the silver team will need to identify corporate priorities and the order in which business units are restored to agreed levels of service. Each team may consider itself the most important, requiring the silver team to determine what meets corporate objectives most effectively.

Gold strategic

Consisting of an organization's most senior executives the role of this team is to deal with strategic issues emerging from an incident. At their most basic these issues are concerned with ensuring that incident response does not spill over into areas of a business unaffected by a particular incident. Dealing with a major incident may require significant expenditure. The senior management team will be responsible for such authorization. Another vital task is for high-level media and stakeholder representation. The senior management team provides a port of last resort for issues that cannot be resolved by the coordinating centre. However, it is not expected to have an active role in the operational coordination of responding to an incident.

Although the bronze, silver and gold incident command structure has been adopted by a number of organizations, there is no single way of organizing for a crisis. The idiosyncrasies of organizations will require structures reflecting their different needs. BT's structure, for example, sets out responsibilities at the centre and in the regions. There is a two-tier hierarchy with supporting documentation explaining roles, levels of authority and checklists for the main incident manager and the forward control manager, who have key functions. Regional coordinators also have a clear understanding of what their role is and how they fit into the overall command-and-control structure. Everyone concerned will have received some training; exercises are run regularly and participants will draw on their experience of real invocations. Currently, all operational managers at Thames Water may, in theory, be called upon to act as an 'event manager' (that is, to manage crisis incidents of differing severity).

Figure 6.6 depicts how one multinational company organized its two-tier structure when faced with a major business interruption. The brief of the executive management team is to coordinate activities on two fronts – crisis management and mitigation – that encompass external communications with media and regulators, as well as internal communications with support functions in the organization.

The brief of the business management team is to coordinate the business recovery teams for the business units. The recovery teams have a focus on the supply chain and will work to a recovery plan to maximize contact with customers, suppliers and other relevant stakeholders.

The particular arrangements for handling incidents or crises vary between

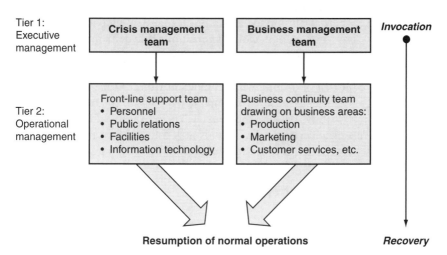

Figure 6.6 Example command-and-control structure to manage incidents

organizations. What they share, however, is a recognition of the need for teams to specialize in a controlled way. There is a need for strategic, tactical and operational activities to be separated in some way. The detail may differ from industry to industry and from scenario to scenario, but there must be some means of ensuring a coordinated response.

Effective teamwork, leadership and contingency planning are all essential ingredients of effective crisis management. Inevitably, a disproportionate amount of research effort has focused upon incidents involving many injuries or multiple fatalities. Such incidents lend themselves to research as they come into the public domain. There are resulting dangers that crisis management is perceived to be a discipline restricted to such events, or that managers within other industries fail to learn the lessons. Flin's (1996) comprehensive analysis of incident command provides a short analysis of a range of multiple fatality accidents from stadium disasters and fires to airplane crashes and concludes that these:

> were all situations in which incident commanders were faced with extremely difficult decisions, characterised by ambiguous and conflicting information, shifting goals, time pressure, dynamic conditions, complex operational team structures and poor communications. . . . Despite the broad spectrum of incidents types and conditions . . . there is sufficient commonality in the roles of various incident commanders to merit an integrated examination of their selection, their training . . . coping with stress, decision-making and team management.
>
> (Flin, 1996: 37)

Strip away the colour labels of the Home Office's (1997a, 1997b) incident command structure and we are left with the recognition that there are at least three distinct, basic roles to be undertaken during any incident. For the emergency services, there is an implied assumption that dealing with incidents is their *raison d'être*. For commercial organizations, incident management is, hopefully, a rare event and team members will be less practised at it. The role of the crisis management team for the commercial organization will also be to remove the burden of dealing with an incident from routine operations; in other words, it will seek to ensure that unaffected parts of the business will be able to continue trading. Because incidents will occur rarely and be associated with high levels of uncertainty, individuals may find incident management a stressful experience and it is to a consideration of this that we now turn.

Decision-making under stress

Defining stress

Major incidents are likely to prove a stressful experience for people, threatening health and potentially hindering an organization's response. The study of stress and crisis decision-making has provided the focus for many studies yet still it seems that:

> The concept of stress is elusive because it is poorly defined. There is no single agreed definition in existence. It is a concept which is familiar to both layman and professional alike; it is understood by all when used in a general context but by very few when a more precise account is required, and this seems to be the central problem.
>
> (Cox, 1978: 1)

Cox's (1978) view is as apt today as it was when it was first written. Within the academic literature, there are various approaches to the study of stress, each with its particular definition of the term. Cranwell-Ward (1990) identified two broad approaches from her study of stress in management: those that related to the *causes* of the stress and those that related to the *effects* induced by it. A third approach is the transactional model, defined below (Cox, 1978; Fisher, 1986; Brown and Campbell, 1994). The transactional or interactional model of stress is developed from the work of Lazarus, Cox and their colleagues (Cox, 1978; Lazarus, 1966, 1999; Lazarus and Launier, 1978; Lazarus and Folhman, 1984): 'the physiological and psychological reaction which occurs when people perceive an imbalance, between the level of demand placed upon them, and their capability to meet those demands' (Cranwell-Ward, 1990: 10).

This definition is close to the one used by Cox (1978) in his observation that:

> Stress . . . can only be sensibly defined as a perceptual phenomenon arising from a comparison between the demand on the person and his ability to cope. An imbalance in this mechanism, when coping is important, gives rise to the experience of stress, and to stress response. The latter represent attempts at coping with the source of stress.
>
> (1978: 25)

This interactional model posits that an individual interacts with his or her environment and that, whilst the environment can affect the individual, so too can the individual affect the environment. In both cases, there is seen to be an imbalance between the demands placed upon the individual and their perceived abilities to cope with these demands. Both groups of authors emphasize the continuing nature of this process and both emphasize the role of cognitive appraisal in determining the perceived imbalance and therefore stress. For Lazarus (1978), the evaluation process occurs in two stages. The first stage, or primary appraisal, occurs when the individual first evaluates the event or demand and focuses upon the negative outcomes that can result from the interaction. The secondary stage occurs when the respondent seeks to evaluate the potential responses that can be made to the negative outcomes that were previously determined.

Stress and incident management

Given the difficulties associated with managing crisis incidents, the notion of stress, and increasingly more specifically Post-Traumatic Stress Disorder (PTSD), as a potential impairer of individual and thus organizational performance, is becoming an important consideration (see, for example, Elliott and Smith, 2000).

Within the study of crises, prominence has been given to PTSD, although it must be pointed out that occupational stress has increased in importance for human resource managers. A number of studies have been concerned with the traumatic experiences of military personnel or emergency services staff acting in the role of rescuers (see, for example, Elliott and Smith, 2000). PTSD emerges from an experience of an event outside the usual bounds of experience, such as threat to oneself, loved ones, home, or close involvement in a major incident. Symptoms may include re-experiencing the trauma, avoiding stimuli associated with the trauma and persistent increased arousal in the form of:

- thoughts/feelings
- activities/situations
- psychogenic amnesia
- lack of interest
- detachment/estrangement

The implications for effective incident management of individuals experiencing some or all of these symptoms are obvious. Yet few organizations consider stress when creating continuity plans, despite the evidence that staff will tolerate the dislocation associated with crisis incidents for a short period only. This toleration may well be determined by factors such as pre-incident culture and the extent to which an organization's support staff are called upon to commit more time and energy to their employer than usual. This has implications for all operational staff but, more critically in this context, for staff participating within crisis management teams. As we have seen major incidents will be characterized by uncertainty, lack of information, time pressures and a tendency towards rigidity in decision-making. Within such a context, organizations must ensure that the most appropriate individuals are selected and managed effectively.

The types of incident that come quickly to mind are fires and explosions but these represent the tip of the iceberg. The failures of information systems, prolonged transport breakdown and failures of suppliers will also create uncertainty within time constraints. Although little research has been undertaken, it seems probable that the blockade of UK oil refineries during September 2000 will have caused high levels of uncertainty for a range of organizations. For retailers, demand rose sharply at a time when supply to stores was difficult (Mellish, 2000).

Box 6.5 Employee mobility

An insurance company owns two main offices in France: one near Paris, another at Lyon. In case of the loss of either office, it plans to switch staff to the other one. As the two cities are more than 300 km apart, the plan assumes that staff are able to spend the week away from their homes. Not only will working routines be affected, but so will domestic arrangements. Anecdotal evidence suggests that, whilst employees may be willing to accept such a major upheaval for a very short period, their patience will be short-lived.

In another case, an organization was forced to relocate its staff, temporarily, from a West End office to the East End of London, disrupting the daily routines of hundreds of staff. The organization reported higher levels of absenteeism and, subsequently, higher turnover.

When Commercial Union's headquarters was severely damaged in 1992, the management team quickly recognized that enthusiasm for a two and three-quarter hour journey to the temporary headquarters, each way, each day, changing trains twice *en route*, would soon wane, however dedicated its staff were. To support staff it gave regular updates on progress, to reassure them of concern for welfare. Commercial Union also agreed to reimburse any additional travel costs incurred; flexi-time arrangements for staff were introduced including the possibility of days off.

Stress and the individual

At a basic level, an individual's response to stress appears to be dependent upon two factors. First, an individual's personality characteristics may modify any response to stress. Training and experience may play a vital mediating role, indicating that organizations must consider methods of developing staff skills. In the case of J Sainsbury's handling of the oil blockade and the extra demands placed upon staff, the existence of a clear process played a key role. Staff had rehearsed responses to similar scenarios (i.e. panic buying at the millennium) and could rely on a process that was familiar to them and to colleagues (Mellish, 2000). The second factor concerns the nature of the traumatic experience itself and the recovery environment. An individual's perception of the nature of an experience will be key because, as Lazarus argues, only an individual can describe a particular event as stressful to himself or herself. However, it seems clear that certain situations are more likely than others to lead to a negative 'stressful' response, almost irrespective of individual characteristics. Organizational crises, characterized by lack of information, uncertainty and limited time for decisions, are just such situations. The duration of an incident may also play a part. Mellish (2000) identifies the role played by the 'Dunkirk Spirit' in J Sainsbury's crisis response. Had the incident been prolonged that spirit might have been broken.

Evidence has suggested that previous exposure to some of the hazards encountered may also reduce the perceived threat, and thereby reduce the experience of stress (Warr, 1990). Fire-fighters are exposed to heights and smoke-filled rooms, pilots to water-filled simulators; indeed the use of simulated crisis exercises within organizations of all types (discussed later) might be seen as one useful means of preparing staff for handling an incident (Elliott and Smith, 2000).

A number of possibilities for organizations emerge from these studies. Effective intervention may include three basic groups of practice:

- the identification of 'hardy' individuals during recruitment, selection and training
- staff development to raise individual capabilities and thereby reduce the perceived threat of a situation
- providing a supportive recovery environment

The first is difficult, both politically and practically, and may be interpreted as placing blame upon the individual. Further, whilst it may have relevance to the emergency services, the notion that a hardy personality is a requirement for many other jobs might be challenged. The second and third groups recognize management's role in this area and avoid individual blame. The effects and duration of the symptoms of PTSD will be critical factors in impairing organizational effectiveness. Counselling via a detailed debriefing has long been advocated, particularly for the emergency services. However, recent research has suggested that in some cases debriefing has the effect of forcing individuals to re-live traumatic events with dire consequences (Raphael *et al.*, 1995; Rick and Briner, 2000).

Managers and supervisors should be trained to identify the symptoms of psychological distress and to provide immediate support including the monitoring of individuals who may be potentially at risk from the effects of stress and PTSD. Most practically, the evidence is (see Elliott and Smith, 1993, 2000) that training plays a major role in preparing staff for incident management, in terms of raising their capabilities and readying them for the demands of crisis management. The HSE (2001) has provided much guidance on the causes of stress at work and, whilst their concern is with occupational stress, their findings have some relevance for our subject.

The HSE checklist provides a useful means of summarizing this section. There is a danger that stress is considered to arise from fire, explosion or threat to life. It will do so in some cases, yet stress may arise from more mundane scenarios. Role ambiguity, excessive demands, poor relationships and a perception of lack of control may cause stress on a daily basis. These are more likely to arise at times of crisis and should therefore be considered by continuity managers. Key considerations include ensuring that excessive demands are not placed on staff, even during times of crisis. Whilst the 'Dunkirk spirit' may come to the fore initially, fatigue may break it. The

Box 6.6   Causes of stress

Occupational stress

Key causes of occupational stress and their remedies:

1. Poor management culture

    Improved by:
    - commitment to promoting the health of employees
    - value and respect for employees
    - support for staff raising problems about their work

2. Excessive demands upon staff

    At a manageable level of demand:
    - staff are able to cope with the volume and complexity of the work which is scheduled so that there is sufficient time to do allocated tasks
    - people are not expected to work long hours over an extended period

3. Lack of control

    People feel in control when:
    - they may influence how they do their work; and control is balanced against the demands placed upon them

4. Poor relationships

    Good relationships evolve when:
    - there is good communication, with employees understanding what's expected and employers reacting to any problems being experienced by the employees
    - employees are not bullied or harassed

5. Poor management of change

    Good change management will be characterized by:
    - an organization communicating the reasons why change is essential
    - an organization having a clear sense of purpose
    - the organization having a timetable for implementing change, which includes realistic first steps
    - the organization ensuring a supportive climate for employees

6. Lack of training, support and failure to take account of individual factors

    Examples of good practice:
    - employees receive adequate training to do their jobs
    - employees receive support from their immediate line management, even when things go wrong
    - the organization encourages people to share their concerns about health and safety and, in particular, work-related stress
    - the individual is fair to the employer – they discuss their concerns and work towards agreed solutions

7. Role ambiguity

> *Examples of where people understand their role are when:*
> - they know why they are undertaking the work and how this fits in with the organization's wider aims and objectives
> - jobs are clearly defined to avoid confusion.

The Health and Safety Executive (HSE) is working towards standards of good management practice in these areas.

Source: Adapted from HSE Guidance (2001)

---

uncertainty associated with interruptions of all sorts will increase the likelihood of role ambiguity. Training can play a major role in reducing the threat of role ambiguity and in identifying the demands placed upon any particular role. An advantage of the HSE's checklist of factors is that it provides an indicator of how stress may arise.

We have argued that the planning process is more important than the plan and that testing, maintenance and auditing are vital elements of this. They can ensure that personnel develop relevant skills and are exposed to the potential stressors of a real business interruption.

Testing, maintenance and auditing

Business continuity management depends on up-to-date information within plan documents, which provide the basic tools for effective interruption response and will provide better preparation for staff involved in incident response. Mintzberg and Waters' (1985) view of strategy as 'a pattern in a stream of decisions' or strategies 'as patterns or consistencies in such streams' recognized that a distinction must be made between what organizations intend to do (as set out in plans, be they strategic or continuity plans) and what they do. Strategy is distinguished between those actions that were intended (planned) and those which emerged (realized). For plans to shape behaviour fully requires absolute certainty and does not allow for the bounded rationality of managers.

As discussed in Chapter 5 (see Figure 5.4 for a depiction of Mintzberg and Waters' emergent properties of strategy), intended strategy refers to the plan. The many arrows refer to the behaviour of individuals and teams, which, cumulatively, add up to the organization's behaviour. Marks & Spencers' long-standing reputation for customer service provides a good example. That reputation is founded on every interaction between members of staff and customers. Together, these interactions prove the decisive test of customer service. Achieving this consistently requires selecting and training the right staff, maintaining a positive disposition, systems and processes for handling difficulties and a real top management commitment. Each arrow may be thought of as representing one interaction and the successful retailer must ensure consistency in millions of such interactions every week – no mean feat. In the context of continuity management these arrows may be thought of as sheep and the continuity management team, using their plans, may be thought of as the sheep dog, steering the flock towards safety. The metaphor of the sheep dog is useful as they are well trained but are also flexible, able to adapt to differing circumstances. The purpose of the plan is to help managers steer a safe course in response to an interruption. The purpose of testing, auditing and maintenance is to ensure that plan documents can support this, rather than to impose a bureaucratic stricture on the business continuity process. The imposition of a bureaucracy would impede an organization's response and make the context worse for individual managers.

Operational management of business continuity

In this section, the assimilation of BCM into day-to-day management is considered. This is the fourth stage of our framework (see Figure 6.1) and we give it the label operational management.

The operational management of BCM falls broadly into two areas: testing, and maintenance and auditing

Testing

Testing is a generic term for a number of activities that are designed to evaluate whether BC plans direct business resumption efforts as expected. As Doemland (1999) observed, the purpose of testing and auditing is to ensure the continuing readiness of a plan. Contact information is a particularly good example, as such data may become dated quickly, making plans dependent upon such databases worthless.

There are four basic premises for testing:

- ensuring the organization can walk before it tries to run
- reducing complacency – the 'we have a plan' attitude
- improving maintenance and auditing
- maintaining awareness

Importantly, testing provides a way of reducing uncertainty, both as to what could happen and how an organization will react to recover business activities. Testing provides a benchmark for the BCM process in terms of how successful initiation was, the appropriateness of planning for business continuity and the degree of success in overcoming resistance to change. Testing provides an opportunity to shift the view of BCM as being a theoretical necessity to being a practical one by extending involvement throughout an organization. The planning process (see Chapter 4) should have determined the type and frequency of tests. A key difficulty is that testing will be subject to the range of demands facing an organization.

Preparing for tests

Before a test, the BC manager must decide what is to be tested and how it is to be tested. This involves two decisions: setting the context and setting the scope of response. Setting the context for the test in the form of a scenario (perhaps one identified in the planning process) is intended to address specific causes of interruption and to trigger the invocation of plans. Typical scenarios may include:

- chemical/hazard spill
- Information Systems shutdown
- logistics interruption
- loss of a building (totally, temporarily, indefinitely)
- loss of key customer
- loss of utilities (power, telecommunications, water)
- loss of a key supplier
- threat to reputation

Setting the scope for the response refers to the frequency of testing (quarterly, yearly, etc.) and whether tests are announced or unannounced. Announced tests serve to evaluate the procedures within a plan. Unannounced tests are designed to evaluate whether employees can respond to an unexpected event and implement plans as originally intended. As Doemland (1999) notes, such tests may also provide a means of assessing an individual's capacity for decision-making under stress. Generally, announced tests are undertaken more frequently. Setting the context and scope of the test is important because it underpins the expectations and criteria against which the efficacy of the test will be assessed.

Types of tests

Desk check tests are the simplest and most frequent form of tests. The author of the plan simply checks the contents of the plan to ensure that information, such as named employees and telephone numbers, are up to date. In addition, the desk check should consider whether the plan reflects the organization's operations as they currently stand. If, for example, a department has taken on new responsibilities within an organization, this may necessitate revisions, which are undertaken in the maintenance phase discussed later in this section. The rapidity of organizational change influenced by staff turnover as well as environmental shifts requires a regular, if not ongoing, monitoring of business unit responsibilities. Some organizations (such as the AA) carry out desk checks with two persons, in order to ensure that the limitations of a single person's knowledge does not hamper the verification of the plan.

Walk-through exercises are similar to desk checks in their execution but involve all named participants (which will vary between plans and organizations). The participants are brought together to role-play their defined resumption procedures alongside those of others. In this way, issues such as the timing of activities, reporting lines and coordination between incumbents can be verified. Often, the walk-through is undertaken to meet a specified disruption scenario. From these exercises, business continuity coordinators can initiate maintenance to ensure that coordination is enhanced when the plan is invoked in a real situation.

Simulation exercises widen participation to all those who are to be involved in business recovery. Such tests are conducted with prior notice to all employees concerned. In this type of test, an interruption, such as a building fire, provides a scenario in which employees do not have access to normal facilities and must recreate the working environment in an alternative location. In addition, role-plays are used to ensure that business continuity activities such as customer services, public relations and legal affairs can operate under simulated conditions of a disaster. Throughout the exercise, a team of observers is responsible for recording how recovery activities were undertaken, whether they conformed to procedures laid down in plans and whether problems or omissions in the plan become apparent. Since a simulation exercise is designed to test the integration of plans from the zero hour to 72 hours or more, often a system of 'accelerated time' is used, whereby the simulation requires all steps to be completed in a quarter of the time normally required. Where this approach is taken, activities are not 'completed' but 'acknowledged', whereby the personnel responsible will simulate the procedure in the correct order and register its 'completion' with the manager responsible for coordinating the overall recovery process (normally the BC manager).

Function/operational testing is limited in scope to one or two departments/functions. In such a test, normal facilities are closed and employees must recreate their working environment in an alternative location, such as another company building or at the premises of a third-party supplier. The purpose of these tests is to ensure that a function can be recovered to another location in the time-scale set down in the BC plan, and to ensure that sufficient resources are available to resume adequately a minimum level of service. For instance, a function test may reveal that employees were able to move a telephone sales department to an alternative site quickly, only to find that insufficient telephone lines and computer terminals were available. During the test, observers are in place to note such anomalies and areas for improvement.

Full/live exercises are the most extensive and expensive form of test. Consequently they are normally only undertaken on a yearly or bi-yearly basis. This is the largest-scale test and involves the invocation of the main BC plans and functional BC policies to deal with a scenario, which normally involves a move to another site where operations are to be resumed and organizational preparedness is evaluated. Live exercises differ from other tests because participants are not given prior notice of the invocation. Accordingly, this ensures that, are far as is possible, the test is the most rigorous that could be achieved without facing a real disaster. The dependencies and links between different plans are a focal point of this type of testing. For example, individual plans may have time-lines of recovery that are, in isolation, consistent and coordinated. In a full test, it may be the case that variations in the time-lines of recovery between different functions conspire to hamper recovery efforts.

In addition, the full test raises organization-wide awareness of the impact that a disaster could have. When an entire facility has to invoke its plans and cease normal operations, this is the ultimate test of whether the two most vital recovery resources – plans and personnel – can work together effectively. Only then can BC managers and coordinators fully evaluate the effectiveness of pre-planning, decision-making, coordination and awareness-raising. Normally, senior management approval is required before such tests can take place and the timing of these events may coincide with quieter periods in the calendar (although a successful resumption during a quiet period could be misleading).

Post-test evaluations

The post-test evaluation should be conducted by the BC managers, coordinators and independent observers (where used). With specific reference to the plans and bearing in mind the context and the scope of response, the following issues should be considered:

- Did the plans help or hinder recovery efforts?
- Did people deviate from the plan and, if so, what was the effect of this?
- Were recovery time objectives (RTOs) achieved?
- Where and when did delays occur?
- What did staff do well?
- What did staff do badly?
- How did the expectations differ from what actually happened?
- Were functional policies/plans integrated sufficiently to achieve recovery?
- What are the priorities for change?
- How should changes be implemented?
- Could the observation process be improved?

Questionnaires can be used to gather information from participants and to demonstrate that the users of plans have some input into how they are formed, developed and presented. In addition, questionnaires can be valuable for measuring attitudes towards BCM over time. If questionnaire surveys are carried out regularly, this provides important information to the BCM team about changing attitudes toward BCM. The results could highlight that the barriers to change (see Chapter 5) have not been removed, prompting improvements to training, communication and control-and-reward systems. Depending on the outcome of the post-test evaluation, maintenance and auditing will follow.

Maintenance and auditing

Maintenance is a generic term for a number of activities that are designed to evaluate whether BC plans are up to date, i.e. their relevance. Maintenance, like testing, should be undertaken regularly to ensure that plans accurately mirror the organization's structure and operations. As a plan is only as effective as its most recent test, so too is it as relevant to organizational needs as its most recent maintenance. Maintenance can be triggered in two ways: testing (as above) or periodic reviews.

The BC manager and those at a departmental/functional level responsible for ensuring that plans are not out of date undertake periodic reviews. In many ways, periodic reviews are similar to desk check tests, and in some cases this type of test will be used as the most regular form of maintenance.

Auditing is a generic term for a number of activities that are designed to evaluate whether BC plans are appropriate, i.e. meet the specific needs of a changing organization. This activity has wider connotations and implications, and may require a new BIA and BIE (Chapter 4). If testing has shown that plans have failed to meet major recovery objectives, a fundamental review of provisions may be required. In particular, where an organization has grown in such a way that it now has new information systems, departments, facilities, or has been involved in merger or acquisition, maintenance will be insufficient to ensure that plans are appropriate.

BCM as a continuous organizational process

Plans are live documents. If they are not sustained, improved and, when necessary, changed, the investment in BCM will be wasted. Moreover, if a plan is perceived to be of little help both during tests and in real invocations, support for BCM will falter. BCM often starts as a minor project, with little investment yet with major strategic importance; a failure to engage support from the organization will increase the barriers to change BCM intends to reduce. Moreover, BCM should be considered to be more than a project, which implies a small-scale temporary activity. Few organizations can invest in BCM on a large scale at start-up, but this does not mean that, as time passes, BCM should not become a normal part of every activity within an organization. This is why we refer to BCM as a process: it is ongoing, continual, organization-wide and normalized.

Continuity plans

There can be no simple prescription for the content of business continuity and major incident plans. At one level, the major incident plan is concerned with the coordination of an organization's response to a significant interruption. It provides a process for activating those mechanisms required to ensure that the continuity response is conducted in the best interests of the entire organization. At another, the major incident plan will probably be a short document identifying roles and responsibilities of the strategic, tactical and operational groups as well as indicating where key information is located. Detailed plans will lie at the operational level, for each business unit, team or support function. Personnel may have plans for a range of alternative scenarios, from outlining support for staff in the event of a major relocation following the loss of a building, through to using last month's BACS payroll data in the event of a loss of current employee information.

Crisis communications

How might corporate image and reputation help or hinder an organization's crisis response? The wealth of material dealing with crisis from a communications perspective indicates that its importance is well understood (see, for example, Stone, 1995; Regester and Larkin, 1997). It is not the purpose of this chapter simply to repeat what is available elsewhere. The books identified above provide useful prescriptions for crisis communications. Rather, we intend to consider some of the broader issues concerned with crisis communications. The underlying philosophy of our approach is that sound preparation builds resilience. Nowhere is this more true than with regard to crisis communications. An organization's historical context, expressed in the form of the established corporate reputation, can be seen as a crucial factor in determining the efficacy of crisis communications. As Shrivastava observed:

> Crisis communications is not a short-term, one-shot public relations effort, or a one-way transfer of pertinent information from organizations to the public. Instead it should be viewed as establishment of permanent long-term communicative relationships with multiple internal and external stakeholders. Communication implies not only the transfer of information, but an exchange of information and underlying assumptions, and discourse aimed at reaching a common understanding of issues.
>
> (1987: 5)

This reputational context will be determined by the fit of crisis communications with a number of factors including:

- ongoing marketing communications
- relationship with the media
- history of previous incidents (expressed in terms of the affected organization and its broader industrial sector)
- previous experience of successfully dealing with events
- stakeholder relationships
- organizational culture and structure

Ongoing marketing communications refers to branding, advertising and promotional issues. Perrier water's close association with 'naturally pure' was struck an almost fatal blow when it was contaminated with benzene. Perrier was perceived as a secretive, awkward organization with poor media relations preceding the crisis. Cunard was vilified for its tardy handling of passenger complaints when its expensively refitted luxury liner was not ready in time for a cruise. Disgruntled passengers received extensive media coverage damaging the company's image. Contrast that with the plaudits received by P&O when affected by a similar problem. In May 2000 P&O's brand new, £200 million cruise ship *Aurora* limped back into port after breaking down one day into her maiden voyage. *Aurora*'s 1,800 passengers were bitterly disappointed at the cancellation of their once-in-a-lifetime holiday cruise. Clearly, maintaining customer confidence in this luxury market demanded a quick, super response. Passengers were quickly offered a full compensation package, which included a refund on their ticket as well as another free cruise of an equivalent value costing P&O's insurers an estimated £6 million.

Reputation may be damaged when stars paid to endorse particular brands are implicated in a scandal. When O.J. Simpson was alleged to have murdered his wife, Hertz Rent A Car ended a ten-year-long advertising campaign featuring the sportsman. Michael Jackson's paid endorsement of Pepsi terminated shortly after he was alleged to have been involved in impropriety. Star endorsement in such scenarios is double edged with negative associations potentially replacing positive ones.

Effective crisis communications, it is suggested, can be nourished by a reservoir of goodwill, built up with the media and customers alike. Such resources cannot deal with a crisis on their own, but they can provide a powerful platform from which to launch an effective crisis communications strategy.

Effective communications requires getting the right message to the right stakeholder group. During the pre-crisis stage, this requires that organizations identify:

- who their stakeholders are
- what problems the crisis causes for them
- what their initial perceptions of the organization are
- the best means of communicating with them
- the message or information that they require

Increasingly, utility companies maintain detailed databases of customers so that they can quickly identify the likely consequences of an interruption. Such databases may include at-risk groups, be they elderly residents, young families or major industries requiring significant resources. Some databases record when groups may have been affected by previous interruptions, or where influential environmental groups or politicians are located. From a self-interested point of view, this provides a useful warning of public embarrassment. Such monitoring requires significant investment and commitment. A growing dimension of marketing concerns the development of relationships within industrial and consumer markets (Egan, 1995). Relationships are increasingly seen as the key to success and it may be a truism to say that most relationships founder when truly tested. An increasing amount of evidence suggests that strong loyalties can be developed where there is a long record of assistance during crises.

The means of communicating must be closely linked to the content and purpose of a message. For example, personal telephone communications is the mode chosen by hospital trusts to communicate with patients who have received the wrong treatment or have been treated by a medic with an infectious disease. A personal touch is important and the target group is well defined. Product recalls of consumer goods are usually handled via the print and broadcast media, depending upon the threat of the difficulty and the likely public interest. Radio may be used for urgent, local warnings such as major pollution scares. During winter, local radio is often the best source of information on the effects of snow. It is difficult to be prescriptive as the demands of every interruption will differ. Further advice can be found in Regester and Larkin (1995) and Lagadec (1993).

Summary

This chapter has sought to provide some insight into the key issues associated with incident management. The adhocracy has been put forward as the model crisis management team. Carefully selected, well-trained, multi-skilled and able to draw on up-to-date documents, the crisis management team needs to retain some flexibility. Distinction between gold, silver and bronze level activities highlights the different roles needed to manage with an interruption effectively. Other key issues during the operational crisis stage concern staff health and welfare, and effective communications. Change will affect different staff in different ways and supervisory staff must be aware of the symptoms. Similarly, those with a coordinating role must consider ways of either reducing the burden upon individuals or else implement practical steps to support staff. Although crisis communications are seen as a key part of response, it has been argued that pre-crisis investment in this area will reap rich rewards. Training, maintenance and auditing will play a key role in exposing staff to potential stressors, raising capabilities and identifying communication needs. They help ensure that the best possible support is available to staff called upon to deal with an interruption. They also provide an opportunity for staff to experience in some way the possible stressors of incident management. This, as we have argued, will reduce the negative aspect of stress. Finally, we have considered, briefly, the essentials of communications management. In this, we have sought to emphasize that good communications is built up from firm foundations and is unlikely to appear out of the ether following an interruption.

References

Belbin, R.M. (1981) *Management Teams: Why They Succeed or Fail*, Oxford: Butterworth-Heinemann.

Brown, J.M. and Campbell, E.A. (1994) *Stress and Policing: Sources and Strategies*, Chichester: John Wiley.

Cameron, K.H. (1994) 'An international company's approach to managing major incidents', *Disaster Management* 3(2).

Carley, K. (1991) 'Designing organizational structures to cope with communication breakdowns: a simulation model', *Industrial Crisis Quarterly* 5(1): 19–57.

Cox, T. (1978) *Stress*, London: Macmillan Education.

Cranwell-Ward, J. (1990) *Thriving on Stress*, London: Routledge.

Doemland, T. (1999) 'Awareness through auditing, testing and training', in A. Hiles, and P. Barnes (1999) *The Definitive Handbook of Business Continuity Management*, Chichester: John Wiley.

Egan, C. (1995) *Creating Organizational Advantage*, Oxford: Butterworth-Heinemann.

Elliott, D. and Smith, D. (1993) 'Coping with the sharp end: recruitment and selection in the Fire Service', *Disaster Management* 5(1): 35–41.

Elliott, D. and Smith, D. (2000) 'Opening Pandora's box', in E. Cole, D. Smith and S. Tombs (2000) (eds) *Managing in the Risk Society*, Cambridge: Kluwer.

Fisher, S. (1986) *Stress and Strategy*, London: Lawrence Erlbaum.

Flin, R. (1996) *Sitting in the Hot Seat*, London: John Wiley.

Ginn, R.D. (1989) *Continuity Planning: Preventing, Surviving and Recovering from Disaster*, Oxford: Elsevier Advanced Technology.

Government Centre for Information Systems (CCTA) (1995a) *An Introduction to Business Continuity Management*, London: HMSO.

Government Centre for Information Systems (CCTA) (1995b) *A Guide to Business Continuity Management*, London: HMSO.

Hiles, A. and Barnes, P. (1999) *The Definitive Handbook of Business Continuity Management*, Chichester: John Wiley.

Home Office (1997a) *Business as Usual: Maximising Business Resilience to Terrorist Bombings*, London: Home Office.

Home Office (1997b) *Bombs, Protecting People and Property*, 3rd edn, London: Home Office.

HSE (2001) 'Health and Safety Executive guidance notes on stress' [on-line] http://www.hse.gov.co.uk/pubns/stress2.htm, accessed 4 June 2001.

Lagadec, P. (1993) *Preventing Chaos in a Crisis*, Maidenhead: McGraw-Hill.

Lazarus, R.S. (1966) *Psychological Stress and the Coping Process*, New York: McGraw- Hill.

Lazarus, R.S (1999) *Stress and Emotion: A New Synthesis*, London: Free Association Books.

Lazarus, R.S. and Folhman, S. (1984) *Stress, Appraisal, and Coping*, New York: Springer.

Lazarus, R.S. and Launier, R. (1978) 'Stress-related transactions between person and environment', in L.A. Pervin and M. Lewis (eds) *Internal and External Determinants of Behavior*, New York: Plenum.

McFadden, T. (1993) 'World Trade Center', *New York Times* 6 February: 5.

Mellish, S. (2000) 'J Sainsbury and the fuel crisis', *Continuity* 4 (4): 3–6.

Mintzberg, H. (1983) *The Structuring of Organisations*, Englewood Cliffs, NJ: Prentice Hall.

Mintzberg, H. and Waters, J. (1985) 'Of strategies, deliberate and emergent', *Strategic Management Journal* 6: 257–72.

Pauchant, T. and Mitroff, I. (1988) 'Crisis-prone versus crisis avoiding organizations: is your company's culture its own worst enemy in creating crises?', *Industrial Crisis Quarterly* 2: 53–63.

Pauchant, T. and Mitroff, I. (1992) *Transforming the Crisis-Prone Organisation*, San Francisco: Jossey-Bass.

Perry, K. (2000) 'Cruise down the Swanee: *Aurora*'s maiden voyage halted', *The Guardian* 3 May: 5.

Raiffa, H. (1968) *Decision Analysis*, Reading, MA: Addison Wesley cited in C. Smart and I. Vertinsky (1977) 'Designs for crisis decision units', *Administrative Science Quarterly* 22: 640–57.

Raphael, B., Meldrum, L. and McFarlane, A.C. (1995) 'Does debriefing after psychological trauma work?', *British Medical Journal* 310: 1479–80.

Reason, J. (1997) *Managing the Risks of Organizational Accidents*, Aldershot: Ashgate,

Regester, M. and Larkin, J. (1997) *Risk Issues and Crisis Management*, London: Kogan Page.

Rick, J. and Briner, R. (2000) *Trauma Management vs. Stress Debriefing: What Should Responsible Organizations Do?*, London: HSE Books.

Shrivastava, P. (1987) 'Are we ready for another Three Mile Island, Bhopal, Tylenol?', *Industrial Crisis Quarterly* 1(1): 2–4.

Smart, C. and Vertinsky, I. (1977) 'Designs for crisis decision units', *Administrative Science Quarterly* 22: 640–57.

Smith, D. (2000) 'Crisis management teams: issues in the management of operational crises', *Risk Management: An International Journal* 2(3): 61–78.

Stone, N. (1995) *The Management and Practice of Public Relations*, London: Macmillan.

Strohl Systems (1995) *The Business Continuity Planning Guide*, King of Prussia, PA: Strohl Systems.

ten Berge, D. (1990) *The First 24 Hours*, Oxford: Basil Blackwell.

Turner, B. (1976) 'The organizational and interorganizational development of disasters', *Administrative Science Quarterly* 21: 378–97.

Turner, B. and Pidgeon, N. (1997) *Man-made Disasters*, 2nd edn, London: Butterworth-Heinemann.

Warr, P. (1990) 'The measurement of wellbeing and other aspects of mental health', *Journal of Occupational Psychology* 63: 193–210.

Further reading

Elliott, D. and Smith, D. (2000) 'Opening Pandora's Box', in S. Cole, D. Smith and S. Tombs *Managing in the Risk Society*, Cambridge: Kluwer.

Flin, R. (1996) *Sitting in the Hot Seat*, London: John Wiley.

Morwood, G. (1998) 'Business continuity: awareness and training programmes', *Information Management and Computer Security* 6(1): 28–32.

Smallman, C. and Weir, D. (1999) 'Communication and cultural distortion during crises', *Disaster Prevention and Management* 8(1): 33–41.

Study questions

1 (a) What are the different types of test?
   (b) What are their advantages and disadvantages?
2 Consider Barclays Bank negative publicity in 2000–1. What were the factors behind this? What advice would you give to Barclays to avoid such negative publicity in the future?
3 What are the elements of an effective crisis management team?
4 How might stress influence decision-making capabilities?

7 Business continuity
Where next?

Introduction

It has been a key argument of this book that business continuity concerns more than IS security, from which the discipline emerged. The ubiquity of IS and our dependence upon it makes it a natural focus for continuity efforts. However, as we enter the twenty-first century the range and types of business interruptions are likely to grow. What is the role of business continuity likely to be in the new millennium? Throughout this book we have sought to distinguish between the trigger and consequence. Buildings, information systems, hardware and other assets are only means to an end, that is, means of satisfying customers. The typology of crisis introduced in Chapter 4 provided some insight into the potential range of interruptions (see Figure 4.4). Mellish (2000), for example, described how Sainsburys activated their plans for dealing with the so-called millennium bug when faced with a fuel crisis caused by a blockade of UK oil refineries. A plan developed to deal with the millennium bug fitted the needs of a potential crisis triggered by angry lorry drivers.

The concern of this chapter is with the future challenges facing business continuity management. Our starting point is to consider the challenges posed by developments in the political, economic, social and technological environment. These aspects of the business environment provide important 'push' and 'pull' factors for continuity management. Business continuity may have its roots in the protection of computer systems but we hope that, through the many examples cited throughout the preceding chapters, we have illustrated how the discipline is maturing and changing. We therefore wish to stress that, despite beginning this chapter with the challenges posed by developments in the new economy and e-commerce, we are concerned with the organization in a holistic manner and interested in how physical systems can be threatened by virtual systems and vice versa. The Internet and e-commerce merely emerge as the most significant technology-push factors affecting organizations and business continuity now and probably during the next decade. However, they are not the only significant changes in the business environment and others are discussed later.

The chapter begins with a consideration of how the new economy provides a new context for continuity management. The implications of e-commerce for the continuum of business continuity practice are examined. From the outset it is argued that e-commerce represents only one of the most obvious challenges for continuity management. Later themes are, however, inextricably linked with the Internet or at least with interdependence. The Internet provides the technical dimension of many of the changes that together form a 'postmodern' world. Interest in reputation management, for example, has grown rapidly as organizations recognize that poor images can be beamed around the world instantly; for example, in the case of Firestone and the Ford Motor Company during autumn 2000. The rise of consumerism and activism has also been fuelled by new technologies, whether hackers target Microsoft's software or employ technology to organize campaigns. These themes do not provide an exhaustive list but draw on our anticipation of the most important and imminent developments that organizations should be aware of.

The new economy

The explosive growth of Internet-based business, the rise in value of technology-based companies and the fact that high technology companies listed on the Nasdaq[1] in the USA now consistently attract more investment than those on the New York Stock Exchange make it clear that the new economy has dawned. The new economy is shaped by the manner in which financial markets and commentators regard and value companies. Its chief feature appears to be extreme share price volatility and uncertainty. Indeed, whole sectors such as pharmaceuticals and financial services, that have always been very profitable areas, have been relegated to second-class citizen status for investment as they are not seen to be a part of the new economy.

At the company level, the development of this new economy creates strategic issues that companies have to contend with. At the level of corporate strategy, the board has to be clear about the direction of a company. However, this is not easy at a time of fundamental change and when those who comprise the board do not have a deep knowledge of the new technology and its capabilities. Skapinker (2000) points out two additional issues of strategic concern to boards. The first is how to value companies – old methods do not work any longer, particularly when companies that have not made a profit have such huge and volatile valuations, evidenced by Freeserve which was sold by its parent company for a much lower figure than its original valuation.

The second issue concerns how conventional companies should respond to the new challengers on the Internet. Large, established companies appear to have particularly difficult challenges in this respect. Moss-Kanter (2001) found two patterns of company behaviour regarding exploitation of the Internet. 'Pacesetters' embraced the Internet early and exploited it as a channel. Alternatively 'Laggards' described companies unable to support change processes internal to the organization that would move employees to embrace the Internet as another point of contact with consumers. Many large companies reported that they had spent substantial sums of money on Internet sites without deriving any benefit. One company reported spending $100 million on 1,000 websites without any quantifiable benefits (Moss-Kanter, 2001). The issues that inhibit action to embrace the Internet will clearly vary across industries and for different brands. It is clear that organizations may experience resistance internally from constituencies such as salesforces (Moss-Kanter, 2001), who regard new channels as a threat. For franchised organizations there may be resistance from franchisees who might regard the Internet as a threat to sales at 'brick and mortar' sites – for example, the reaction of the franchisees to the launch of the Body Shop website (Body Shop International, 2000). Finally, established organizations have to be cognizant of the balance of power within their industry. Today retailers increasingly wield power in fast-moving consumer goods industries, requiring caution from manufacturers intent on establishing their own websites as part of a multi-channel strategy. Large retailers may retaliate should a manufacturer wish to sell direct to the consumer. Unusual partnerships may emerge such as that between Amazon and Wal-Mart announced in March 2001. Organizations may need to consider the remuneration of key staff, with Yahoo! executives choosing equity holdings in place of salaried positions: dramatic falls in market value have led to an exodus of key personnel (Hutton, 2001).

What is clear is that the new millennium and new technology have thrown up incredible opportunities (economic growth through technological change and productivity increases), extreme uncertainty and many challenges. How companies respond to these will depend upon the strategy they adopt and we argue that crisis management and business continuity will have to occupy central roles in formulating corporate strategy. Directors clearly play a crucial role in determining that these issues are dealt with from a continuity perspective. Yet, few if any companies today have BCM[2] represented at board level, even though the current conditions provide a strong case for such representation to become normalized. The value-based mindset, introduced in Chapter 1, indicated that some organizations have attempted to integrate business continuity by ensuring a structural link to the board via a senior director. In better-practice companies it was not unusual to find that business continuity managers would be invited to brief the board on specific strategic issues (Herbane *et al.*, 1997).

The effect of globalization and normalization of business continuity requires that it becomes a transnational activity as R&D has become in sectors such as telecommunications and pharmaceuticals. This means that plans from different regions should be as integrated as the operations they seek to protect. Accordingly, business continuity planners will need to be aware of organizational, cultural and national differences for plans to maintain their potential.

E-continuity

In Chapter 1 three different business continuity mindsets were identified. It was argued that, during the early years of the twenty-first century, business continuity would become 'normalized' in certain types of environment, becoming an integral part of the management task. It was also argued that practice would be influenced by an organization's experience of interruptions, management style and approach to technology and strategy. Thus, some organizations would develop a more sophisticated approach to continuity management than others. A continuum of practice was put forward, bounded by polarities of either 'standard practice' or 'better practice', depending on the scope of preparations and how embedded business continuity had become within the organization. This model was developed from earlier research (see Herbane *et al.*, 1997). The term 'better practice' was employed to emphasize that, despite the suggestion of polarities, there was no intention to suggest that the best practice of 1997 constituted an end-point. Figure 7.1 provides a modified version of the BCM continuum that considers how the Internet will force organizations to modify their BCM focus, progressing from a disaster recovery focus through a value-based continuity focus, to an e-continuity focus. This will be driven primarily by a realization that there is no end-point in pursuing organizational preparedness. Indeed, the philosophy of continuous improvement and the learning organization have been used as an analogy for the learning that needs to occur about BCM. The field is in its infancy and the possibilities are endless.

'E-continuity' refers to the provision of BCM services to e-commerce sites as well as the virtual networks, which they spawn. Indeed, it is salutary that the Year 2000 problem effectively became a non-event in most countries, only to be replaced by disruption to e-commerce sites in early January 2000. What

'Standard practice'	'Better practice'	Continuous improvement
Old	New	Virtual
Disaster recovery	**BCM**	**(e-continuity?)**
IT focus	Value chain focus	Virtual value chain focus
IT staff	Multi-disciplinary team	Intra-organizational teams
Existing structure	New structures	Virtual structures
Protect core operations	Protect entire organization	Protect virtual organization
Sustain current position	Create sustainable advantage	Compelling performance
Parochial view	Open system view	Virtual system view
Recovery emphasis system	Prevention emphasis	Up and down the virtual value

Figure 7.1 From disaster recovery to e-continuity

both businesses and consumers suddenly discovered was that, once your main supplier's site was targeted and shut down, your own business could not operate – 'e-continuity' is being driven by changes in economic sectors as fundamental as those experienced during the industrial revolution.[3] Indeed, the Internet exposes the fact that no organization can exist on its own, a fundamental concept in crisis management thinking.

Figure 7.1 illustrates how, as organizations become more reliant on virtual networks, the focus of BCM has to shift in an appropriate way to capture the networked nature of business. Thus, strategic analysis has to take into account virtual value chains and external networks. No longer will it be appropriate to focus solely upon staff within the organization but intra-organizational teams have to be considered; a virtual systems view will need to replace thinking about conventional organizational boundaries and continuous improvement focus needs to be considered both up and down the virtual value system.

Providing continuity for virtual value chains

A key issue for business continuity will be the provision of continuity for virtual value chains. The virtual value chain refers to the new opportunities for value creation, facilitated by ICT and the Internet in particular (see Box 7.1). It has been argued that commerce on the Internet creates a 'market space' in addition to the normal marketplace in which business transactions take place (Rayport and Sviokla, 1995). Rayport and Sviokla present the case of a virtual value chain, which runs parallel to the value chain that defines the conventional activities of the company. Three conditions are necessary before the virtual value chain can yield value.

- First, companies have to use information systems to coordinate the activities in their conventional value chain in such a manner that those activities become *visible* as a process.
- A second condition is that of '*mirroring capability*' in which physical activities are substituted by virtual ones, creating the infrastructure of the virtual value chain.
- Third is the creation of *new customer relationships* – it is during this stage that real value can be added by revolutionizing product offerings.

Continuity plays a role in all aspects of the three conditions of building a virtual business, but particularly during the stage of establishing customer relationships, as this is when customers are receiving a product or service that has utility. A break in continuity during this phase of the virtual value chain destroys value for both the client company and the provider of the virtual service. During the stage where visibility is established client organizations are not themselves affected should a website not be accessible. Similarly, where a company still provides a service through conventional channels, the

---

Box 7.1 Oracle

Many users of database technology will be aware that Oracle now offers new products over the Internet as well as through conventional channels. If you wish to make use of their trend analysis software for research purposes, or XML software for authoring web pages, you will discover that these are only available online. This is a new trend in the delivery of software to consumers of such products. The trend originates in the wave of innovation that the Internet has enabled. New e-business applications are currently being brought to market. These include Blue Martini (integration of online and offline sales channels), diCarta (contract management software) and Dorado (Kehoe, 2001). Dorado is a pioneer in software provision in financial services. The company does not sell software licenses as it would traditionally do. Instead, it sells access to web-based services on a usage fee basis. The company has made inroads into providing web-based solutions to mortgage banks and lenders in the US. Among its clients is Chase Manhattan Mortgage Company, which uses an e-commerce platform to enable 1,300 loan officers at branches to create their own, customizable websites. The company uses this as an element of its Internet marketing strategy.

Source: Kehoe (2001, [online]
http: //www.dorado.com/news/releases2000061401.html)

---

client organization has the option to consume the service through such channels. Such options may not exist in the final stage of establishing new customer relationships. This leads us to consider the implications of some developments in e-commerce.

Implications of the growth of e-commerce

The new economy is exemplified by the rapid take-off of e-commerce. By e-commerce we mean that there are effectively three processes of importance. Consumers usually experience the sales side of e-commerce, be this in the form of business-to-consumer or business-to-business sales. However, to enable sales, the e-company has to acquire raw materials, and transform these into saleable goods. On the purchasing end of e-commerce, a key activity emerges in the form of managing the supply chain in such a manner that efficiency is maximized across the entire chain, but particularly in logistics and distribution. On the sales side, customer relationship management becomes essential, calling for new electronically based administrative tools and possibly even a call centre through which to make all this possible.

The main strategic risks that are associated with doing business on the Internet have been divided into the following (Clemons, 2000). First, structural risk arises from business models that do not heed industry structure and profitability in certain industries or sectors. Thus, we know that in the toy business, profit margins range between 35 per cent and 40 per cent but that this is now known to be too low to sustain the structure of online toy companies when their investment in e-commerce technology, advertising, warehousing and fulfilment costs are factored into their business model. Clemons (2000) points out that most large retailers, such as e-Toys and Amazon.com, are still acquiring customers and paying to win market share. Risk is also present in the fact that online retailers have less latitude with pricing as the web makes both costs and pricing much more transparent than would conventionally be the case, forcing retailers of consumer goods to sell at cost or below the optimum price for their products. Indeed, the troubled e-Toys discovered that it would be more profitable for them to launch a range of own-label toys that would yield around 75 per cent margin. Alas, at the time of writing this chapter, it would appear that this vital piece of learning will not be put into practice but that others will learn from the mistake made by e-Toys.

Second, e-commerce puts at risk established relationships within a value system. Clemons (2000) refers to this as channel risk. Most companies make use of distribution networks to reach the consumer. We are all aware, through making use of intermediaries such as travel agents, that many such organizations are threatened by the existence of online sites owned by the airline companies themselves, who increasingly sell directly to the consumer. Conversely, if you wish to run an online company, it is imperative that you choose partners who will prove to be dependable. For example, the difficulties that characterized fulfilment services at the ToysRUs.com warehouses in the US during Christmas 1999/2000 caused a strong reaction against the company. Once packages did leave the warehouse many still did not reach their destination promptly. The negative publicity and consumer reaction to this forced the company to reconsider their strategy and choose a partnership with Amazon.com in the hope that they could piggyback on Amazon's capabilities.

Sourcing risk involves over-dependence upon one or a few critical suppliers. This may also be associated with the transfer of critical information to a strategic supplier (Clemons, 2000) that may decide to start up in competition. Finally, risk of strategic uncertainty arises when trends are misread or misunderstood and preparations are made on incorrect assumptions. Rapid technological changes make this a more likely event for online business than for conventional companies. How to determine the behaviour of buyers in the online world would require a crystal ball at present and this makes it difficult for companies to respond. Overall, therefore, it is clear that e-commerce requires a completely new set of strategic capabilities which may usefully draw their inspiration from the tools and techniques of BCM. We discussed some of these tools in Chapter 4.

In terms of security, e-commerce raises an interesting conundrum for organizations: as IT infrastructure becomes more complex and organizations more networked, it becomes sensible to outsource the design and management of e-commerce solutions to specialists but place at a slight distance control over security. Such a situation played itself out on Wednesday, 5 April 2000, when the London Stock Exchange (LSE) did not open for trading until 15: 45, creating havoc on the last trading day of the tax year (BBC, 2001). The incident apparently arose because of technical problems inside the electronic share dealing system itself and the then chief executive of the exchange, Gavin Casey, admitted the following day that they did not fully understand what went wrong to cause the outage. The LSE outsources responsibility for the computerized system to Andersen Consulting who worked through the night to correct system errors. It appears that two of the processing systems were not synchronized and that this could have been induced by the sheer volume of trade generated the previous day by the dramatic swings and volumes of trade in the US market. Data was corrupted and the exchange could not make use of incorrect share information. Even the back-up systems were not useful as they relied upon the same corrupted information (*Financial Times*, 2000a: 8).

The LSE outage demonstrates how tightly coupled technological systems have become today, and how much more vulnerable companies will become because of the convergence of technology. Over the next decade e-commerce and globalization will be major influences on continuity management – indeed, one could argue that this has already happened when one considers the huge increase in Internet-based crime or business interruptions.

Managing the virtual value system

It is important to understand how the growth of e-commerce will transform the way business is done. The most important implication of e-commerce concerns changes in company supply chains or value systems, creating, as we noted earlier, a virtual value chain. In the case of some organizations there is no doubt that a virtual value chain can exist alongside the conventional one. For example, the UK grocer Tesco's success in pioneering an e-commerce arm is such that there is speculation of its flotation in the near future. A number of companies from the 'old' economy are now fighting back to get a presence on the Internet. Such companies have the advantage of having sufficient transaction volumes to make e-commerce viable. There are partnerships between companies from the old and new economies such as that between the chemicals group Du Pont, with Internet Capital Group (ICG) which manages business-to-business sites (*Financial Times*, 2000b).

All companies involved in commercial or financial transactions depend to some extent upon intermediaries that are crucial in enabling such transactions to occur or to be successfully completed. Such intermediaries might bring together purchasers and suppliers in the case of business-to-business transactions or alternatively consumers and retailers or other service providers in consumer transactions. The service provider or manufacturer might in the past have relied very heavily upon advertising media or networks to facilitate the sale of goods or services to consumers or, in the case of business transactions, to enable purchaser and supplier to conduct a transaction. At the heart of these relationships is the communication of valuable information. It is now evident that the Internet increasingly places such relationships under threat. And if they are not threatened, they are at least irrevocably changed. It is clearly evident in the case of consumer transactions, where traditional intermediaries, in the form of retailers with a physical presence, have discovered that consumers have shunned them in favour of e-commerce companies that sell the same product or service. Consumers appear to make the shift to e-commerce companies once they are convinced that the traditional supplier cannot add value above and beyond that offered by the e-commerce company. The value added need not only be financial but is often not tangible in cases where consumers might wish to have direct contact with a product to test it physically. The process whereby intermediaries become excluded from transactions has become known as 'disintermediation', whereby supplier or other intermediaries are 'removed from the information chain' (Suskind, 2000).

The global automotive and pharmaceutical industries are two sectors of the 'old economy' where the implications of the shift to the new economy are slowly unfolding. 'Disintermediation', or the elimination of some suppliers, will certainly be one outcome of the new technology. Early into the new millennium, both General Motors and Ford declared their intentions to become involved in Internet-based exchanges through which they would be sourcing automotive component supplies. They declared that this would enable savings well into billions of dollars (Burt, 2000). Nasser, Chief Executive of Ford Motor Company, expects the Internet to unleash dramatic changes on normal business practice within the motor industry:

> nothing short of a total reinvention of this company. . . . It will transform how we think, how we operate, how we design and manufacture. Above all, it will change how our dealers communicate and connect with customers.
>
> (cited in Burt, 2000: 1)

Nasser considers a fundamental change in relationships in the industry is likely including:

- Direct selling to consumers via the Internet.
- Shift in power relationship between consumers, dealers and manufacturers. For example, the US Priceline.com acts as a mediator between consumers, dealers and automakers, making transparent issues of supply and demand to the consumer. With a closer relationship between consumer and manufacturer and dealer, consumers are benefiting from a flow of more and better quality information via the Internet, enabling them ultimately to make better value purchases of cars.
- Dealers might become surplus to requirements unless they demonstrate

to consumers how they add value. Indeed, many dealers do participate in the Priceline.com scheme primarily as this helps them, in turn, to manage inventory.

'Disintermediation' therefore has the following implication:

• Where there is increasing convergence between electronic systems of companies and their suppliers, there is a greater need for collaboration in respect of managing the continuity of business systems. All organizations making use of such technology will become a part of the total system and will therefore become exposed should systems fail.

This situation is one which is already fairly commonplace in the financial sector, where a new mindset in respect of system security is required to complement the new means of conducting business (Herbane *et al.*, 1997). It is now accepted by investment banks that, should they wish to do business with another organization and there are convergence implications, they have to submit to inspections of their business continuity or contingency arrangements before contracts are even considered.

Companies such as Ford and General Motors have very quickly been joined by other automotive suppliers in setting up on-line exchanges. This trend is echoed in other sectors too. In the USA, in 2001, pharmaceutical companies involved in drug delivery systems (including Johnson & Johnson) and educational providers (University of Columbia, London School of Economics and others) have indicated that they intend to provide their products via the Internet.

Supply chain issues

In making an analysis of the supply chain changes that might occur due to the Internet we are less concerned with the strategic content of these changes than with the implications of such changes for security. It is clear that the most important security issue becomes who owns which part of the converged telecommunications chain, and who is responsible for safeguarding its integrity. In all of the writing on e-commerce, this aspect is almost always overlooked. The only occasion when it is mentioned is indeed when there is a crisis, such as the interruption to the London Stock Exchange's automated systems. Internet portals clearly present sellers with the opportunity to get products to the right place and at the right time; the chance to streamline the buying and selling process, as well as to deliver efficiency of trade. In terms of continuity, the dilemma that portals present to most of the sellers in the network is three-fold:

• How to ensure that the portal of choice is the one with the best continuity and security in place to prevent an outage such as those suffered by

Yahoo! and Amazon. Yahoo!, for instance, provides an innovative business service in the form of Yahoo! Store through which companies may use the site to run an online store and thus achieve visibility. This is popular with many small companies as transaction costs of having an online presence are kept low and the user has the knowledge that the site is run professionally.

- How to choose a portal that will continue in business! In the US there is doubt about the long-term financial health of many of the health sector portals such as DrKoop.com and PlanetRx.com.
- What internal arrangements might be made to ensure that the company can continue to withstand an attack on company e-commerce sites, which might emerge through the network itself. This is the one part of the chain where a company can have some control.

Chapter 4 highlighted the importance of understanding the dependencies within a company's value system. The same is true of Internet portals. Such increased dependence is set to become even more complex as companies make use of web-hosting. Web-hosting involves the commoditization of software and refers to software companies enabling the downloading of applications to remote data centres. This market is forecast to grow from $2 billion in 1999 to around $29 billion in 2004 (*Financial Times*, 2001). The advent of this service means that user companies become dependent upon telecommunications companies for managing the physical network and to software companies for customizing applications, creating a further complexity in managing systems.

The implications of these developments in virtual networks appears to us to be that some regulation of the continuity of Internet-based companies will need to occur. To some extent this, like all other aspects of the Internet, has been left to the market to determine, as the US legal case being fought over privacy on the Internet illustrates. Given all the attention recently focused upon the Year 2000 problems, it seems ironic that governments have not grasped the importance of ensuring continuity of companies that so fundamentally require electronic networks for their smooth operation.

Security and the new economy

The number of incidents that involve computer viruses such as the 'love bug' and the attack on providers such as Yahoo! during the early months of 2000 demonstrate that the rush to establish control over portals as gatekeepers to the new economy has meant a neglect of security issues. This can be very costly. The Computer Security Institute in the US and the San Francisco Federal Bureau of Investigation's Computer Intrusion Squad surveyed US companies during 1999 and estimated that financial losses due to 'cyber-crime' doubled to more than $226 million during that year (*Financial Times*, 2000b). Approaching 74 per cent of the 600 organizations polled had suffered financial loss due to computer crime. The nature of the crimes are also of interest (sabotage, theft of proprietary information and financial fraud) when one considers that these crimes were committed from both inside and outside the organizations (*Financial Times*, 2000b: 4). The most costly of these, however, appear to be those committed via the Internet, with several of the highly visible e-commerce companies suffering huge losses in early January 2000. At present business-to-business Internet companies appear to be relatively safe but as these organizations grow larger, they too will be subjected to unwanted 'outages'.

The reliance of organizations on mainframe computers saw the emergence of disaster recovery as a discipline from the 1970s onwards. Within this context business continuity has been approached as a discipline to deal with a broad range of operational risks. Implicit has been the view that business continuity practitioners are well placed to support boards of directors in controlling the group of operational risks identified by the Institute of Chartered Accountants in England and Wales' guidance notes for *Implementing Turnbull* (Jones and Sutherland, 1999). It is clear, however, that sharp differences exist in the minds of business continuity practitioners about what their role should be. On one side are those who emphasize the recovery of the technical systems aspect of business continuity. Such a mindset can be seen from the glossary of terms in Doswell's (2000) guide to business continuity management. This 'nuts and bolts' or technology approach is concerned with identifying potential points of failure and preparing contingency plans to recover them in line with corporate objectives. An alternative, augmented, approach incorporates the 'nuts and bolts' but is not driven by them. Instead it focuses upon value and business continuity and is driven by business objectives (see Figure 7.2).

Business continuity has evolved from a focus limited to technology to a much broader, value-based approach. The latter has not replaced the former, it has evolved from it, as depicted in Figure 7.2. The core elements remain but have been augmented in a number of ways. Where the technology phase was driven by IT personnel, the value-based phase is characterized by its employment of staff from a range of business disciplines. Where the technology phase is located firmly in the IT or IS department, the value-based approach places responsibility for continuity management with line business units, supported by a dedicated business continuity team. This symbolizes that continuity management is not an IT or facilities issue alone, but is concerned with continuing value adding activities. A higher profile and closer links to the core business activities arguably ensures that continuity management can be invoked to deal with any interruption, as was the case for J Sainsbury (see Box 7.2).

The perceived link between internal business continuity management and external reputation management is characteristic of the value-based approach. An earlier chapter referred to the example of P&O's rapid response to compensate customers aboard the cruiser *Aurora* and limit

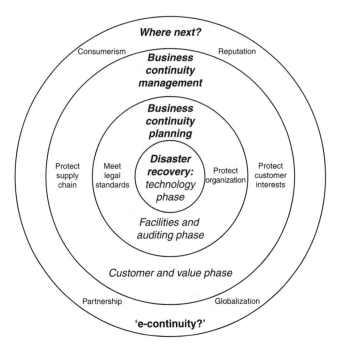

Figure 7.2 Augmenting business continuity

damaging publicity. The importance of reputation management grows all the time, a feature of the media society (Pilger, 1998). The corporate rebrandings and renamings of Monsanto to Pharmacia or British Airways' and British Gas's dropping of the label 'British' from their names represent corporate attempts to shape public opinion. We return to a discussion of reputation management as a theme for the future later in this chapter.

Future themes

Figure 1.2 (Chapter 1) suggested not only that business continuity has constantly evolved but also that this process continues. This section considers a range of themes, divided into the main political, social and economic issues that will provide push factors in the evolution of BCM.

Political

Global web crime – efforts at protection and regulation

The year 2000 should not be noted for the lack of chaos caused by the millennium bug as much as for the jolt given to significant online companies such as Yahoo! and Amazon.com by denial of service attacks. The major

---

Box 7.2   Multiple uses for recovery scenarios

As a major UK retailer of groceries, J Sainsbury prepared comprehensively for possible interruptions during the millennium. Preparations were not restricted to IT failure but were concerned with a wide range of scenarios and could be invoked to deal with many forms of interruptions, as was demonstrated during the UK fuel protests of September 2000 when protestors blockaded UK oil refineries.

Those involved were professional drivers unhappy at the cost of fuel and the levels of duty tax levied by the UK government. The effects were immediate. Fears of shortages encouraged drivers to purchase more fuel than usual. A combination of higher than usual demand and supply difficulties led to a debilitating national shortage of fuel.

During the fuel crisis J Sainsbury invoked a continuity plan developed for dealing with the threat of the millennium bug. Although J Sainsbury experienced difficulties because they were without supplies to their 230 petrol stations, more significant was the sharp increase in demand for staple products like bread, milk, baby food and nappies. Demand for many goods was reaching Christmas levels, placing excessive strain upon unprepared suppliers who were also short of fuel supplies.

The continuity team that dealt with the crisis drew on members from across the organization. It had good communication links with the UK government, suppliers and with its own stores. It heavily influenced all external communications, recognizing that consumer panic buying would simply exacerbate the situation.

Source: Mellish (2000)

---

developments we have witnessed in terms of regulation in recent months have been efforts to focus on how to control the dark side of the Internet! The most significant of these will turn out to be those that are global in nature. During October 2000 the Organization for Economic Co-operation and Development (OECD) led calls for a global effort to enforce Internet security. The OECD appears to be setting itself up as a coordinating body, the aim of which would be to encourage information sharing world-wide (Grande, 2000).

Corporate governance

A key driver of continuity services is regulatory intervention. Within the UK, companies are expected to demonstrate satisfactory risk management and internal control mechanisms. The Turnbull Report (1999) represents the latest step in the evolution of the UK's self-regulatory regime. Where earlier reports were concerned with strengthening audit controls and the roles of non-executive directors following a number of scandals (for example, Maxwell, Polly Peck, Bank of Credit and Commerce International), Turnbull was concerned with board responsibilities for a wide range of risks from market and financial through to operational risks, a convenient catch-all.

At the risk of generalizing, business and government in the USA regard themselves as remarkably free of the kind of intervention that Turnbull and Cadbury represents. Culturally there is a preference for specific, tight industry regulation that has to be enforced, rather than the British model of 'gentlemanly codes'. Food and Drugs Administration (FDA) agencies will come down hard on businesses should they not comply. On Friday, 16 February 2001 the pharmaceutical company Schering-Plough announced that they had to shut down some factories in North America as their practices were found not to comply with FDA production guidelines. The company issued a statement indicating that the FDA would be tying approval for a new allergy drug to successful resolution of their quality control problems (*Financial Times*, 2001). The size and complexity of US industries cause federal regulations to become very important. This does not mean that all companies comply with the letter and spirit of the law. For example, in February 2001 it was revealed that many manufacturers of seafood products did not comply with regulations, and that the FDA did not audit these companies as tightly as they did pharmaceutical companies. The presence of many small companies in this industry presented a 'logistical nightmare'.

Economic

Partnership and prevention

A growing feature of strategic management concerns partnership. Increasingly, the supply chain is recognized as the fundamental unit of competition. Frey and Schlosser (1993) indicate the limitations of traditional competitive bidding within the automotive supply chain, the antithesis of partnership. Put simply, the competitive bids system discourages research and development investment because there is a real risk that such costs will not be recovered. For Womack *et al.* (1990) the adversarial nature of supply chain relations within this industry was identified as a key factor in the decline of the Anglo-US car industry, whilst supplier partnerships were seen as key to the success of the Japanese car industry.

Increasingly, business continuity recognizes that any one interruption will impact upon a number of organizations. Where organizations are tightly coupled, as in just-in-time manufacturing systems, cross-organizational impacts will be virtually immediate. Interruptions may arise where the activities of organizations meet. For example, control of the UK railways is divided between Railtrack, who maintain and build the railway track, and the train companies who manage the trains. The immediate causes of the

Paddington crash in 1999 (in which thirty people died) included the layout of the track and signals (Railtrack's responsibilities) and staff reductions and extended working hours (the railway companies' responsibility). Following the Paddington crash and the subsequent Hatfield crash, the consequences were immense. Railtrack was forced to invest millions in an immediate track improvement scheme; the resulting disruptions forced train cancellations and delays to the cost of the railway companies; virtually every company dependent upon staff commuting by train (e.g. every London-based corporate headquarters or institution) saw an increase in absenteeism or lateness as staff struggled to get to work.

The railways provide the most obvious example of how the repercussions of an interruption may be widespread. However, few interruptions are firmly bounded. The outbreak of foot and mouth in the UK during early 2001 had a major impact upon the farming industry. Livestock hauliers have also lost their livelihoods. Yet the economic costs to tourism were even greater as large tracts of British countryside were closed. The ripples of crisis spread wide. Increasingly, the liability of, response toward, and prevention of, crises of this type will require attention in partnership-type arrangements. Business continuity plans will not only span organizations, but span across them. This is one of the key tasks facing the discipline and can only evolve from a value-based approach. Where a sharp focus upon technical systems and buildings exists the potential for partnership is limited.

Continuity service providers

On the supply side, changes in the BCM industry structure itself are of great importance. Consolidation continues with large players acquiring scarce skills and offering a one-stop continuity shop, from the 'lan-in-a-van' situation during the 1980s and 1990s, to the provision of 'e-continuity' services today. The market has matured greatly over the last two decades – in the UK the disaster recovery services industry grew by 10 to 15 per cent per year during the 1990s. Indeed, the UK business continuity management industry is at an interesting point in its development, with business continuity consultancy services predicted to overtake hardware-focused disaster recovery services soon. International Data Corporation estimates that the market is likely to grow as follows:

- The market for business continuity services is set to increase from £138 million in 1996 to £287 million in 2000.
- Growth in hardware recovery services will reach a compounded annual growth rate in 2001 of 7.5 per cent.
- Expenditure on electronic vaulting (the storage of electronic data as an outsourced service) will constitute a new growth area, reaching £45 million a year in 2001.

(International Data Corporation, 1997)

The potential for the data storage industry to expand beyond storage for industry is potentially also huge, should the 'democratization of data' continue (Lyman and Varian, 2001). Lyman and Varian predict how business in the future will be affected by the greater access to data by individuals made possible by the decreasing real cost of data storage and communications. They conducted research on data storage and found that, despite the growth of industry giants in data storage, such firms store only around 16 per cent of the total digital storage internationally; 56 per cent is stored on individually owned personal computers.

The outlook for the data storage and services industry is therefore very rosy at present. In part this is due to the trends outlined above, but also to the commercial explosion of the web. The Internet has boosted the earnings potential of data storage companies such as EMC, one of the most successful companies of the past decade (Hemp, 2001). The average rate of profit and revenue growth for the company over the last fourteen consecutive quarters has been 20 per cent. Box 7.2 demonstrates how the market has changed and will continue to move away from a highly fragmented industry dominated by smaller players, to one which is controlled by larger companies. Changes in how companies are using technology (web-hosting and the emergence of application service providers) mean that the higher overheads associated with having the correct infrastructure and knowledge competencies will increasingly erect higher barriers to entry to smaller companies, Box 7.3

The BCM market still has a mix of smaller and corporate providers but consolidation will increase. A number of smaller companies such as Guardian DR have listed on the London Stock Exchange and are no longer independently owned. Large consultancy and computer groups have also become very active in the area, notably Andersen Consulting, IBM and the like. Indeed, what is instructive is that the product offerings of such organizations appear to be mainly influenced by technological developments such as convergence between client and supplier systems, or Internet-based trade. For instance, American International Underwriters (AIU) have launched an Internet liability insurance product covering losses incurred through computer attacks (*South China Morning Post*, 2000). A number of firms in the industry also appear to be working on setting up international security assessment standards for Internet-based business. These standards should help to protect critical information and will be used to define insurance products to cover the product exposure of companies involved in such transactions. Whilst corporate governance and the needs of individual businesses will continue to be the major drivers of BCM, it is clear that the Internet and technology convergence will also have an increasing influence on BCM. It is to some extent inevitable that the negative aspects of using the Internet will have a very big impact on the regulatory environment, reinforcing demands that some control be exercised over the cyber environment. Attacks on Internet sites during early 2000, the increasing number of viruses that affect computer users, as well as concerns over the criminal use of the Internet, have led

---

Box 7.3   The rise and development of EMC

EMC began life as a manufacturer of motherboards. Based in Hopkinton, MA, USA it was worth $120 million by 1988. In 1989 Michael Ruettgers was appointed CEO and, due to quality control problems with their existing manufacturing operation, he decided to redirect the company towards data storage instead of motherboard production. By 1992 he was appointed CEO and accelerated the company's concentration on data storage, doing battle with the likes of IBM and many other, smaller competitors. The company has grown through its ability to anticipate and capitalize on changes in the data storage industry. This it has done by being customer-focused and using input from these stakeholders to make changes to EMC products and services. For instance, in the early 1990s the company, through talking to large clients, realized that corporations wanted to move away from decentralized computing with data stored on local area networks back to centralized storage. This led them to move into open storage, where different servers are linked to a single storage system (Hemp, 2001). At present the company is set to capitalize on the growth of the networked information storage market which is undergoing rapid growth. IDC estimates that, in this market, EMC had a total market share of 30.5 per cent in 2000. This market grew from $2.8 billion in 1999 to $6.7 billion in 2000. EMC recently also reported that it was increasingly selling into international markets. A company spokesman reported in January 2001 that international markets represented about 64 per cent of future business opportunities, with non-US revenue accounting for 60 per cent of total revenue in 2000.

Source: Foremski (2001)

---

in the USA to demands for government surveillance of the medium. There are new rules to enable digital wire-tapping by the FBI. The measure is aimed at tracking the physical location of cellular phones but could potentially be used to monitor Internet traffic (Waldmeir, 2000). The law that enables this practice is the 1994 Federal Communications Assistance for Law Enforcement Act which mandates that telecommunications companies must design their networks to enable monitoring. Privacy activists, including the American Civil Liberties Union, were, during May 2000, engaged in challenging the provisions to engage in digital wire-tapping that would enable e-mails and other Internet communications to be scrutinized. During November 2000 the US Justice Department released a report on the FBI's 'Carnivore' surveillance system that gave the software a clean bill of health but the Illinois Institute of Technology Research Institute (IITRI), the body that had reviewed the software, admitted their concerns at the lack of provisions that would ensure the FBI did not abuse the system and the power they had.

Social

In recent years it has become evident how powerful and well-organized organizational stakeholders can affect companies. January 2001 saw the culmination of a concerted effort by animal rights activists to close down the Huntingdon Life Sciences (HLS) animal testing laboratories, based in Cambridge, UK. Whatever the rights and wrongs of animal testing, and despite evidence of past malpractice, the HLS laboratories provide a valuable and legal service to the pharmaceutical industry. The anti-HLS campaign demonstrates the vulnerability of organizations to seemingly powerless groups. The main effort has been to target key investment groups, including the company's bank, the Royal Bank of Scotland (formerly NatWest) which was due to consider an overdraft facility to the company during January 2001. Other examples abound of how stakeholders, including the mass media, can have a powerful effect on how companies deal with issues of service or product quality.

'Information and ambiguity'

The Internet is commonly perceived as a fast way to communicate and gather information. For organizations, this represents as much of a threat as a benefit. Disinformation (cf. FUD), rumours and protests may quickly spread across nations and time zones, thereby requiring crisis communications to be ready to address incidents as they happen (in order not to exacerbate the situation or compound a crisis) and adopt Internet crisis communications strategies in addition to their regular crisis communications strategies. Several issues spring to mind:

1   regular Internet scanning to ensure that organizations are quickly aware of false/malicious information
2   policies toward newsgroups, discussion forums and unofficial sites
3   strategies to respond effectively to this information in the electronic domain as well as regular media
4   knowledge of differences in legal systems where negative information may be sourced
5   dealing with incidents instigated by rival companies.

'Consumerism and continuity' or 'The accidental accused'

Consumer affairs programmes (e.g. *Watchdog*) and magazines such as *Which?* highlight the enormous appetite that the UK public has for the 'outing' of reckless (or worse) companies trading in the UK. However, recently, a number of companies have found that they have had to respond to (and been seen to be to blame for) problems with products and service, when the problem may reside with the supplier. Although the companies concerned may have continuity plans that deal with supplier crises, the downstream organization has publicly 'taken the rap' for the incident. In the media, the culpable party is not always the one that is chastised, and with the increased integration between products, this is likely to continue. For instance:

- Digital operators have faced extensive media criticism when 'Tivo' failed to integrate fully with EPG (electronic programme guides) for Sky digital and OnDigital satellite television services.
- DVD software (i.e. films) which does not follow the DVD forum code, and thereby fails to operate on budget DVD players – hardware manufacturers face media criticism.
- Internet Service Providers offer erratic/slow service – telephone companies, such as BT (ironically), receive blame for opening exchanges.
- Organic farmers in the Third World are found to be less than organic – in the UK, the retailer Iceland has faced public/media criticism.

Reputation management

Two hundred years ago the vast majority of the world's population was virtually self-sufficient in essentials; risk and safety from food contamination was a personal responsibility. A feature of commerce in the twenty-first century is the growing separation between producer and consumer; the scale, complexity and remoteness of food production all contribute to the potential for contamination. Consumers are forced to place their trust in producers and regulators to ensure the safety of the produce they consume. Trust has been eroded because of fears arising from the threat to health posed by BSE, the extravagant use of antibiotics, and the uncertainty surrounding the growing use of genetically modified foodstuffs. At a macro level, popular and media concern about food production methods in agriculture, processing plants and additives is growing. At a micro level there appears to have been an increase in product contamination incidents. Some involve malicious product tampering such as the lacing with cyanide of Johnson & Johnson's Tylenol painkiller drug. Other incidents may arise from errors in production or from the use of contaminated raw materials as happened with the contaminations experienced by Perrier (in 1990) and Coca-Cola (1999).

The proliferation of the means of communication has changed the context in which communications occur. Managers are deluged with information, problems are widely disseminated. Some commentators describe this as the 'age of information' although, more cynically, Pilger (1998) refers to a media age in which information is distorted or sanitized by the media and organizations. The social reports published by companies including Merrill Lynch, Barclays and Shell indicate the importance corporations place on publicizing a 'socially responsible face'. The management of reputation has gained increasing relevance to organizations in the 'media age' (see, for a full discussion, Riel, 1995; Fombrun, 1997; Gray and Balmer, 1998; Balmer and Soenen, 1999; Fombrun *et al.*, 2000).

Elliott *et al.* (2001) in an analysis of Perrier (1990) and Coca-Cola's (1999) response to product contamination crises offers some insight into the process of reputation management. First, organizations need to communicate in an open and consistent manner. A disjointed approach to communication can create serious problems for a company as witnessed by Perrier. Communications should be unambiguous and free from attempts at the projection of blame elsewhere. Scapegoating is often viewed with considerable suspicion by the media and other observers.

Second, contingency plans must be tested. Developing such plans without testing them or providing training for staff will severely inhibit their effectiveness. A core element of such a planning process should involve media training for key staff and the creation of media-friendly background information which can be given out in the early stages of the crisis. There was little evidence of such plans in the responses of either Perrier or Coca-Cola. It seems inconceivable that Coca-Cola did not possess such plans, suggesting that it was a failure in their implementation that lay behind the poor crisis response.

A third issue concerns the role of trust in stakeholder management. Organizations that appear to prioritize profit over safety will find that their attempts to manage their image will be plagued by a persistent lack of trust amongst stakeholders. This process is not something that can be established during a crisis but should be an integral part of a company's strategy. Organizations must be aware of the variety of stakeholder groups, their interests and power in planning for and when managing crisis events. Some utility companies maintain databases of vulnerable groups who might require special attention should there be an interruption in supply (e.g. hospitals, residential care homes, etc.). Politicians or vociferous pressure groups may also be listed in order that potentially embarrassing media coverage can be anticipated. Since the Brent Spar difficulties, Shell has employed environmental activists as consultants to provide input at board level.

Closely linked to stakeholder management is historical context which combines the record of media relations, perceptions of openness and ongoing marketing communication activity. Certain product attributes may be more vulnerable to threat, such as 'natural purity'. Alternatively, there is the context in which an incident occurs. For Perrier, the disillusionment of key investors and weak links with the media isolated the company from potential allies during the crisis. Media support for Johnson & Johnson was vital in their recovery from the Tylenol incidents. For Coca-Cola, the coincidence of the contamination with the high-profile dioxin problems in Belgium created an ultra-sensitive environment for their own difficulties. Continuity plans, including crisis communication blueprints, can only assist an organization's crisis response. Effective crisis response requires ongoing environmental scanning in order that such plans can be used in a flexible manner and adapted to the particular circumstances of each incident. For the global company there are likely to be many local difficulties that have the potential to trip them up.

Finally, the recognition of a company's intangible assets is an important, but neglected, aspect of the strategic management process. All too often, organizations fail to take account of their intangible asset base when developing contingency plans for crisis events. As the cases discussed here illustrate, the reputational costs of a crisis can be considerable (see Box 7.4).

A number of practical lessons may be learnt from the experiences of Perrier and Coca-Cola:

- Product contaminations do not necessarily result in a full-blown crises. Poor media relations, and disillusioned investors were key factors in allowing the escalation to develop into a full-blown crisis for Perrier. The coincidence of a scare with the Belgian dioxin contamination was unfortunate for Coca-Cola, yet the frequency of such scares is increasing rapidly. Coca-Cola's response, in public perception, was that of a distant corporation with little real interest in Western European consumers. Globalization requires that companies manage information flows to ensure that they remain abreast of 'local key issues'.
- Second, where national or product divisions exist, an overall coordinating structure within a crisis management team is necessary to distinguish between strategic, tactical and operational matters (as discussed in Chapter 6).
- Third, effective communication is based on a thorough understanding of all stakeholders and their needs during a crisis. This understanding will be translated into messages communicated. Perrier and Coca-Cola's initial responses created an impression of self-interest to the detriment of customer care.
- Fourth, communicating the message requires a good understanding of context. For Perrier, an unsympathetic media, coupled with a fickle customer base concerned with health and purity, provided an unfavourable context. Coca-Cola's scare was inextricably linked to the dioxin contamination and the associated political furore. Effective communications and public relations require significant intelligence and environmental scanning (see Stone, 1995; Regester and Larkin, 1997; Elliott *et al.*, 2001).

Internet and reputation

The Internet provides great opportunity for companies to communicate directly with consumers, facilitating a 'militant tendency' to organize against companies, whether warranted or not. Indeed, the ability to communicate with customers is one of the most important facets of truly building a loyal customer base through establishing a sense of community. Unfortunately this positive aspect of the Internet has an associated weakness in that electronic

Box 7.4   Reputational crisis – Coca-Cola emulates Perrier?

In early 1990 Perrier experienced a major business interruption from a crisis triggered by suspected contamination. On 2 February the US Food and Drugs Administration notified Perrier that minute traces of benzene had been found in its product. However, it was not until 12 February that Perrier recalled its American stocks. Perrier perceived of the problem as affecting the USA only, despite rumours that the French source had been polluted. British supermarkets began to remove Perrier water from their shelves in the absence of clear communications from the company. On 14 February Perrier announced a world-wide recall of Perrier water.

Perrier's management of the crisis was widely criticized for a number of reasons. First, the length of time taken by the company between identifying a problem and acting. This indicated that there was no crisis plan. The crisis was pushed through public and media pressure and was allowed to pass beyond the control of the Perrier Group. There was an apparent lack of a coordinated response with a response in the UK and USA targeted at reassuring consumers and media. The response of Source Perrier was focused upon poorly thought-through attempts to reassure investors. Perrier's handling of the disaster was described as: 'uneven at best, ranging from head in the sand refusal to talk, to announcements in arch corporatese, to bursts of pique'. Another commentator called it 'the caveman approach to public relations'.

Perrier had ignored warnings of contamination that had circulated for some six months preceding the crisis. There was no clear view of who the key stakeholders were at each stage of the crisis or the message that should be targeted towards each group. There was evidence of significant differences in opinion regarding the strategic direction of the Perrier Group, between key shareholders and the management team, personified in its chairman, Leven. Such division may cause problems for an organization at the best of times. During a crisis it may of course create a common sense of purpose or, alternatively, one party may exploit the troubles to meet their own objectives. Perrier had developed a strong brand image, founded on natural purity. Its crisis communications do not appear to have considered this. Its post crisis communications included messages emphasizing the technical nature of the production process, which might be perceived to be at odds with the natural purity of the water. As Raymond Perrier (no relation) pointed out, 'The images of peasants filling empty bottles from gushing springs was destroyed.' There is much evidence that the behaviour of the different divisions of the Perrier Group was uncoordinated. This added to the potential for contradiction and reinforced, in the minds of the media and financial institutions, the view that Perrier was poorly managed. The lack of a proper business continuity plan was clear.

Sources: Crumley (1990), Elliott *et al.* (1993), *Economist* (1999)

Coca-Cola

In June 1999 the suspected contamination of Coca-Cola prompted the largest product recall in the company's history. Although the 'contamination' affected much of Western Europe, the events were centred on Belgium. Fears of contamination occurred in the midst of a major health scare in which the Belgian government's handling of the dioxin contamination of chicken and eggs had been widely criticized and had led to the resignations of the Ministers for Agriculture and Public Health.

Almost 200 people reported feeling ill after drinking Coca-Cola. Although the symptoms were limited to consumers in France and Belgium, the suspect plants supplied the Netherlands, Germany, Luxembourg, Spain and Switzerland. Government bans, across north-western Europe, created the impression that Coca-Cola was reluctant to act. Control of the crisis passed to government agencies creating an impression that Coca-Cola was uncaring.

Defective carbon dioxide and a fungicide were identified, initially, as the immediate causes of the contamination, although the evidence for this was mixed. Most important was that the identification of these 'causes' was interpreted as an attempt by Coca-Cola to deflect blame for the contamination onto two suppliers. Coca-Cola's crisis response was perceived as lacklustre and was extensively criticized. The *Economist* (1999) described this response:

> Coca-Cola's public-relations error is to have seemed keener to protect its own back than to allay the understandable fears of consumers . . . the firm's legal-sounding insistence that there were no 'health or safety issues' and that the drinks 'might make you feel sick, but are not harmful' were hardly going to reassure people. . . . A statement on June 16 from Douglas Ivester, the firm's chairman, expressing his regret, arrived hopelessly late.

It is likely that analysts at Coca-Cola's Atlanta headquarters were not fully aware of this recent history and thus of the likely strength of concerns. The quick introduction of government bans may have been excessive in the light of the real hazard to health, as identified later. However, given resignations less than two weeks earlier, it would be a brave politician who failed to act quickly and assertively. It seems that, as with Perrier ten years previously, Coca-Cola did not fully appreciate the implications of the potential for damage associated with an alleged contamination. Ivester later admitted that he did not capture the depth of the problem early enough and that he had relied on subordinates to manage the incident, rather than seizing the opportunity to reassure government ministers early enough.

Sources: Kielmas (1999), *Economist* (1999), Elliott *et al.* (2001)

billboards or chatsites also provide disaffected consumers with the power to communicate negative news about organizations to vast numbers of consumers, often sparking copy-cat actions. Moss-Kanter (2001) reports how in

1999 a Toshiba customer created a website to publicize how poor the company's aftersales customer service was. The customer had allegedly bought two VCRs which were discovered to be defective and Toshiba representatives did not repair the machines properly. The company representative had also apparently refused to apologise and the website contained an audio recording of this. The company responded to this public 'outing' with an apology and compensation but by then the damage was done – the website had received 7 million visits and sparked off copy-cat sites.

Summary

Chapter 7 has outlined some of the potential developments for business and continuity management. It is our view that the future of business continuity rests in the imaginations of the business continuity managers of today and tomorrow. A key development will concern a shift in focus away from hardware protection to an approach which recognizes that the tangible and intangible assets of an organization exist as means rather than as ends. The notion of service continuity has proved to be a powerful one in the public services, and it might be reflected in customer continuity, or possibly stakeholder continuity, for private sector organizations. What is clear is that change will continue in terms of technology, society, regulation and customer expectations. The role of the continuity manager is here to stay. We have argued that effective continuity requires commitment, access to the senior echelons within an organization but, perhaps most importantly, a mindset in which organizational assets are seen as a means to an end. Within such a mindset, creative solutions to continuity problems will always be possible.

In this last chapter our intention has been to be thought-provoking rather than to provide a comprehensive list of issues for the future. We possess no crystal ball! A key task for business continuity professionals is to ensure that, as a process, BCM becomes normalized within organizations. Devoting Chapter 5 to this subject is an indication of its importance. Chapters 3 and 4 provide a framework for conducting business continuity planning and analysis. The frameworks within these chapters represent a tool box to be used flexibly rather than a strictly prescriptive process, which must be adhered to at all costs. Chapter 2 considered some of the legal and regulatory drivers of business continuity. Chapter 6 identified a range of issues pertinent to managing an interruption. Throughout we have sought to balance the demands of an academic textbook with examples which will also advise and guide practice. It will be clear that we believe that business continuity is here to stay. Our identification of a value-based mindset in Chapter 1 highlights that we consider that BCM can add value, and that it should be thought of as an integral part of the management process.

Notes

1 The US-based stock exchange that lists primarily technology stock. It has internationalized in recent years and is available as a screen based and Internet based service.
2 To some extent the debate on whether BCM should have board representation echoes that of whether Risk Management should have board representation. In some companies Risk Management takes care of much the same issues that BCM does – particularly in insurance-related businesses.
3 The 'love bug' virus that affected both domestic and corporate computer systems during May 2000 is a good example of this.

References

Balmer, J.T. and Soenen, G.B. (1999) 'The acid test of corporate identity management', *Journal of Marketing Management* 15: 69–92.
BBC (2001) [on-line] (http: //news.bbc.co.uk/hi/english/business/newsid_702000/702573.stm, accessed 7 February 2001.
Body Shop International (2000) *Annual Results*, London: Body Shop International Plc.
Burt, T. (2000) 'Fast-track drive on the road to e-commerce', *FT Auto Survey*, 29 February: 1.
Clemons, E. (2000) 'Gauging the power play in the new economy, mastering RISK, Part eight', *Financial Times* 23 March: 1–4.
Crumley, B. (1990) 'Fizzzzz went the crisis', *International Management* 45(3): 5.
Doswell, B (2000) *Guide to Business Continuity Management*, Leicester: Perpetuity Press.
Economist (1999) 'Coca-Cola: bad for you?', *Economist* (USA) 19: 62.
Elliott, D., Smith, D. and Sipika, C. (2001) 'Message in a bottle: learning the lessons from crisis, from Perrier to Coca-Cola', University of Sheffield mimeo.
Financial Times (2000a) 7 April: 8.
Financial Times (2000b) 'Mastering risk, Part eight', 23 March 1–4.
Financial Times (2001) 16 February: 15.
Fombrun, C. (1997) *Reputation: Realising Value from the Corporate Image*, Boston, MA: Harvard Business School Press.
Fombrun, C., Gardberg, N. and Sever, J. (2000) 'The reputation quotient: a multistakeholder measure of corporate reputation', *Journal of Brand Management* 7(4): 241–55.
Foremski, T. (2001) *Financial Times* 'Siebel beats estimates in fourth quarter', 24 January: 26.
Frey Jr, S.C. and Schlosser, M.M. (1993) 'ABB and Ford: creating value through cooperation', *Sloan Management Review* autumn: 65–72.
Grande, C. (2000) *Financial Times* 'Innovators are back to net a second e-fortune', 17 October: 8.
Gray, E. and Balmer, J.T. (1998) 'Managing corporate image and reputation', *Long-Range Planning* 31(5) 695–702.
Hemp, T (2001) 'Managing for the Next Big Thing: EMC's Michael Ruettgers', *Harvard Business Review* January: 130–41.
Herbane, B., Elliott, D. and Swartz, E. (1997) 'Contingency and continua: achieving excellence through business continuity planning', *Business Horizons* 40(6): 19–25.

Hutton, W. (2001) 'Yahoo – comment', *The Observer* 11 March: 23.

Jones, M.E. and Sutherland, G. (1999) *Implementing Turnbull: A Boardroom Briefing*, London: Institute of Chartered Accountants in England and Wales.

Kehoe, L (2001) 'E-business to the rescue of the Valley', *Financial Times* 21 February: 11.

Kielmas, M. (1999) 'Interest in recall covers rises: Coca-Cola scare fuels awareness of risks', *Business Insurance* 33(28): 18–22.

Lyman, P. and Varian, H (2001) 'The democratization of data', *Harvard Business Review* January: 137.

Mellish, S. (2000) 'When a BCP really comes into its own', *Continuity* 4(4): 4–6.

Moss-Kanter, R. (2001) 'The ten deadly mistakes of wanna-dots', *Harvard Business Review* January: 91–100.

Pilger, J. (1998) *Hidden Agendas*, London: Vintage.

Rayport, J. and Sviokla, J. (1995) 'Exploiting the virtual value chain', *Harvard Business Review* November–December: 75–85.

Regester, M. and Larkin, J. (1997) *Risk Issues and Crisis Management*, London: Kogan Page.

Riel, V.C. (1995) *Principles of Corporate Communications*, London: Prentice-Hall.

Sipika, C., Smith, D. and Elliott, D. (1993) 'Message in a bottle: Perrier', *Proceedings of the World Academy of Marketing*, University of Istanbul, pp. 559–63.

Skapinker, M. (2000) 'FT survey', *FT Director* 31 March.

South China Morning Post (2000) 15 March [on-line] http: //www.globalarchive.ft.com/ search-components/index.jsp, accessed 15 March 2000.

Stone, N. (1995) *The Management and Practice of Public Relations*, London: Macmillan.

Suskind, R. (2000) 'Internet services will step forward to take the initiative, FT Survey', *FT Director* 21 March: VIII.

Thomas, R. (1999) 'Developing an ethical image: managing your reputation via corporate branding', *Journal of Brand Management* 6(3): 113–26.

Turnbull, N. (1999) *Internal Control: Guidance for Directors on the Combined Code*, London: Institute of Chartered Accountants in England and Wales.

Waldmeir, P (2000) 'Monitoring poses threat to cyber-anonymity', *Financial Times* 11 May: 4.

Womack, J.P., Jones, D.T. and Roos, D. (1990) *The Machine that Changed the World*, New York: Rawson Associates.

Further reading

Clair, J.A. (1998) 'Reframing crisis management', *Academy of Management Review* 23(1): 59–76.

Financial Times (2000) 'Mastering RISK, Part eight', *Financial Times* 1–4.

Gray, E. and Balmer, J.T. (1998) 'Managing corporate image and reputation', *Long-Range Planning* 31(5): 695–702.

Jones, M.E. and Sutherland, G. (1999) *Implementing Turnbull: A Boardroom Briefing*, London: Institute of Chartered Accountants in England and Wales.

Pearson, C.M. and Rondinelli, D.A. (1998) 'Crisis management in central European firms', *Business Horizons*, May–June: 50–60.

Study questions

1 How will business continuity evolve during the next five years? You may choose to use the headings, political, economic, social and technological to help structure your answer.

2 How will e-commerce affect your organization?

3 Prepare a 1,250 word report identifying and highlighting the likely concerns of key stakeholders, affected by an interruption in the following:

- an international oil company
- a general hospital
- a large grocery retailer
- a manufacturer of computer memory chips

4 Find examples of two organizations, one which you consider to have effectively managed its reputation in the aftermath of a crisis, and another which has been less effective. What are the key differences in their response? What advice would you give to the less effective organization?

Index